Apparel Making

in fashion design

Injoo Kim
University of Cincinnati
Mikyung Uh
Idea Fashion Institute
Seoul, Korea

Fairchild Publications, Inc.

Executive Editor: Olga Kontzias
Editor: Joann Muscolo
Art Director: Nataliya Gurshman
Production Manager: Priscilla Taguer
Production Services: Monotype Composition, Inc.

Copy Editor: Donna Frasetto
Interior Design: Delgado Design, Inc.
Cover Design: Delgado Design, Inc.
Technical Drawings: Injoo Kim
Fashion Illustrations: Hoesun Jung
Assistant Illustrator: Eunkyung Kim

Library of Congress Catalog Card Number: 2001088928

ISBN: 1-56367-216-2

GST R 133004424

Printed in the United States of America

Contents

Contents

9) The Sleeve   327

Preface

Flat pattern is the study of garment construction in two-dimensional form. Pattern-making skills help the designer to observe the three-dimensional form and accurately translate that form into the two-dimensional component. The understanding of pattern making skills allows the designer to successfully create silhouettes for garments that "come to life" when constructed three-dimensionally.

Pattern making combines all the best elements of design, technical understanding and creativity. There are fundamental concepts, such as an understanding of mathematics and proportions, which are essential to the creation of innovative designs. By successfully applying technical skills to the flat pattern, observations of shape and form are accurately translated into wearable garments. Once learned, these skills can be applied to a multitude of design concepts expressive of the designer's ideas.

Although these are guidelines to the process of flat pattern, there is a great amount of creativity and flexibility. Because designers are always expanding their creative horizons, the understanding of pattern making fundamentals allows for greater ease in the design process and opens up more variations to garment design. Knowledge about flat pattern makes the design possibilities for garments almost limitless.

The goals of this book are as follows:
To introduce the concept of a sloper. The instructions will be easy to follow and these slopers will fit as perfectly as possible with minor alterations for different body shapes. The most common alteration questions and problems will be thoroughly discussed.

To present clear step-by-step instructions and diagrams for the methodology and principles used in pattern drafting.

To cover in detail the whole production process of making a garment from pattern generation to construction, including lining, interfacing, and markers.

To demonstrate the composition of one complete garment per chapter, emphasizing the essential aspects of flat pattern design for this specific garment.

To expose the reader to all the design and pattern variations possible in each garment constructed.

To encourage creativity in (interchanging, combining) individual garment parts to construct clothing with a variety of style lines and design features. Flat sketches will be included at the end of each chapter to suggest design variations.

This book is, in part, a response to the questions asked in my flat pattern classes and workshops for professionals. It is also a compilation of the methods and techniques necessary/important to students and industry professionals learning pattern drafting. It offers a complete picture of the process of individual garment construction following the exact techniques used in the apparel industry today. My professional experiences from industry and teaching both in Asia and the U.S. will be brought together in one comprehensive book.

This book is organized into eleven chapters. Chapter 1 demonstrates how to measure accurately the parts of the body necessary for a pattern draft. Included in this chapter are size and standard measurement charts. Specific techniques for grading accurately for size differences also will be fully explained. A grading chart will be included for each body part measured. Chapters 2 through 10 will cover skirts, pants, culottes, blouses, and the one-piece dress. Each chapter begins with the introduction of a basic sloper for a specific article of clothing. These basic patterns will be accurately fit and have easy-to-follow instructions. The second section of each chapter explains in detail the whole production process of making a garment from pattern generation to garment construction, including lining, interfacing, and markers. The balance of the section of each chapter will cover the techniques for altering separate pattern pieces, using a sloper to create a variety of possible style lines and design features for individual silhouettes.

The unique factor of this book is in the presentation of each garment as a whole concept. My teaching and workshop experiences have made it clear to me that students of pattern drafting and garment construction should first learn the concepts of making an individual item of apparel such as a pant, skirt, or a dress. Once that knowledge has been mastered, students will be able to interchange different parts of various garments and understand the versatility of using design and construction techniques in limitless ways. In addition, the presentation of basic slopers for each garment will include the process of alteration for an accurate fit, based on extensive personal research in Asia, Europe, and America.

Since this book is divided into chapters by individual garments themselves rather than by the parts of a garment, an index is provided for finding specific information about separate pattern pieces. This index makes it easy to find whatever details of instruction are needed, such as collars, sleeves, and pockets. This type of "how-to-book" may be used by anyone interested in the accurate and detailed process of individual garment construction and pattern drafting.

Acknowledgments

I wish to acknowledge the following people for all their help on making this book possible.

Alex Kim, my husband, who gave me extensive advice in producing the technical drawings. The students at the University of Cincinnati in my Flat Pattern classes who tested my instructions. Kathy Reinhart who helped me write the English translation of this book. My colleagues in the University of Cincinnati's School of Design who offered their support and encouragement of my endeavors.

Marty Plumbo, assistant Professor in the Digital Program at the University of Cincinnati, who helped lay out the text and illustrations as well as reviewing the text itself. Eunkyung Kim, a graduate student, who patiently produced illustrations to my exact specifications and never complained.

Olga Kontzias, Executive Editor of Fairchild Publications, and Joann Muscolo, the editor, who both gave me excellent advice and direction in enhancing and expanding the Korean version of this book for publication in the United States. Thanks also to the reviewers of this book. Their comments were very useful in helping me finalize the content of this manuscript. They are Nancy Staples, M. Jo Kallal, and Elaine Zarse.

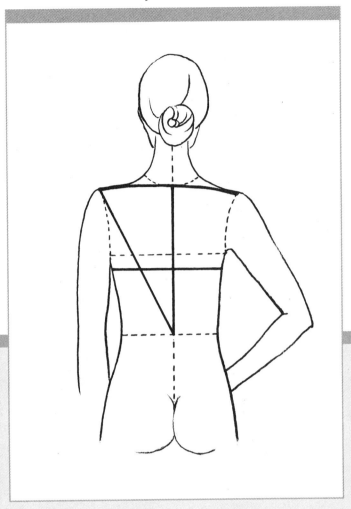

Chapter One

HOW TO MEASURE

To ensure a perfect fit, it is crucial that body measurements be accurate. When measuring, adhere to the following guidelines. When measurements are made by another person, make certain that they follow these procedures.

MEASURING IN GENERAL

- The subject should wear leggings, tights, or panty hose.
- The subject should stand straight, look directly ahead, with the feet placed together and flat on the floor, and arms slightly raised away from the body.
- Record all measurements as they are made on a measurement form.
- Measure without ease but not too tightly.
- When measuring circumferences, the tape measure should be parallel to the floor.
- When measuring vertically, the tape measure should be perpendicular to the floor.
- To measure the waist, tie a string or piece of yarn around the waist at its smallest circumference to mark the natural waistline, generally 1" above the navel.
- To measure the side seams, use pins or tape to mark each side seam from the waistline to the hip line.

* **Note:** The side seam is positioned slightly forward in the front.

MEASURING CIRCUMFERENCES

1. Bust Circumference

Measure completely around the torso, from the bust point at the fullest part of the bust. Make certain that there is no ease in the tape measure and that it is parallel to the floor.

2. Waist Circumference

Measure completely around the waist, at the center front on the smallest part of the waistline. Make certain that there is no ease in the tape measure and that it is parallel to the floor.

3. Hip Circumference

Measure completely around the body, from the intersection of the hip depth line and the side seam to the fullest part of the hip. Make certain that there is no ease in the tape measure and that it is parallel to the floor.

4. Ankle Circumference

Measure the distance around the ankle, just above the most prominent ankle bone.

5. Biceps Circumference

With the subject's arms unflexed, measure the distance around the biceps at its fullest part. Make certain that there is no ease in the tape measure and that it is parallel to the floor.

6. Wrist Circumference

Measure the distance around the wrist, just below the most prominent wrist bone.

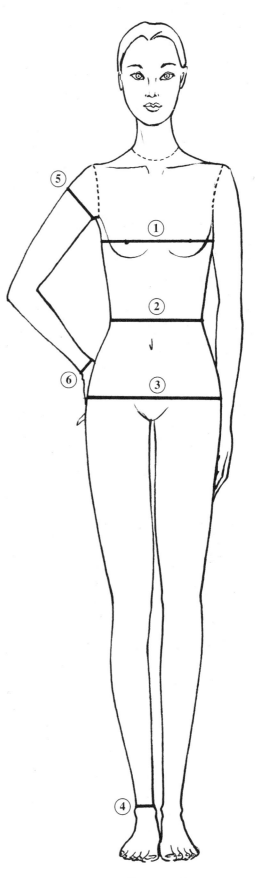

Illustration 1.1

MEASURING LENGTHS

1. Shoulder Length

Measure from where the neck and shoulder meet to the shoulder tip.

2. Front Length

Measure from where the neck and shoulder meet to the waistline, passing through the bust point.

3. Front Shoulder Slope

Measure the angle formed by a line extending from the shoulder tip to the front center point of the waistline.

4. Bust Point Length

Measure from where the neck and shoulder meet to the bust point.

5. Bust Point Width

Measure the distance between the bust points.

6. Sleeve Length

With the subject's hand on the hip, measure from the center of the shoulder tip down through the elbow to the bones of the wrist.

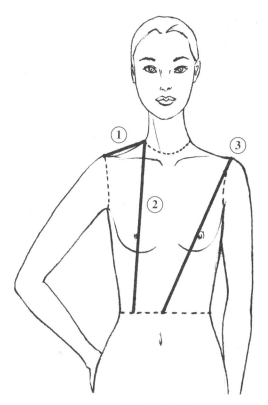

Illustration 1.2

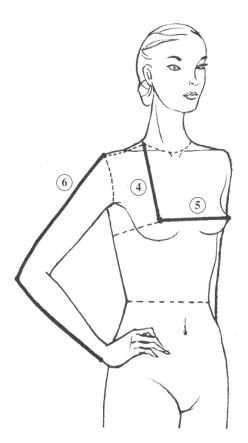

Illustration 1.3

BACK MEASUREMENTS

1. Center Back Length

Measure from the spinal vertebra nearest shoulder level to the vertebra nearest waistline level. Make certain that there is no ease in the tape measure and that it is perpendicular to the floor.

2. Armhole Depth

Measure down 1" from the armpit, then transfer this mark around to the center back. Next, measure the distance from the topmost neck vertebra to the mark.

3. Back Shoulder Slope

Measure the angle formed by a line extending from the shoulder tip to the back center point of the waist-line.

4. Back Shoulder Width

Measure the length of the curved line formed between the shoulder tips, passing through the spinal vertebra nearest shoulder level.

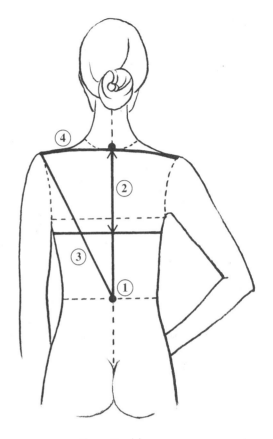

Illustration 1.4

MEASURING DEPTHS

1. Hip Depth (Hip Line)

Mark the fullest part of the hip perpendicular to the side seam with a pin or cellophane tape, then measure from the waistline to the mark. If the stomach or thigh measurement is greater than the hip measurement, record these measurements also.

2. Crotch Depth

With the subject sitting on a flat surface, spine straight, and at a right angle to the sitting surface, measure from the waistline to the surface. Make certain that the tape measure is perpendicular to the floor.

3. Knee Length (Knee Line)

Measure on the side seam, from the waistline to the top of the kneecap.

4. Ankle Length (Pant Length)

Extend a tape measure from the waistline straight down to the ankle.

5. Crotch Length

With the subject's legs spread 6" apart, place the tape measure at the center front waistline, then pull it through the legs and back up to the center back waistline.

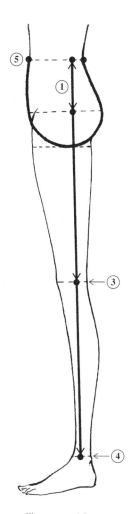

Illustration 1.5

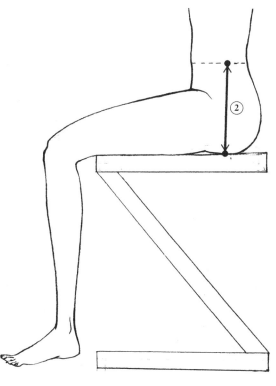

Illustration 1.6

Chapter Two

GENERAL INFORMATION

GRAIN LINE

Grain lines are marked on pattern pieces to indicate how they are to be placed on the fabric from which they will be cut. By aligning the grain lines on a pattern piece with the straight grain of the fabric, the angle of the grain on that piece in the finished garment is determined. The angle of the grain line dictates how the fabric will hang when placed around the body. There are three possible angles for any given grain: straight, cross, and bias.

Straight Grain
The grain line of the pattern is parallel to the selvage of the fabric. This is the most commonly used grain line placement. Garments made of fabrics cut on this grain will hang correctly.

Cross Grain
The grain line of the pattern is perpendicular to the selvage of the fabric. Although garments made of fabric cut on this grain will not hang correctly, it is effective as a decoration for the yoke of a shirt or cuffs, especially with striped fabrics.

Bias
The grain line of the pattern is placed on the bias at about a 45° angle. Garments made from fabric cut on the bias will drape softly, but will also require much more fabric. Design details such as collars, cuffs, and yokes are especially effective when cut on the bias, using striped or plaid fabrics.

Drawing 2.1. Grain line angles.

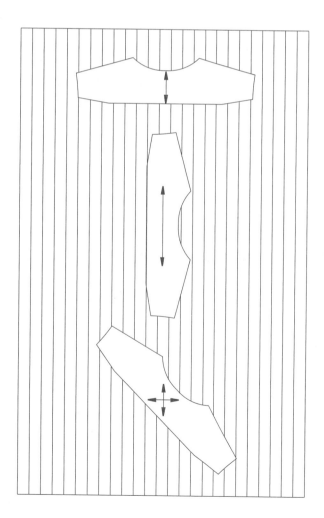

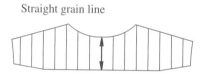

Straight grain line

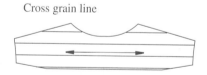

Cross grain line

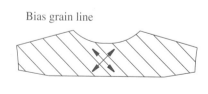

Bias grain line

Drawing 2.1

SEAM ALLOWANCES

A lthough there are standard seam allowances for every type of garment, these can vary depending on the type of garment and the fabric used. Begin by marking each corner of the garment with a right angle to easily determine the width of the seam being sewn. It is important to keep seam allowances consistent in order to avoid confusion during construction.

Drawing 2.2. Standard seam allowances.

- Side, shoulder, and center back seams = $5/8$".
- Armhole, neckline, extension, waistline, and sleeve cap seams = $3/8$".
- Hem = $1\frac{1}{4}$" to 2".

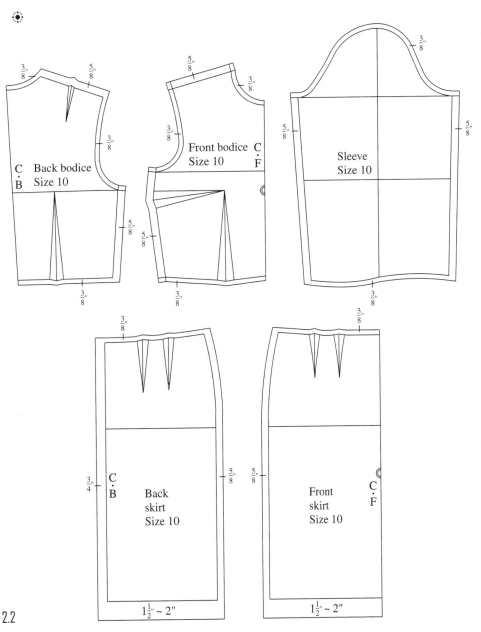

Drawing 2.2

NOTCHES

otches are markings that indicate how the different pattern pieces of a garment are matched to each other, as well as the placement of their darts, zippers, seam lines, hems, and other design details. They are marked before the pattern pieces are cut out, then matched again before the seams are sewn. Notches are made by aligning the seams of two pieces then creating a notch at the corresponding location on each piece. The marks are made inside the seam allowances, at right angles to the seam lines, and extend all the way to the pattern edge.

Drawing 2.3. Notches.

- Bodice armhole: Placed on the armhole.
- Sleeve cap: Placed on the sleeve cap.
- Hip: Placed on the hip line.
- Dart: Placed at each dart leg.
- Stitch lines: Placed on the seam line.

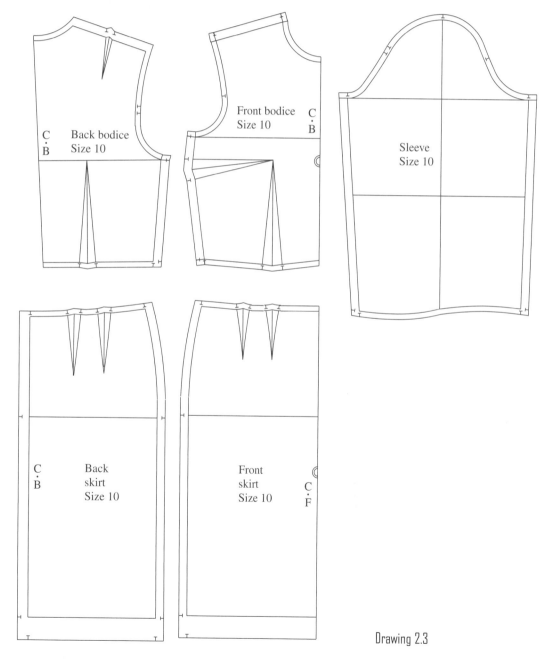

C
·
B   Back bodice
     Size 10

Front bodice   C
Size 10   ·
                B

Sleeve
Size 10

C
·
B   Back
     skirt
     Size 10

Front
skirt
Size 10   C
           ·
           F

Drawing 2.3

EASE

As patterns are being developed, it is important to allow extra measure, or "ease," at key locations for comfort and movement. The amount of ease added to a pattern will effect both the fit and silhouette of the finished garment. Relatively small amounts of ease result in closer-fitting garments with more defined silhouettes, whereas larger amounts of ease result in looser-fitting garments with baggier silhouettes.

Although ease amounts can vary widely, the ranges that follow represent the ease amounts generally used for the pattern types listed.

❖

Pattern Type	Location	Measurement
Blouse One-piece	Bust	3"
	Waist	1½"
	Hip	1½"
Skirt	Waist	1"
	Hip	1½"
Pant	Waist	1"
	Hip	1" to 3"
Jacket Coat	Bust	5"
	Waist	3½"
	Hip	3½"

TRUING

Generally, it is necessary to "true-up" the various hems, curves, connecting points, and darts on a pattern to ensure that the pieces connect with smooth transitions from one to the next. Typically, this process involves the reshaping and straightening of any edges left unfinished after pattern manipulation.

Drawing 2.4. Truing examples.

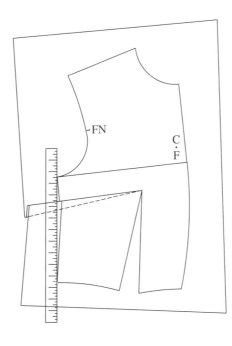

Drawing 2.4

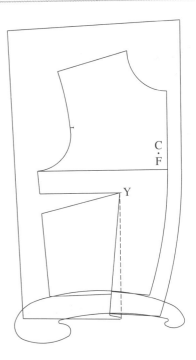

LABELING

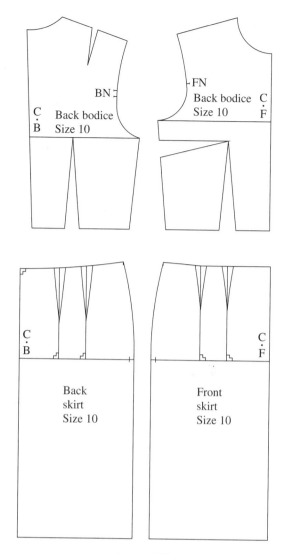

Once finished, patterns are labeled with certain key pieces of information to aid in their identification and use. Finished pattern pieces are commonly labeled to indicate the pattern piece, pattern type, size, center back and front, and the total number of that piece to be cut.

Drawing 2.5. Labeling on the slopers.

Drawing 2.5

BLENDING

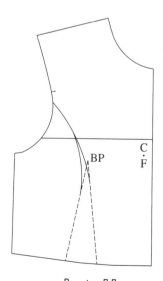

Blending is the process of rounding lines between points and smoothing the transitions between lines so that the finished garment will better match the contours of the body. Certain style lines require blending to smooth out pointed features.

Drawing 2.6. Blending the princess line.

Drawing 2.6

SLASH AND SPREAD

Illustration 2.1

S lash and spread is used to vary the shape of the garment by adding fullness to the silhouette. This fullness can take the form of either volume added to the entire shape or flare added at one end. The amount of fullness added can create many interesting design effects, and thus depends on the desired design. Two variations of the slash and spread method commonly used in this way are one-sided, and two-sided.

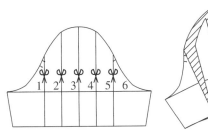
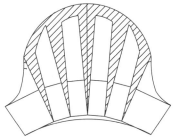

Drawing 2.7. One-sided.

To add fullness at one edge of a pattern, slash from that edge to, but not through, the opposite edge, then spread each slash line as necessary for the desired fullness.

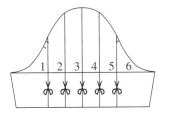
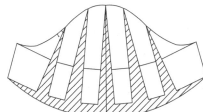

Drawing 2.7

Drawing 2.8. Two-sided.

To add fullness across two opposing edges on a pattern, slash from one edge through the opposite edge, then spread each slash line as necessary for the desired fullness.

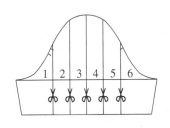
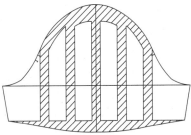

Drawing 2.8

SLASH AND CLOSE

he slash and close method is used to transfer a dart. First, a slash line is drawn from the dart point of the dart to be transferred to the edge to which it is to be transferred. Then, the slash line is slashed and spread open, closing the initial dart and forming a new one on the target edge.

✦

Drawing 2.9

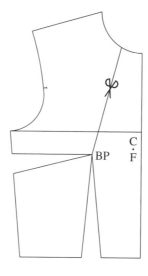
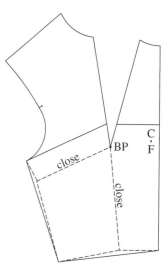

Drawing 2.9

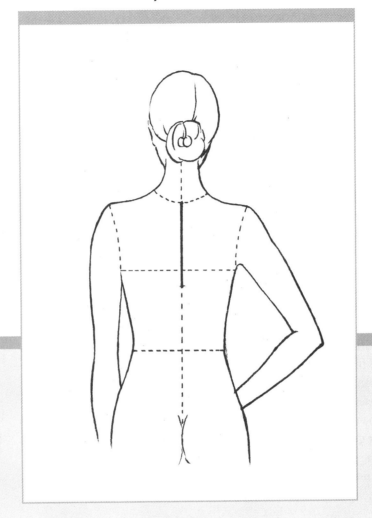

Chapter Three

THE SLOPER

INTRODUCTION TO THE SLOPER

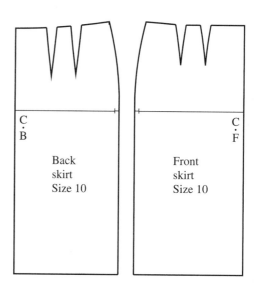

The sloper is the foundation of all flat pattern creation. Using specific body measurements, a sloper can be created to simulate a garment being constructed for any body shape, thus enabling designers to make patterns quickly and accurately. Once completed, variations in size and style often necessitate adjustments to the sloper. These are generally determined by constructing a muslin based on the sloper and then testing it for accuracy and comfort.

There are two methods of sloper development: the short measure method, and the proportional method. Using the short measure method, accurate measurements are taken for each part of the body to achieve a perfect sloper. This requires precise measurement, which can be difficult for beginners. In contrast, the proportional method requires only that key measurements be taken, from which the remaining measurements (for details such as neckline and armhole sizes) can then be derived.

The method of sloper generation presented in this chapter is based on the proportional method. However, a few steps from the short measure method have been used to aid in achieving an accurate fit.

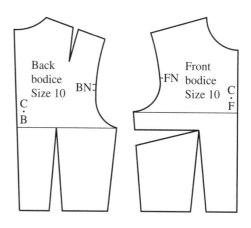

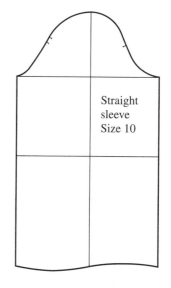

Drawing 3.1

SKIRT SLOPER

$\mathcal{I}$n developing a skirt sloper, it is first necessary to determine the hip measurement, because this generally is the largest measurement of the lower torso and must be accommodated by the skirt opening when the garment is being put on. Owing to the natural curvature of the lower torso at the abdomen and hip, there is an excess of fabric between the hip and waist that must be removed for proper fit. The shaded areas in the illustration below indicate this excess between the waist and the hips, both at the side seams and at the front and back.

⁕

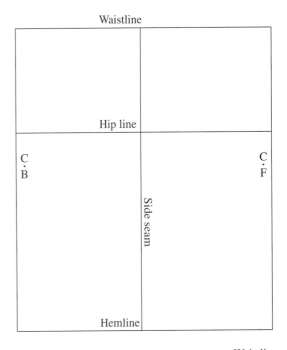

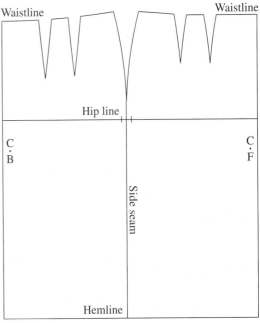

Drawing 3.2

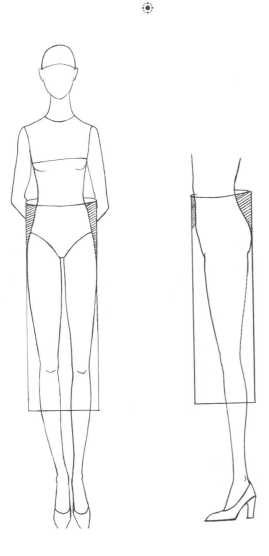

Skirt Sloper Measurements

- Skirt length: _____
- Hip depth: _____
- Hip measurement: _____*
- Waist measurement: _____

* If the thigh measurement is larger than the hip measurement, use it as hip.

Drawing 3.3 Foundation.

- AB = Hip depth.
- AC = Skirt length.
- BB' = Half of the hip measurement plus $^3/_4$" for ease.
- AA' = BB'.
- CC' = BB'.
- A'B' = AB.
- A'C' = AC.
- BD = Half of BB' minus $^1/_4$".
- Connect point A' to C'.
- Square up and down from point D, parallel to line AC.
- Label E and F.
- AG = One fourth of the waist measurement plus $^3/_{16}$" for ease minus $^1/_4$" (front and back difference).
- A'H = One fourth of the waist measurement plus $^3/_{16}$" for ease plus $^1/_4$" (front and back difference).

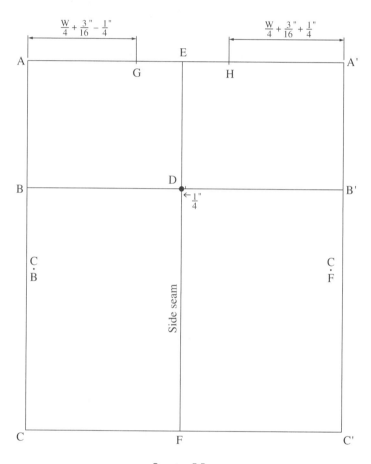

Drawing 3.3

Drawing 3.4

- I = One third of EG.
- Square up $\frac{1}{4}$" from I.
- Draw the hip curve down from I to D, blending into line ED, as shown.
- J = One third of EH.
- Square up $\frac{1}{4}$" from J.
- Draw the hip curve down from J to D, blending into line ED, as shown.

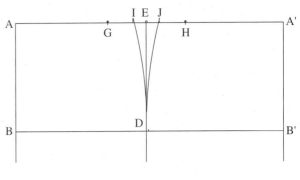

Drawing 3.4

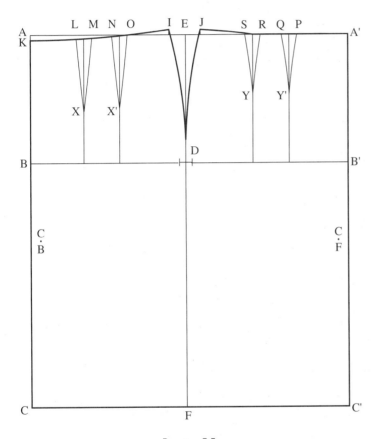

Drawing 3.5

Drawing 3.5. Waistlines and darts.

Back:
- K = Measure down $\frac{3}{8}$" to $\frac{5}{8}$" from A to allow for the back curvature.
- Draw the waistline with a shallow curve, from K to I, beginning square at the center back.
- KL = $2\frac{3}{8}$" for the dart placement.
- LM = IE.
- MN = $1\frac{1}{2}$" space between the darts.
- NO = LM.
- Mark the midpoint of LM, then square down to the hip line (BB').
- Repeat for NO.
- Measure down 4" to 5" and label X and X', as shown.
- Draw the dart legs, shaping the back dart legs in a concave (U) manner.

Front:
- Draw the waistline with a shallow curve, from A' to J, beginning square at the center front.
- A'P = $2\frac{3}{4}$" for the dart placement.
- PQ = JE.
- QR = $1\frac{1}{2}$" space between the darts.
- RS = PQ.
- Mark the midpoint of PQ, then square down to the hip line (BB').
- Repeat for RS.
- Measure down 3" to 4" and label Y and Y'.
- Draw the dart legs, shaping the front dart legs in a convex (V) manner.

Drawing 3.6. Front and back.

- Crease the center of each dart leg by dragging a pushpin down its center while applying pressure.
- Crease dart leg PY, then fold over to match leg QY.
- Crease dart leg RY', then fold over to match leg SY'.
- Crease dart leg LX, then fold over to match leg MX.
- Create dart leg NX', then fold over to match leg OX'.
- True the waistline.

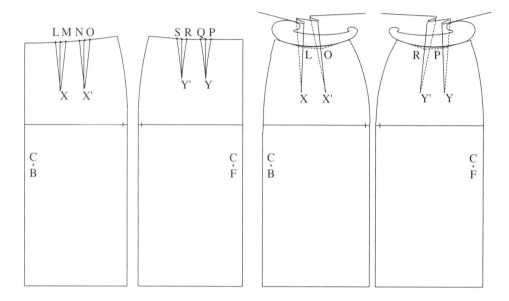

Drawing 3.6

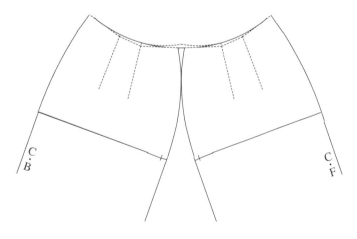

Drawing 3.7

Drawing 3.7

- Match the front and back side seams at the hip curve, making certain that their lengths are matched.
- True the waistline.

- Add the seam allowances:

   Side seams = $^5/_8$".

   Waist = $^3/_8$".

   Center back = $^3/_4$".

   Hem = $1^1/_2$" to 2".

- Mark the notches and grain lines, as shown.

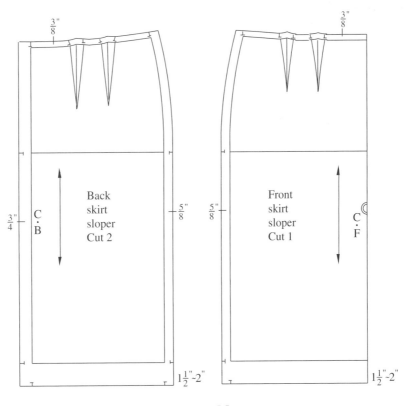

Drawing 3.8

Check Points

After a sloper has been developed and the appropriate seam allowances added to it, a muslin is constructed to its specifications in order to confirm its fit. Any changes necessary are noted on the muslin and then transferred to the pattern for adjustment. Several problems commonly encountered at this stage can be solved, as follows.

Drawing 3.9. Skirt is too tight across the front lower abdomen.

- Determine the amount to be added.
- Add one quarter of that amount to the front and back side seams, at the waistline.
- Add one half of the amount added to each side seam to each waist dart.
- Reshape the hip curve.
- **Note:** If the skirt is too loose across the front lower abdomen, follow the same procedure, but subtract from the side seams and waist darts.

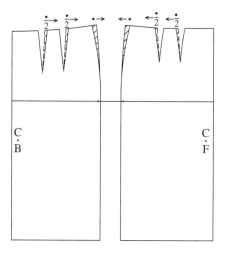

Drawing 3.9

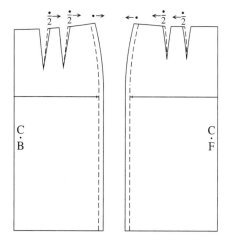

Drawing 3.10

Drawing 3.10. Skirt is too tight overall.

- Determine the amount to be added.
- Add one quarter of that amount along the front and back side seams.
- Add one half of the amount added to each side seam to each waist dart.
- **Note:** If the skirt is too loose overall, follow the same procedure, but subtract from the side seams and waist darts.

Drawing 3.11. **Skirt has an excess of fabric at the sway back.**

- Determine the amount to be subtracted from the skirt back.
- Subtract one half of that amount from the back side seam.
- Subtract one half of the amount subtracted from the side seam from each waist dart.
- Add the amount subtracted from the back side seam to the front side seam.
- Add one half of that amount to each waist dart.
- Lower the waistline as desired for the sway back at the center back.
- Raise the waistline the same amount at the center front.
- Reshape the waistline.

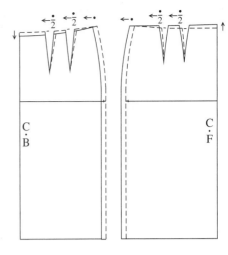

Drawing 3.11

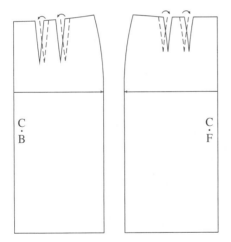

Drawing 3.12

Drawing 3.12. **Adjustment of dart length and placement.**

- Dart length and placement can be adjusted to make a skirt fit more smoothly around the abdomen and hips.
- Mark the specific location on the muslin where the fit of the darts begins to fail, then correct on the pattern after transfer.

BODICE SLOPER

When using the proportional method to develop a bodice sloper, it is necessary to begin with accurate measurements of the bust, waist, and full back length. All remaining measurements, such as the neckline and armhole, are derived proportionally from these key measurements. From them, a tube shape is created that reflects a specific side seam, waistline, and bust line. The contours of the body are then shaped from this tube, using darts to control the excess and to adjust the tube to the contours of the body shape.

The shaded areas in the illustration indicate excess between the initial bodice tube and the body's contours between the waist and the side seam and between the bust and the waist at the front.

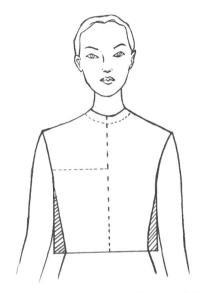
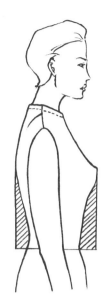

Illustration 3.2

Drawing 3.13. Bodice sloper.

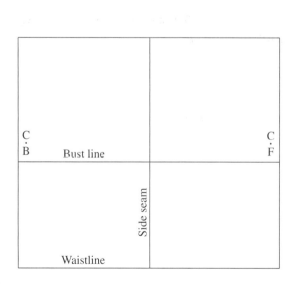

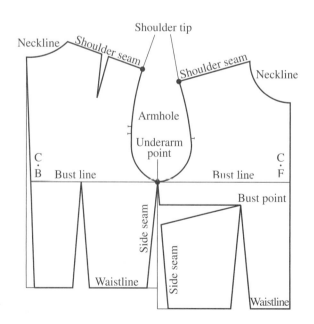

Drawing 3.13

Bodice Sloper Measurements

- Back length: _____
- Bust measurement: _____
- Waist measurement: _____
- Shoulder length: _____
- Bust point length: _____
- Sleeve length: _____
- Wrist measurement: _____

Drawing 3.14. Foundation.

- AB = Back length.
- AC = One fourth of the bust measurement (arm-hole depth).
- CC' = Half of the bust measurement plus $1\frac{1}{2}$".
- Square up and down from point C' to create a line parallel to AB.
- Label A' and B'.
- Connect points A' to A, B' to B, and C' to C.
- D = The midpoint of line CC'.
- D' = The midpoint of line BB'.

- Connect point D to D'.
- CE = One sixth of the bust measurement plus $1\frac{1}{2}$" for ease.
- AE' = CE.
- Connect point E to E'.
- * **Note:** The back ease is $\frac{1}{2}$" larger than the front ease to allow for movement.
- C'F = One sixth of the bust measurement plus 1".
- A'F' = C'F.
- Connect point F to F'.

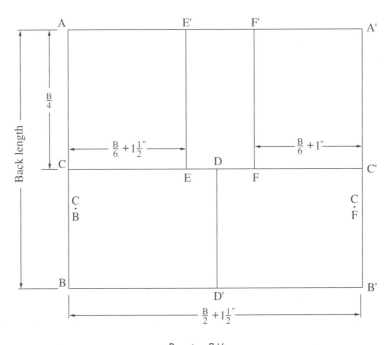

Drawing 3.14

Drawing 3.15. Armhole depth.

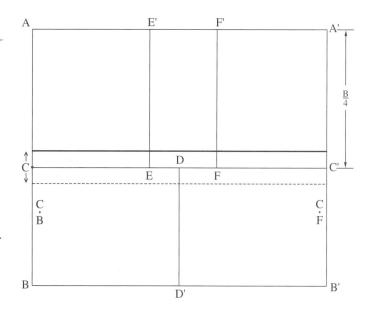

Drawing 3.15

Because the proportional method for creating a bodice sloper is based on the bust measurement, the resulting armhole can be inaccurate at extreme bust sizes—too long for larger busts and too short for smaller ones. Thus, it is necessary to confirm the armhole depth directly on the figure, as follows:

- Measure down 1" from the armpit.
- Draw a line from this mark around to the center of the back.
- Measure the distance from the topmost neck vertebra to the line.
- Correct the armhole depth by raising or lowering line AC by this measurement.

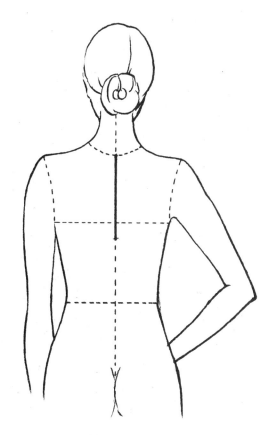

Illustration 3.3

Drawing 3.16. Back and front bodices.

- AG = One twelfth of the bust measurement.
- Square up from point G one thirty-second of the bust measurement and label G'.
- Connect point G' to A with a curved line, ending square to point A.
- Measure down $3/4$" from point E' and label H.
- Square out $3/4$" from point H and label H'.
- Draw the shoulder line by extending a line equal to the shoulder length plus $1/2$" from G' to HH'.
- **Note:** The shoulder line may or may not pass through point H', depending on the shoulder length.
- I = The midpoint of line EE'.
- Connect point I to D.
- Draw a line perpendicular to line ID from point E and label J.
- Divide line JE into thirds and mark.

Armhole curve:
- Start square to point H' and curve down to point I.
- Continue the curve from point I to D, through the two-thirds mark on line EJ, ending square to point D.

Front bodice:
- A'K = One twelfth of the bust measurement.
- A'L = One twelfth of the bust measurement plus $5/8$".
- Square down $1/4$" from K and label K'.
- Draw a line parallel to A'L from point K'.
- Draw a line parallel to A'K from point L.
- Connect point K' to L with a curved line, ending square to point L.
- F" = Square down $1 1/2$" from point F'.
- Draw the shoulder line by extending a line equal to the shoulder length from K', and passing through F". Label M where this line ends.
- Measure up one third of the length of line FF" from point F and label I'.
- Connect point I' to D.
- Draw a line perpendicular to line DI' from point F and label J'.
- Mark the midpoint on line J'F.

Armhole curve:
- Start square to point M and curve down to point I'.
- Continue the curve from point I', through the midpoint of J'F, ending square at point D.

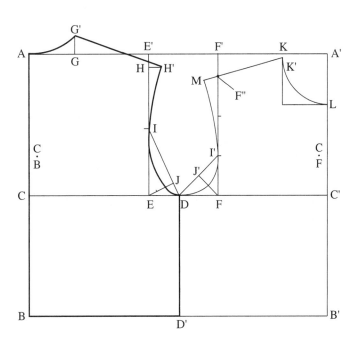

Drawing 3.16

Drawing 3.17. Dart.

Back
- a = The midpoint of line G'H'.
- a' = The midpoint of line CE.
- Connect point a to a'.
- Measure down 3" from point a on the line aa' and label X.
- Measure out $1/4$" on each side of point a.
- * **Note:** Line aX is the center of the shoulder (the total dart intake is $1/2$").
- Draw the dart legs from point X.

Front:
- Y = The midpoint of line C'F.
- Square a guideline down from Y.
- Draw a line equal to the bust point length from K', ending at a point on the guideline, and label N.
- b = Draw a line from N perpendicular to DD' and label b.
- bb' = One twenty-fourth of the bust measurement.
- Connect point b' to N.
- Square down from D' the length of line bb' and label O.
- Square down from B' the length of line bb' and label P.
- Connect line O to P.

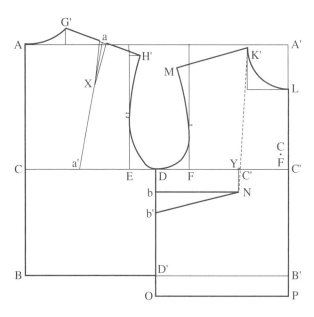

Drawing 3.17

Drawing 3.18. Notches.

- Measure down 5" from point H' on line HD and mark with double notches.
- Measure down 5" from point M on line MD and mark with a single notch.

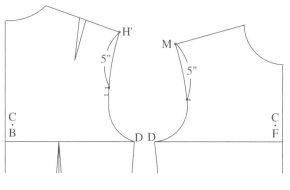

Drawing 3.18

Drawing 3.19. Tight bodice sloper.

- Measure in $\frac{5}{8}$" from point B and label Q.
- Draw the new center back line, connecting point A to Q.
- Measure in $\frac{3}{4}$" from point D' and label R.
- Draw the new back side seam, connecting point D to R.
- Measure in $\frac{3}{4}$" from point O and label S.
- Draw the new front side seam, connecting point D to S.

Back waist dart:
- Square down from point a' to line QR and label a".
- Back dart intake = The length of line QR minus one fourth of the waist measurement plus $\frac{3}{8}$" $(QR - \frac{w}{4} + \frac{3}{8}")$.

- Measure out half of the dart intake from each side of point a" and mark.
- Draw the dart legs from point a' to each mark.
- **Note:** a'a" = Center dart leg.

Front waist dart:
- Square down from N to line SP and label N'.
- Front waist dart intake = The measurement of line SP minus one fourth of the waist measurement plus $\frac{3}{8}$" $(SP - \frac{w}{4} + \frac{3}{8}")$.
- Measure out half of the dart intake from each side of point N' and mark.
- Draw the dart legs from point N to each mark.
- **Note:** NN' = Center dart leg.
- Redraw the final bodice line.

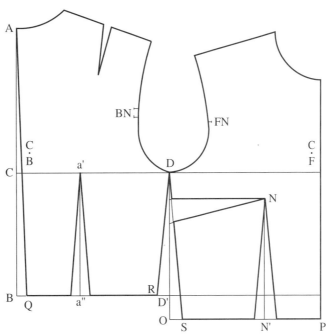

Drawing 3.19

Drawing 3.20. Adjusting dart points.

- The dart points are moved in $\frac{1}{2}$" to 2" from the bust point for a smooth shape through the bust area.

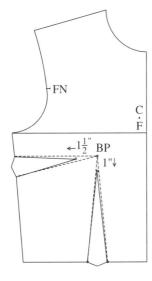

Drawing 3.20

Truing

Drawing 3.21. Waist and shoulder darts.

- Crease the center of each dart leg by dragging a pushpin down its center while applying pressure.

- Crease dart leg AX, then fold over to match leg BX.
- Crease dart leg CY, then fold over to match leg DY.
- Crease dart leg EZ, then fold over to match leg FZ.
- True the shoulder seam and waistlines.

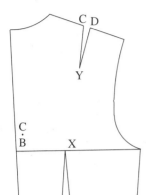
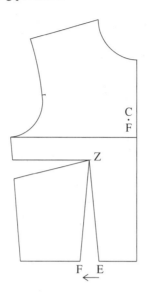
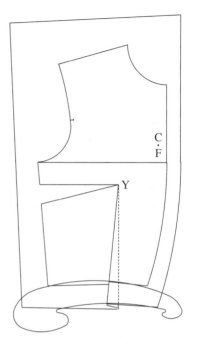

Drawing 3.21

Drawing 3.22. Side dart.

- Crease the center of the dart leg by dragging a pushpin down its center while applying pressure.
- Crease dart leg GZ, then fold over to match leg HZ.
- True the side seam.

Drawing 3.22

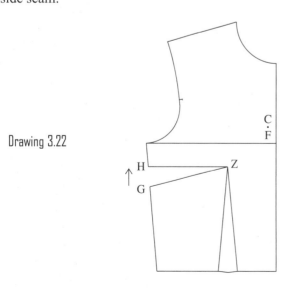
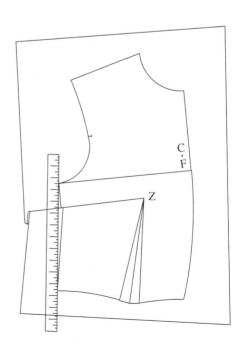

Drawing 3.23. **Side and shoulder seams.**

- Match the front and back side seams, making certain that they are of equal length.
- True the waistline and armhole.
- Match the front and back shoulder seams, making certain that they are of equal length.
- True the neckline and shoulder tip.

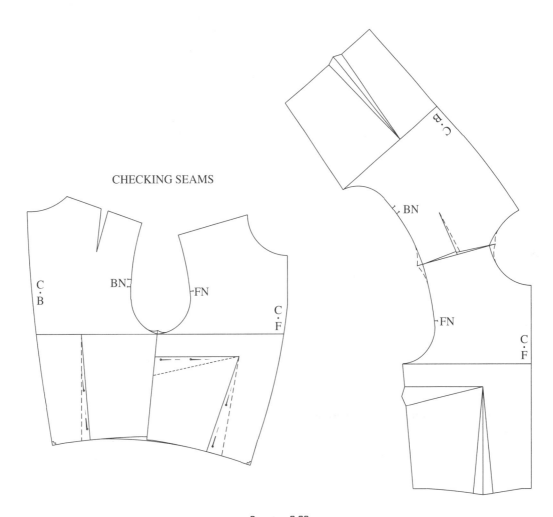

Drawing 3.23.

Drawing 3.24

- Add seam allowances:
    Side seams = $^5/_8$".
    Shoulder = $^5/_8$".
    Waist = $^3/_8$"
    Armhole = $^3/_8$".
    Center back = $^3/_4$".
- Mark the notches and grain lines, as shown.

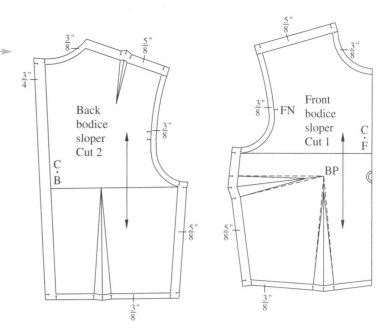

Drawing 3.24

Check Points

After a sloper has been developed and the appropriate seam allowances have been added to it, a muslin is constructed from it to confirm fit. Any necessary changes are noted on the muslin and then transferred to the pattern for adjustment. Several problems commonly encountered at this stage can be solved, as follows.

Drawing 3.25. Armhole is too tight or loose.

- Lower or raise the underarm point at the side seam as necessary.

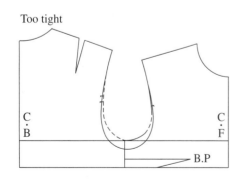

Drawing 3.25

Drawing 3.26. Shoulder is too long or short.

- If the shoulder is too long, measure in or out from the shoulder tip as necessary, then reshape the armhole.

Too long

Too short

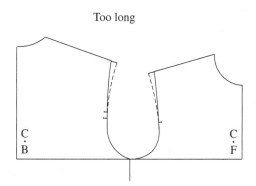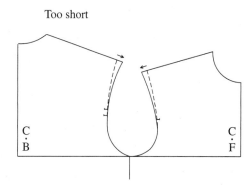

Drawing 3.26

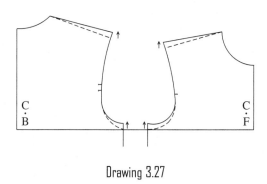

Drawing 3.27

Drawing 3.27. Shoulder is too tight.

- Raise the shoulder tip and underarm point, then reshape the armhole.

Drawing 3.28. Shoulder is too loose.

- Lower the shoulder tip and underarm point, then reshape the shoulder seam and armhole.

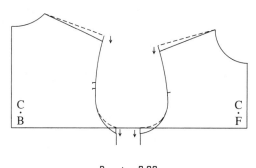

Drawing 3.28

Drawing 3.29. Neckline is too narrow or wide.

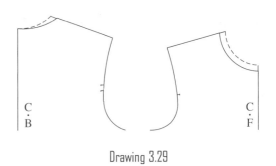

Drawing 3.29

- Adjust the neckline by measuring in or out from the neck on the shoulder line as necessary, then lower or raise the neckline at the center front or back.

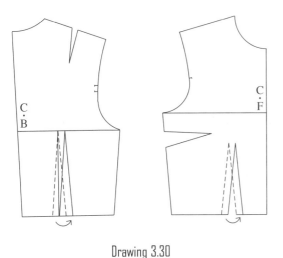

Drawing 3.30

Drawing 3.30. Adjustment of dart length and placement.

- Dart length and placement can be adjusted to make a bodice fit more smoothly around the bust.
- Mark the specific location on the muslin where the fit of the darts begins to fall, then correct on the pattern after transfer.

SLEEVE SLOPER

$\mathcal{I}$n developing the sleeve sloper, begin with accurate measurements of the front and back armholes and sleeve length. The accuracy of the front and back armhole measurements is particularly crucial, as both the cap height and biceps line measurements of the sloper will be derived from these measurements. From these measurements, the tube-shaped sleeve is created, which connects at the bodice, wraps around the arm, then hangs down from the outer edge of the shoulder. The sleeve sloper describes a standardized sleeve, based on an arm extended at a 45-degree angle from the body, achieving a compromise between comfort and style, and lending itself to easy adaptation.

Drawing 3.31. Sleeve sloper.

- AB = Cap height.
- AC = Length to elbow.
- AD = Sleeve length.
- EF/E'F' = Under-sleeve length.
- AE = Back armhole length.
- AE' = Front armhole length.
- EE' = Biceps circumference.

Illustration 3.4

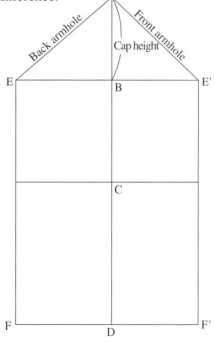

Drawing 3.31

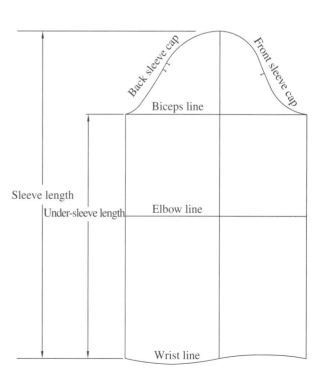

Sleeve Sloper Measurements

- Front armhole: _____
- Back armhole: _____
- Sleeve length: _____
- Biceps measurement: _____
- Wrist measurement: _____

Drawing 3.32. **Measure armhole.**

- Stand a tape measure on its edge and carefully position it along the armhole curve, from the shoulder tip to the underarm point on the side seam.
- Measure the front and back bodice armhole curves separately and record.
- Combine the front and back armhole measurements and record.
- AC' = Back armhole.
- AC" = Front armhole.

Drawing 3.31

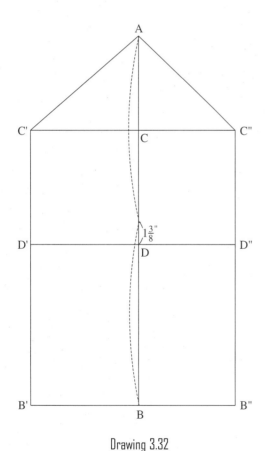

Drawing 3.32

Drawing 3.33. **Foundation.**

- AB = Sleeve length.
- Draw a line perpendicular to AB through point B.
- AC = One fourth of the combined front and back armhole measurements plus 1".
  Example: Back armhole = $8^{1}/_{2}$", Front armhole = 8". AC = ($8^{1}/_{2}$" + 8")/4 + 1".
- Draw a guideline perpendicular to AB through point C.
- AC' = Back armhole measurement.
- Draw a diagonal line from point A that is equal to the back armhole measurement, labeling C' where it intersects the biceps line.
- Square down from point C' the length of line CB, and label B'.
- AC" = Front armhole measurement.
- Draw a diagonal line from point A that is equal to the front armhole measurement, labeling C" where it intersects the biceps line.
- Square down from point C" the length of line CB, and label B".
- AD = One half of AB plus $1^{3}/_{8}$".
- Draw a line perpendicular to AB through point D, then label D' and D" as shown.

Drawing 3.34. **Biceps width and cap height.**

To allow for comfort and mobility, the biceps width on the sloper is generally at least 2" larger than the actual biceps measurement.

- If the biceps measurement is larger than the biceps line (C'C") on the sleeve pattern, extend each side of the biceps line half of the difference.
- If the biceps measurement is smaller than the biceps line (C'C") on the sleeve pattern, shorten each side of the biceps line half of the difference.
- * **Note:** Shortening the biceps line will result in a taller sleeve cap, whereas extending it will result in a shorter one.

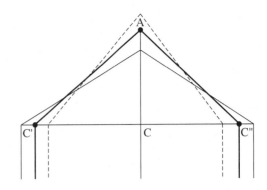

Drawing 3.34

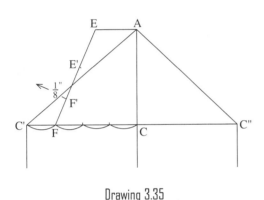

Drawing 3.35

Drawing 3.35. **Back sleeve cap.**

- C'F = One fourth of line C'C.
- Square out from point A one and one-half times the length of C'F and label E.
- Connect point E to F.
- Measure down from point E the length of line AE and label E'.
- Measure up from point F the length of line C'F and label F'.
- Square $\frac{1}{8}$" out from point F'.

Drawing 3.36. **Front sleeve cap.**

- C"G = One third of line C"C.
- Square out from point A the length of C"G and label H.
- Connect point H to G.
- Measure down from point H the length of line AH and label H'.
- Measure up from point G the length of line C"G and label G'.
- Square $\frac{1}{8}$" out from point G'.

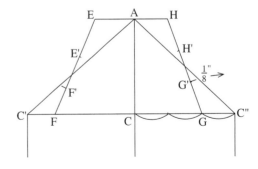

Drawing 3.36

Drawing 3.37. Sleeve cap curve.

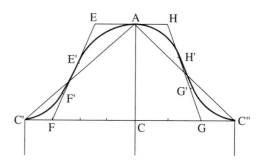

- Connect point A to E' with a curved line.
- Continue the curved line to the mark $1/8$" from F', then on to point C'.
- Connect point A to H' with a curved line.
- Continue the curved line to the mark $1/8$" from G', then on to point C".

Drawing 3.37

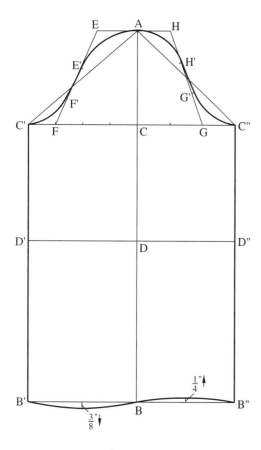

Drawing 3.38

Drawing 3.38. Sleeve hem.

- * **Note:** The back of the sleeve must be lengthened and the front shortened to allow for forward bending of the arm at the elbow.
- Mark the midpoint of BB', then square a line down $3/8$" from the mark.
- Draw a curved line from B' to B, passing through the mark.
- Mark the midpoint of BB", then square a line up $1/4$" from the mark.
- Draw a curved line from B" to B, passing through the mark.

Drawing 3.39. Notches.

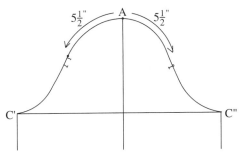

Drawing 3.39

*Note: Between ¼" and 1" of ease should be added to the sleeve cap to provide for comfort and mobility.

- Measure down 5½" on the back sleeve cap (AC') line and mark a notch.
- Continue down the back sleeve cap another ½" and mark a second notch.
- Measure down 5½" on the front sleeve cap (AC") line and mark a notch.

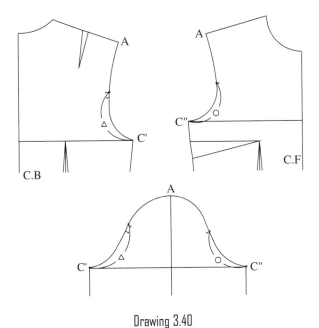

Drawing 3.40

Check Point

Drawing 3.40. Below the notch.

- Measure the distance from the first notch on the back sleeve cap to C'.
- Measure the corresponding back armhole distance on the bodice, from the first notch to C'.
- Repeat for the front as shown.

- If these two measurements are not equal, adjust the sleeve pattern by shortening or extending the biceps line appropriately.
- **Note:** If the difference between the two measurements is greater than $5/8$", the sleeve must be redone.
- Repeat the preceding steps, using the notch on the front sleeve cap and the front armhole on the bodice.

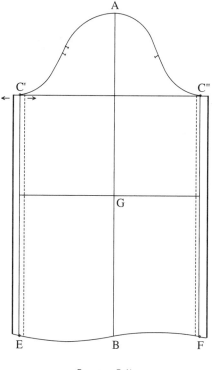

Drawing 3.41

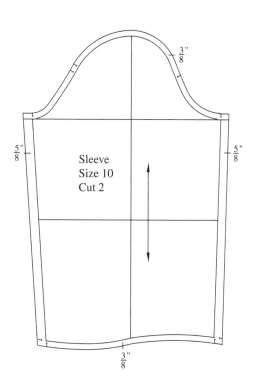

Drawing 3.42

Drawing 3.42

- Add the seam allowances:
    Sleeve cap and hem = $3/8$".
    Side seams = $5/8$".
- Mark the notches and grain lines, as shown.

Tight Sleeve

Drawing 3.43

- Trace the straight sleeve sloper and label points A through G, as shown.
- Measure out ½" from B and label H.
- Connect point G to H with a dashed line.
- Measure the width of the palm, add 1" for ease, then divide by two.
- Measure this distance out from each side of H, labeling I and J.
- Connect point C to I, labeling point K where the line intersects the elbow line.
- Connect point D to J, labeling point L where the line intersects the elbow line.

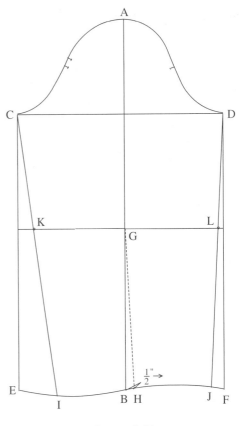

Drawing 3.43

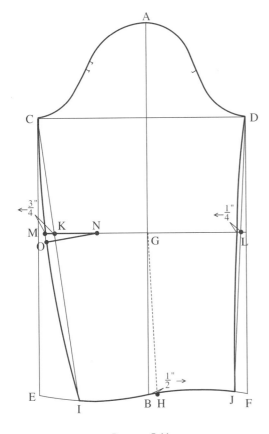

Drawing 3.44

Drawing 3.44

- Measure out ¾" from K and label M.
- Draw a curved line from C to I, passing through M.
- Measure in ¼" from L and mark.
- Draw a curved line from D to J, passing through the mark.

Elbow dart:
- Label N at the midpoint of MG.
- Measure down from M the difference between CI and DJ, and label O.
- Draw the dart legs by connecting N to points M and O.

PANTS SLOPER

*I*n developing a pants sloper, it is first necessary to determine the hip measurement, because this generally is the largest measurement of the lower torso and must be accommodated by the pants opening when the garment is being put on. Owing to the natural curvature of the lower torso at the abdomen and hip, there is an excess of fabric between the hip and waist that must be removed for proper fit.

Drawing 3.45. Pants sloper.

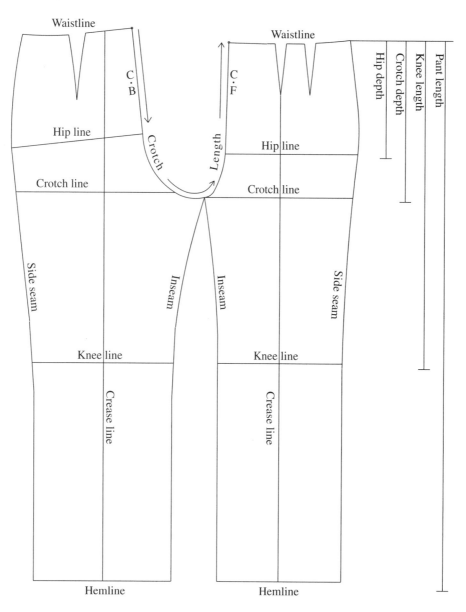

Drawing 3.45

Pants Sloper Measurements

- AB = Pant length: _____
- AC = Hip depth: _____
- AD = Crotch depth: _____
- AE = Length to knee: _____
- Hip measurement: _____*
- Waist measurement: _____
- Crotch length: _____

* If the thigh measurement is larger than the hip measurement, use it as hip.

Drawing 3.46 Pants foundation for front.

- AB = Pant length.
- AC = Hip depth.
- AD = Crotch depth plus 0" to 1" for sitting ease.
- * **Note:** Mature figures need more ease than juniors. The ease can be varied, depending on the pants style.
- AE = One half of line DB minus 2" (knee length).
- Measure down $^3/_8$" from A for waistband height and label F.
- CC' = One fourth of the hip measurement plus $^1/_4$" to $^1/_2$" for ease (hip line).
- FF' = CC' (waistline).
- DD' = CC' (crotch line).
- Connect D' to F'.
- Draw a line perpendicular to AB at E (knee line).
- Draw a line perpendicular to AB at B (hemline).
- D'D" = One twenty-fourth of the hip measurement plus 0 to $^1/_2$".
- Label G at the midpoint of DD".
- Square up and down from point G (crease line).
- Label G' at waist and G" at hem.
- Label M at the knee line.

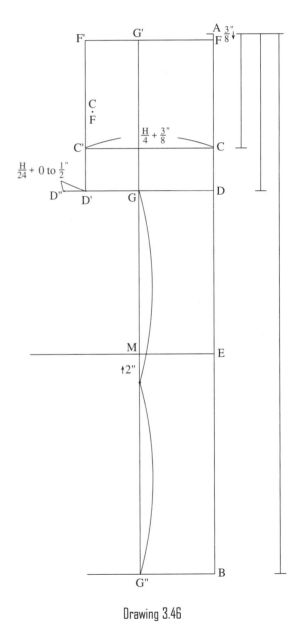

Drawing 3.46

Drawing 3.47. Waistline and crotch curve.

- H = Measure in $3/8$" from point F'.
- D'I = One third of D'F'.
- Connect H to I.

Crotch curve:
- Connect I to D".
- Draw a line from D', perpendicular to ID", and label X.
- Mark a point on D'X that is two thirds its length from D'.
- Draw a crotch curve from I to D", passing through the two-thirds mark.
- HJ = One fourth of the waist measurement plus $1/4$" for ease and $1 1/2$" for darts.
- Measure up $1/4$" from J and label J'.
- Blend J' to the midpoint of the waistline with a slightly curved line.
- Draw the hip curve from J' to C.

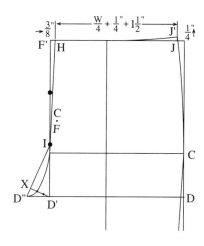

Drawing 3.47

Drawing 3.48. Dart inseam and side seam.

- Measure out $3/8$" on each side of G' and label 1 and 2.
- Measure down $3 1/2$" from G' and label 3.
- Draw the first dart by connecting point 3 to points 1 and 2.
- Measure over $1 1/2$" from point 2 and label 4.
- Measure over $3/4$" from point 4 and label 5.
- Measure down $3 1/2$" from the midpoint of points 4 and 5, and label 6.
- Draw the second dart by connecting point 6 to points 4 and 5.

Inseam and side seam:
- Measure $4 1/2$" to the left of G" and label L.
- Label K at one third of the length of D'D".
- Draw a straight line from L to K, and label N at the knee.
- Connect point D" to N.
- Mark in $3/16$" from the midpoint of D"N.
- Draw a curved line from D" to N, passing through that mark and blending into line NL.
- MN' = MN.
- G"L' = G"L.
- Connect N' to L' with a straight line.
- Connect C to N' with a slightly curved line, blending into line N'L'.

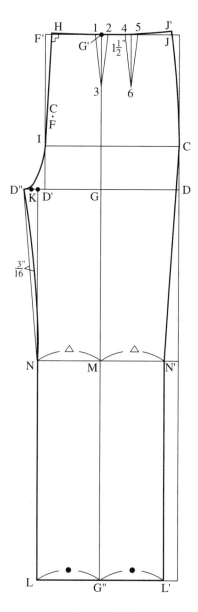

Drawing 3.48

Drawing 3.49. **Back of pants.**

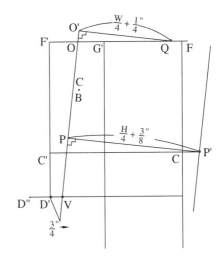

Drawing 3.49

- Draw the pants foundation, following the instructions for Drawing 3.46.
- Measure in $3/4$" from D' and label V.
- O = The midpoint of F'G'.
- Connect V to O, extending through the waistline.
- Extend C'C (hip line) from point C.
- Calculate one fourth of the hip measurement plus $3/8$" (for ease) and mark this distance from OV toward C.
- Draw a line that passes through the mark and runs parallel to OV, labeling P' where it intersects CC'.
- Draw a line from P', perpendicular to OV, labeling P where it intersects OV.
- Q = One fourth of the waist measurement plus $1/4$" from OV on the waistline (F'F).
- Draw a line from Q perpendicular to OV, then label O' at the intersection of this line and OV.

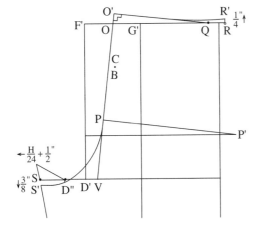

Drawing 3.50

Drawing 3.50. **Waistline and crotch curve.**

- R = Extend line F'Q from point Q and mark $1\frac{1}{2}$" for dart intake.
- R' = Square up $1/4$" from R.
- Blend R' to the waistline (O'Q) with a slightly curved line.

Crotch curve:
- D"S = One twenty-fourth of the hip measurement plus $1/2$".
- SS' = Mark $3/8$" down and draw a 1" line parallel to D"S.
- PS' = Draw the crotch curve from P to S', blending to the 1" line, as shown.

- Y = The midpoint of O'R'.
- Measure out $^3/_4$" (for a total of $1^1/_2$") on each side of Y and label 1 and 2.
- Measure down $4^1/_2$" from Y, parallel to G'G", and label 3.
- Draw the dart legs by connecting point 3 to points 1 and 2.

Inseam and side seam:
- Draw a hip curve connecting point R' to P'.
- MT = The length of MN plus $^1/_2$".
- MT' = MT.
- G"U = The length of G"L plus $^1/_2$".
- G"U' = G"U.
- Connect T' to U' with a straight line.
- Connect P' to T' with a slightly curved line, blending into line T'U'.
- Connect T to U with a straight line.
- Connect S' to T with a straight line.
- Mark in $^3/_{16}$" from the midpoint of S'T.
- Connect S' to T with a slightly curved line, passing through that mark, and blending into line TU.

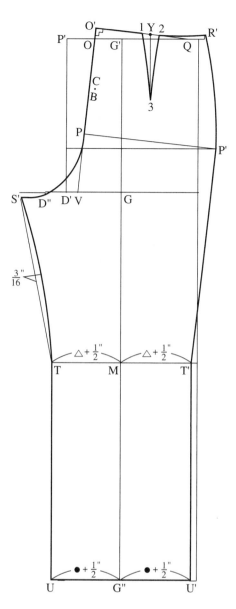

Drawing 3.51

- Add the seam allowances:

    Waistline, center front, and center back = $^3/_8$".

    Side and inseams = $^5/_8$".

    Hem = $1^1/_2$".

- Mark the notches and grain lines, as shown.

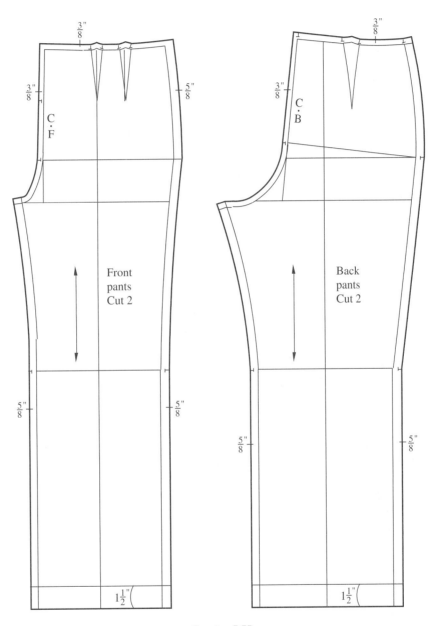

Drawing 3.52

Check Points

After a sloper has been developed and the appropriate seam allowances added to it, a muslin is constructed from it to confirm fit. Any changes necessary are noted on the muslin and then transferred to the pattern for adjustment. Several problems commonly encountered at this stage can be solved, as follows.

Drawing 3.53. Crotch is too tight or loose.

- Increase or decrease the crotch curve length at the inseam on both the front and back pattern pieces, as shown. Then taper gradually from this point into the inseam. Note that adjustment is often only necessary on the back pattern piece.

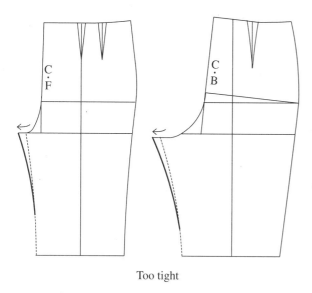

Too tight

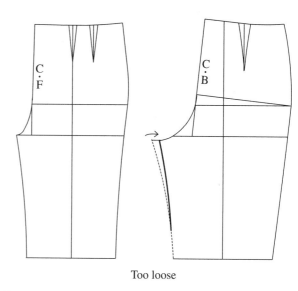

Too loose

Drawing 3.53

Drawing 3.54. Crotch is too short or deep.

- Alter the pattern between the waist and hip lines. If more crotch depth is needed, cut the pattern between the waist and hip lines, then spread the two pieces apart as necessary. If less crotch depth

is needed, fold accordion-style between the waist and hip lines, then bring the folded section either up or down half the amount necessary. Once adjusted, reshape the hip curve and the center front and back seams.

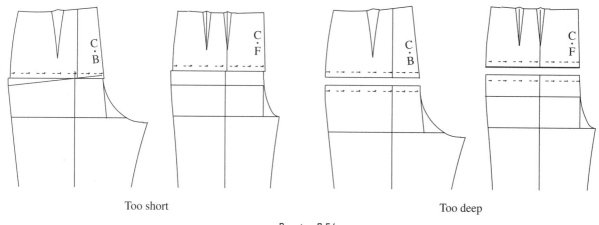

Too short

Too deep

Drawing 3.54

Drawing 3.55. Back seat is too tight or loose.

- Increase or decrease the crotch curve on the back pattern, tapering into the original upper part of the back seat area. The alteration should be restricted to the area between the crotch inseam and the upper thigh area.

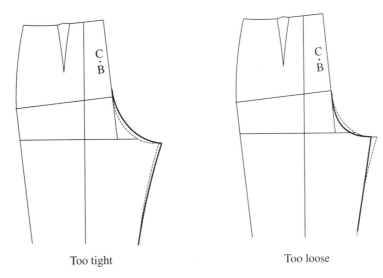

Too tight   Too loose

Drawing 3.55

Drawing 3.56. Waist or hip is too tight or loose.

- Increase or decrease the waist dart intake. Add or subtract at the side seam.

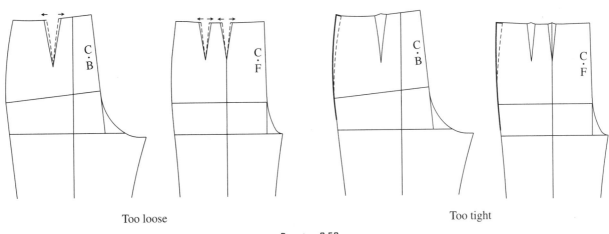

Too loose   Too tight

Drawing 3.56

Drawing 3.57. Large stomach.

- Extend the center front ¹/₂" to 2" above the waist-line, taper in ¹/₂" to 1" on the waist at the center front and the same amount on the waist at the side seam. Draw the new hip curve, blending into the side seam.

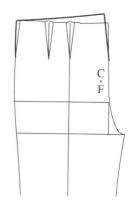

Drawing 3.57

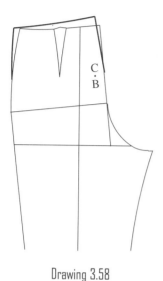

Drawing 3.58

Drawing 3.58. Protruding buttocks.

- Slash from the center back at the hip line to, but not through, the side seam. Spread ¹/₂" to 2" at the center back, then reshape the center back seam.

Drawing 3.59. Flat buttocks.

- Slash from the center back at the hip line to, but not through, the side seam. Fold ¹/₂" to 2" at the center back, then reshape the center back seam.

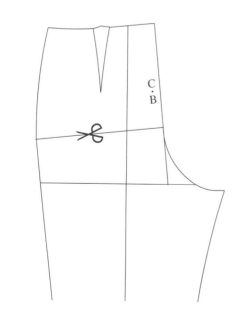

Drawing 3.59

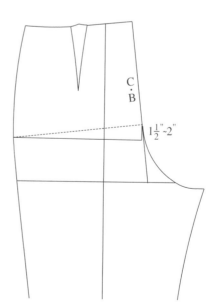

$1\frac{1}{2}"$~2"

Chapter Four

THE SKIRT

INTRODUCTION TO THE SKIRT

$\mathcal{T}$he skirt covers the lower part of the body in a tubular shape, from the waist down to the desired length. Historically, skirt silhouettes have evolved under the combined influences of economics, custom, and social change. The chief influences on a skirt silhouette are its length and the sweep. Changing the position of the waistline, adding design details (e.g., darts, pleats, shirring), and using different types of fabric can all create various skirt styles.

Drawing 4.1. Skirt components.

A. Waistband.
B. Center front.
C. Side seam.
D. Front dart.
E. Hemline.
F. Center back.
G. Back dart.
H. Back zipper.
I. Back slit or pleat.
J. Button.
K. Buttonhole.

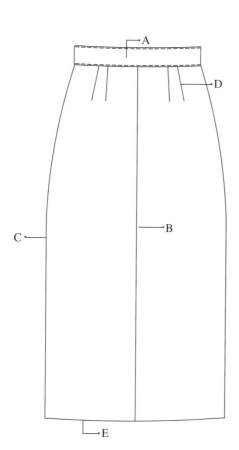
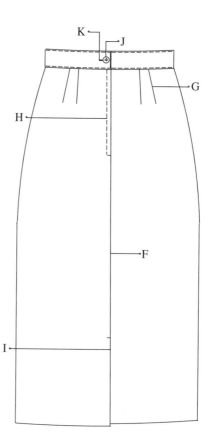

Drawing 4.1

Skirt Length Variations

Changes in the length of the skirt can create a new look and define the occasion for which it is worn. These changes can also be a reflection or an adaptation of a current style or of a style worn in an earlier era.

Skirt Lengths by Style
- Micro-mini skirt length = Mid-thigh or above.
- Mini skirt length = 4″ or more above the knee.
- Natural line/knee-length skirt length = Knee level.
- Midi skirt length = Between knee level and mid-calf (the "Chanel" line).
- Maxi skirt length = Lower calf level.
- Long skirt length = Ankle level.

| Micro-mini | Mini | Knee length | Midi | Maxi | Long |

Illustration 4.1

Common Skirt Lengths

The following chart illustrates the names and typical lengths for various common skirt lengths. Note that this information is also applicable to pants and dress lengths.

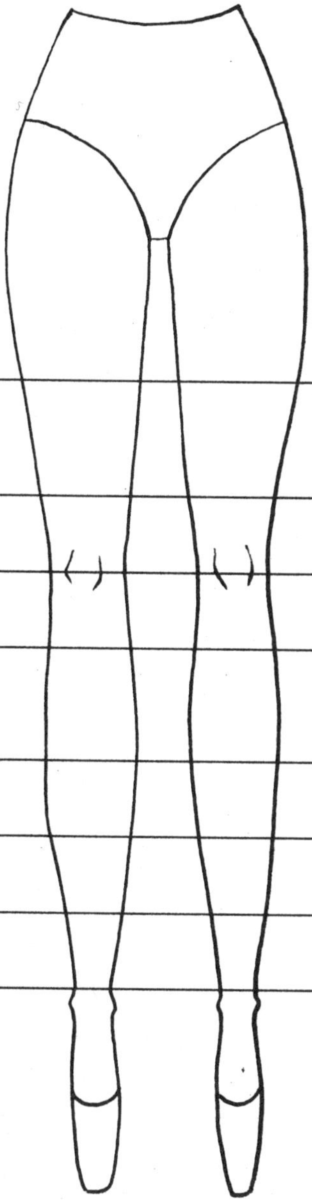

			Short	Average	Tall
Thigh		Mid-thigh	33	34	35
		Above knee	35	36	37
Knee		Knee length	36/37	38/39	40/41
		Below knee	39	41	43
Calf		Mid-calf	44	46	48
		Low calf	46	48	50
Long		Tea length	48	50	52
		Ankle length	50	52	54

Illustration 4.2

Skirt Silhouette Variations

The skirt silhouette can be altered by dart manipulation and the slash and spread method. Skirt silhouettes fall into six categories: straight, A-line, gathered, circular, pegged, and trumpet.

Drawing 4.2. Straight skirt.

- This style has equal hip and hem circumferences. It fits at the waist, then falls straight down from the hips to the hem.

Drawing 4.2

Illustration 4.3

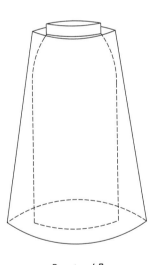

Drawing 4.3

Illustration 4.4

Drawing 4.3. A-line skirt.

- This style has a hem circumference greater than its hip circumference. It fits at the waist and then flares outward from the hips to form an A-shaped silhouette.

Drawing 4.4. Gathered skirt.

- This style has equal waist, hip, and hem circumferences, yet achieves a gathered, or "shirred," effect at the waist.

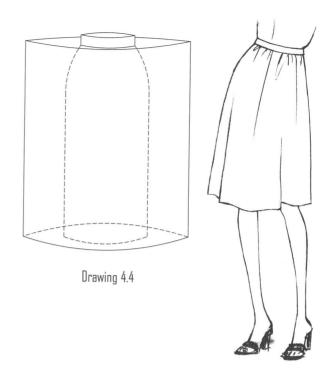

Drawing 4.4

Illustration 4.5

Drawing 4.5. Circular skirt.

- This style flares out from the waistline to a wide hemline circumference. Generally based on 180°, 270°, and 360° circular sections, the finished circular skirt will be fuller, and have varying silhouettes, the greater the section used.

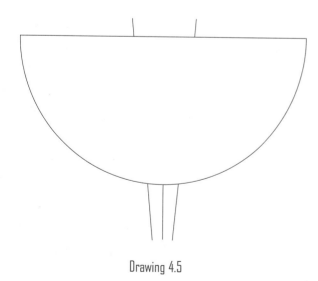

Drawing 4.5

Illustration 4.6

Drawing 4.6. Pegged skirt.

- This style is tapered from the hips so that the hem circumference is less than the hip circumference. The hips may be accentuated by adding gathers or pleats at the waistline.

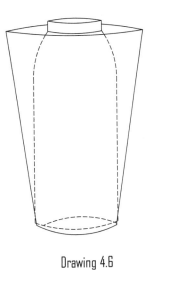

Drawing 4.6

Illustration 4.7

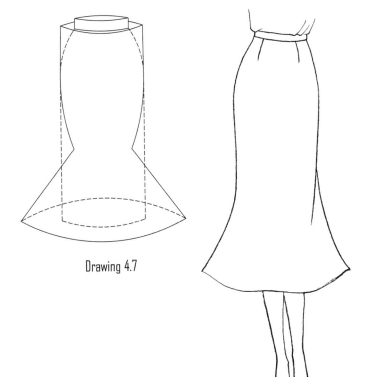

Drawing 4.7

Illustration 4.8

Drawing 4.7. Trumpet skirt.

- This style tapers from a point somewhere below the hip line and then flares out to the hemline. Adding to the hem circumference will increase the flare of the hem.

Waistline Variations

To create different style lines, the waistline on a skirt may be placed at one of three locations: natural, low, or high. Both higher and lower waistlines can vary greatly in placement from the natural waistline. The waistline can also be finished in one of four ways: classic waistband, pull-on waistband, facing, or bias binding.

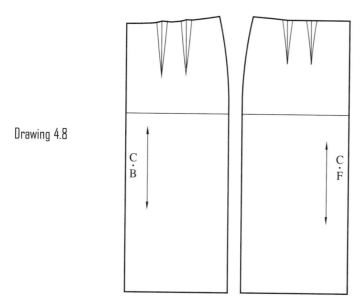

Drawing 4.8

Drawing 4.8. Natural waistline.

- Use the waistline from the sloper, without adjustment.

Illustration 4.9

Drawing 4.9. Low waistline.

- Lower the waistline 2″, or any amount desired.
- Measure in ¼″ from each side seam.
- Reshape the hip curve.

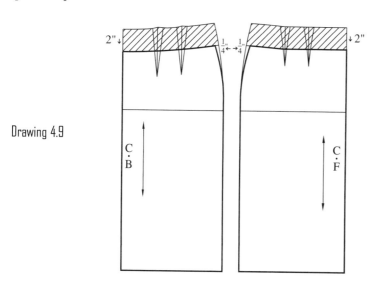

Drawing 4.9

Illustration 4.10

- Square up from the waistline 2¼" at center back and 2" at center front.
- Square up 2" from the waistline at each side seam.
- Draw the new waistline.
- Square up from the dart legs to the new waistline.
- Measure in ⅛" from each dart leg and reshape each dart.

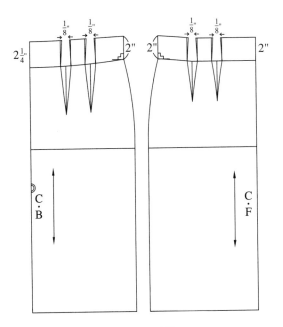

Drawing 4.10

Illustration 4.11

Dart Manipulation

All or part of the waist darts may be transferred to
the hem by first closing them and then opening an
equivalent angle of flare at the hem. The more dart
that is transferred to the hem, the greater the resulting flare at the hem.

Drawing 4.11. One dart transferred to the hem.

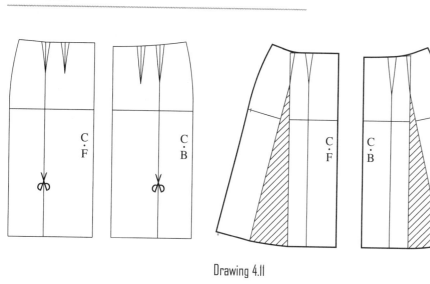

Drawing 4.11

Illustration 4.12

Drawing 4.12. Two darts transferred to the hem.

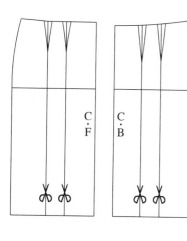

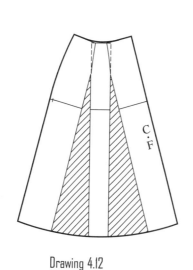

Drawing 4.12

Illustration 4.13

The front and back skirt patterns have different amounts of dart intake, resulting in different hem circumferences and a garment that does not fall and flow properly. Thus, it is always necessary to balance the amount of flare at the front and back hems.

Drawing 4.13. Balancing the front and back hem circumferences.

- Align the front and back skirt pattern pieces at the center front and back.
- Determine the difference between the front and back hems and divide this amount in half.
- Add this amount to the smaller hem circumference.
- Subtract it from the wider pattern piece.

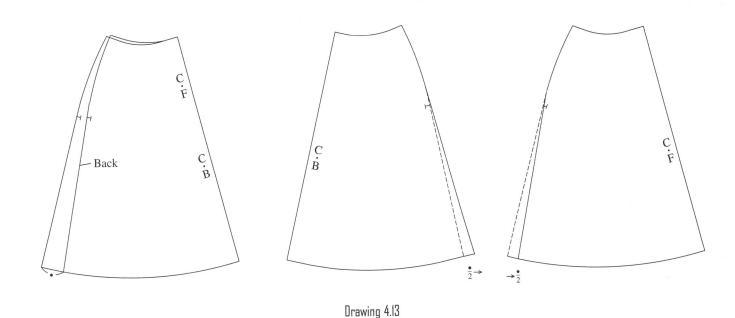

Drawing 4.13

One-Dart Skirt

Generally, placing two darts on pants or a skirt will provide a better shape and fit. The two darts may even be combined, in which case they are generally repositioned on the center of the waistline. When one dart is used, it must be lengthened for a smooth fit.

Drawing 4.14.

- Combine the two darts into one.
- Reposition the new dart at the center of the waist or as desired.
- Lengthen the dart to 4½″ in front and 5″ in back.

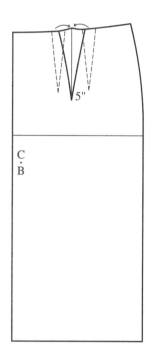
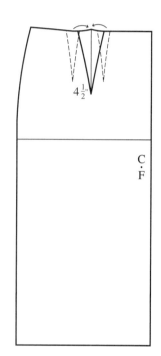

Drawing 4.14

Illustration 4.14

TAPERED SKIRT

$\mathcal{T}$he tapered skirt fits snugly at the waist and hip, and tapers from the hip to the hem. Tapered skirts usually feature a slit at the center back or side seam(s), to allow for leg movement.

Illustration 4.15

Pattern Analysis
- The side seam is tapered from the hip line.
- Darts are shifted toward the side seam.
- The skirt is vented at the center back.
- There is a center back zipper.
- The lining pattern is developed from the skirt pattern.
- Marker directions are provided for garment and lining.

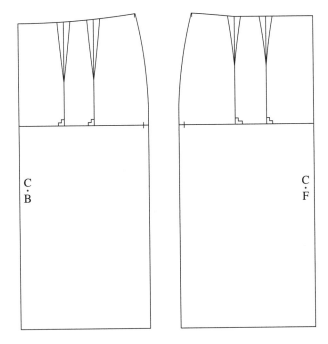

Drawing 4.15

Drawing 4.15. Back and front.

- Trace the skirt sloper.

Drawing 4.16. **Back**

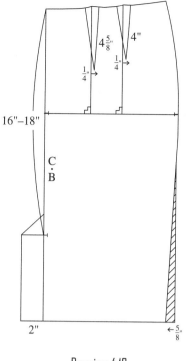

- Redraw the dart closest to the center back $4\frac{5}{8}''$ long and the other dart $4''$ long.
- Move the dart points $\frac{1}{4}''$ toward the side seam.
- Measure in $\frac{5}{8}''$ from the side seam at the hem, then taper the side seam from the hip to the hem.

Vent at center back:
- Measure down $16''$ to $18''$ from the waistline then out $2''$ at the center back and mark.
- Square down to the hem from the mark.
- Shape the top of the vent with a diagonal line, as shown.

Drawing 4.16

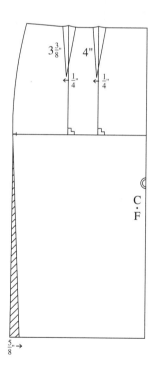

Drawing 4.17

Drawing 4.17. **Front.**

- Redraw the dart closest to the center front $4''$ long and the other dart $3\frac{3}{8}''$ long.
- Move the dart points $\frac{1}{4}''$ toward the side seam.
- Measure in $\frac{5}{8}''$ from the side seam at the hem, then taper the side seam from the hip line to the hem.

Reshaping the waistline:
- Fold the waist darts toward the center back and the center front and reshape the waistline.

Drawing 4.18. **Waistband.**

- Draw the waistband, using the following dimensions:
  Length = Waist circumference plus $\frac{1}{2}''$.
  Height = $1\frac{1}{4}''$.
  Button extension = $1''$.

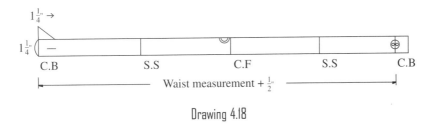

Drawing 4.18

Drawing 4.19. **Finished patterns.**

- Label the pattern pieces and mark the notches and grain lines, as shown.

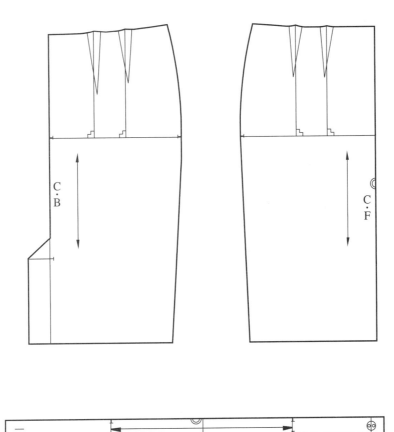

Drawing 4.19

Drawing 4.20. Seam allowances.

- Add the seam allowances:
    Waistline, waistband, slit = $^3/_8''$.
    Center back = $^3/_4''$
    Side seams = $^5/_8''$.
    Hems = 2''.
- * **Note:** Fold the hem up, then redraw the side seam so that the hem follows the taper, as shown.

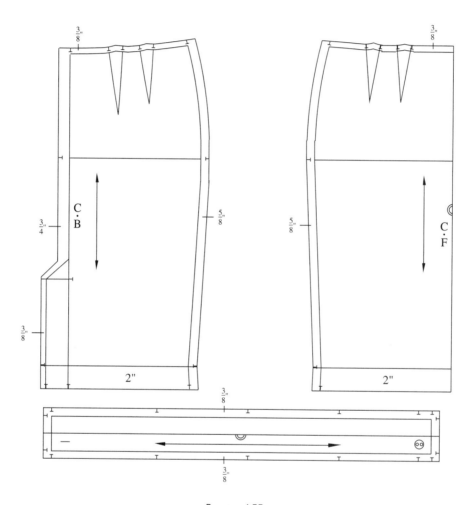

Drawing 4.20

Drawing 4.21. Lining.

* **Note:** Lining patterns are drawn with dashed lines.

Back right side:
- Trace the back right skirt pattern.
- Add $1/8''$ to the side seam.
- Raise the hem $3/4''$.
- Remark the waist darts as 2″-long pleats, as shown.

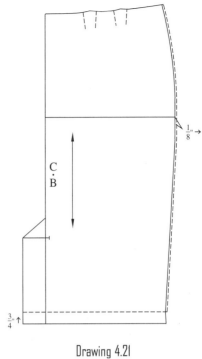

Drawing 4.21

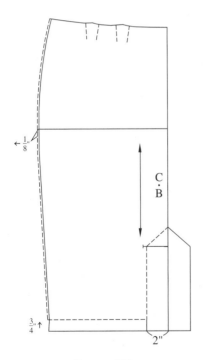

Drawing 4.22

Drawing 4.22.

Back left side:
- Flip the right side pattern over.
- Fold the center back line at the vent and trace the center back line.
- Measure in 2″ from the center back at the hem and draw the vent shape, eliminating the vent from the left side skirt.

Drawing 4.23. Front lining.

- Trace the front right skirt.
- Add $^1/_8''$ to the side seam.
- Raise the hem $^3/_4''$.
- Remark the waist darts as 2″-long pleats, as shown.

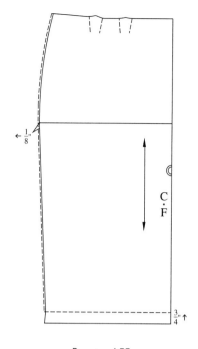

Drawing 4.23

Drawing 4.24. Lining seam allowances.

- Add the seam allowances:
    Waistline and slit = $^3/_8''$.
    Side seams = $^5/_8''$.
    Center back = $^3/_4''$.
    Hems = $1^1/_4''$.

* **Note:** Fold the hem up, then redraw the side seam so that the hem follows the taper, as shown.

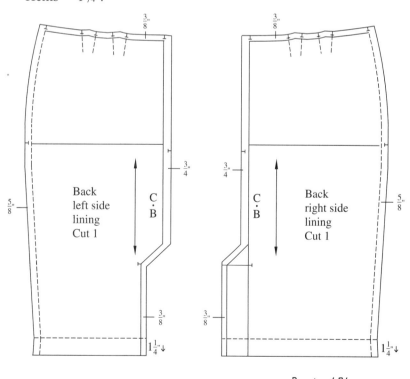

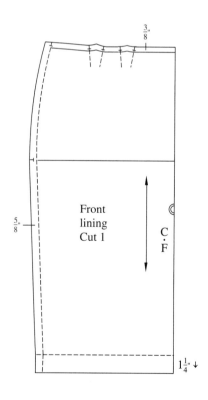

Drawing 4.24

The garment marker is produced by laying all of the pattern pieces out on the fabric. The pattern pieces should be placed so that their grain lines match the straight grain of the fabric. The width of the fabric and sizes of the pattern pieces will dictate how the pieces are laid. Much of this process is handled by computers in industry, but it is still important to be familiar with the relationship between fabric and pattern.

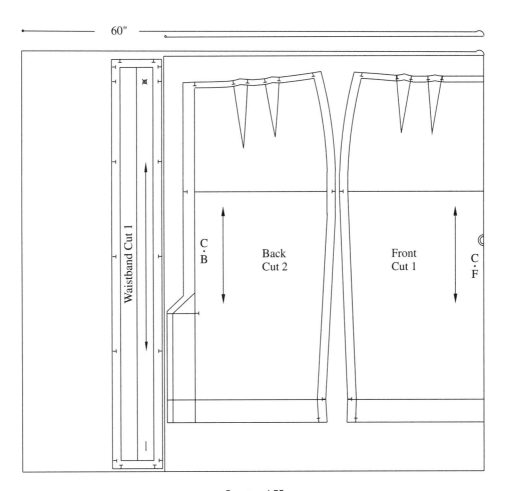

Drawing 4.25

As with the garment marker, the lining marker is produced by laying all of the pattern pieces out on the
fabric. The pattern pieces should be placed so that
their grain lines match the straight grain of the fabric.
The width of the fabric and sizes of the pattern pieces
will dictate how the pieces are laid. Again, much of
this process is handled by computers in industry, but it
is still important to be familiar with the relationship
between fabric and pattern.

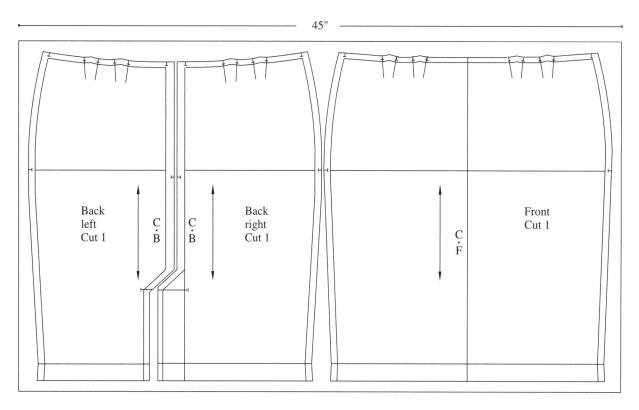

Drawing 4.26

SKIRT CONSTRUCTION

Drawing 4.27. Preparation.

- Attach the interfacing to the wrong sides of the fabric on the zipper placement, to the vent on the left side of the skirt, and to the waistband.

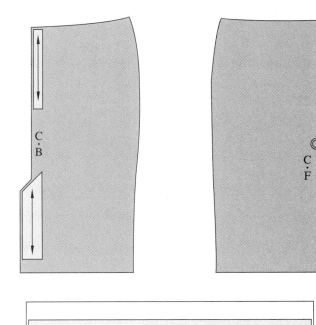

Drawing 4.27

Drawing 4.28.

- Zigzag or serge the seam allowance on the side, back, and hem to keep the fabric from fraying.
- Turn up the hemline, then press.

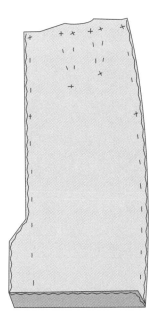 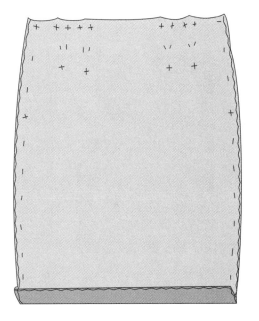

Drawing 4.28

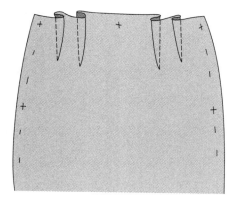

Drawing 4.29

Drawing 4.29. Garment construction.

- Sew the front and back darts, then press toward the center front and center back.

Drawing 4.30.

- Sew the center back seam between the notches and across the top of the vent up to $^3/_8''$ from the cut edge.
- Press and open the center back seam and zipper opening, then press the vent to one side.

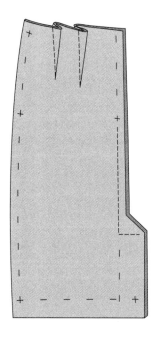 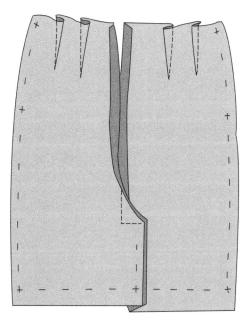

Drawing 4.30

- Press and open the left side of the zipper opening on the center back seam.
- Shift the right seam allowance $\frac{1}{8}''$ over the seam line, then press.
- Align the teeth of the closed zipper with the fold of the right seam allowance and stitch in place.
- With the zipper closed, place the overlap of the garment over the zipper and baste in place.
- Topstitch the left side of the zipper in place approximately $\frac{3}{8}''$ from the center back seam edge, at the bottom of the zipper opening.
- Sew the front and back side seams with the right sides together.

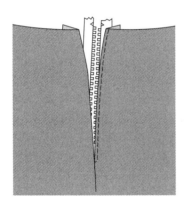 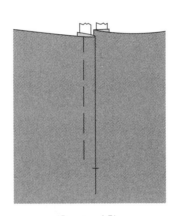 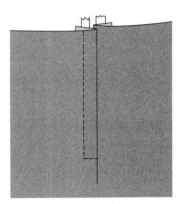

Drawing 4.31

Drawing 4.32. Lining construction.

- Sew the darts as tucks on the front and back panels of the lining fabric.
- Sew the center back seam between the notches and across the top of the vent up to $3/8''$, then serge or zigzag the seam allowances.
- At the zipper opening, fold the fabric over $3/8''$, then fold again $3/8''$ and stitch.
- Sew the side seams and then serge or zigzag the seam allowances.
- Press all seam allowances toward the back of the skirt.
- Fold the hem of the lining up $3/8''$, then fold again $3/4''$ and stitch.

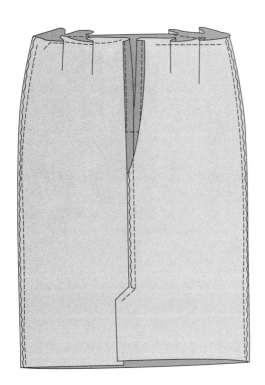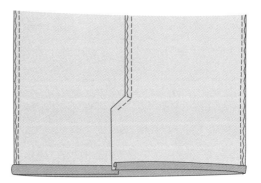

Drawing 4.32

Drawing 4.33. Lining attachment.

- Place the wrong sides of the garment and lining together.
- Match all notches and side seams, then baste together at the waistline.
- Place the extended edge of the waistband on the right side of the garment; pin into place, matching all markings and notches; and then baste together.
- Stitch the waistband to the garment.

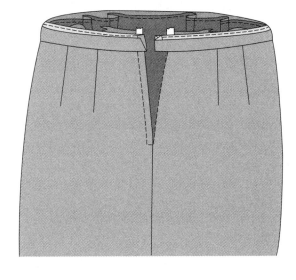

Drawing 4.33

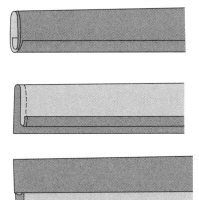

Drawing 4.34

Drawing 4.34. Waistband construction.

- Fold the waistband in half, right sides together.
- Fold up the seam allowance of the noninterfaced side, then press.
- Stitch the sides together from the top to the folded seam allowance.
- Trim the top corner of the side seam at an angle.
- Turn the waistband right side out, then press.

Drawing 4.35.

- Turn up the waistband, then press.
- Fold the seam allowance into the waistband, then press.
- Stitch the waistband closed by "stitching in the ditch" on the right side of the garment.

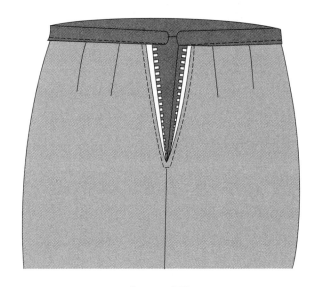

Drawing 4.35

Drawing 4.36. Vent.

Left side vent:
- Sew the seam allowance of the lining to the garment vent with the right sides together.
- Press the seam allowance toward the side seam.
- Turn the right side out and press.
- Fold the skirt hem up under the lining.
- Catch stitch the hem in place.
- The lining will fold over the hem to provide a clean finish.

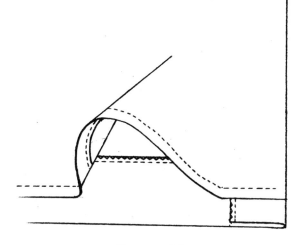

Illustration 4.16

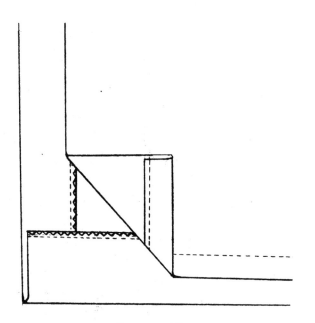

Illustration 4.17

Drawing 4.37.

Right side vent:
- Sew the seam allowance of the lining to the vent overlap of the skirt.
- Turn the right side out, then press.
- Fold the skirt hem to overlap the vent.
- Catch stitch the hem in place.

- Press the hem, then catch stitch in place.
- Tack the lining to the skirt at the hem with a thread chain, from lining to garment, at the side seams.

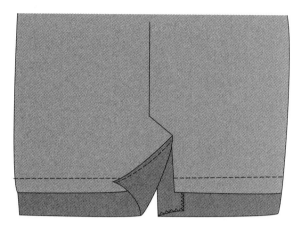
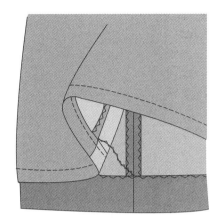

Drawing 4.38

Drawing 4.39. **Fasten the center back of the waistband.**

- Create a buttonhole, then attach a button at waist-band opening.
- Sew the hook and eye into place at the waistband opening.
- Press the entire garment.

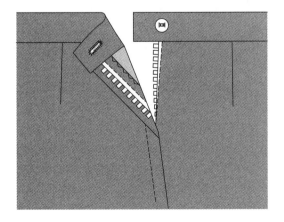
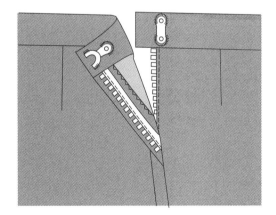

Drawing 4.39

A-LINE SKIRT

$\mathcal{T}$he A-line skirt fits at the waist and then flares outward from the hips to form a silhouette in the shape of the letter "A." This shape is achieved by transferring a portion of the waist dart to the hem. The greater the portion of the dart that is transferred, the greater the resulting flare.

Pattern Analysis
- Portions of the front and back waist darts are transferred to the hem to spread it 2″.
- The remaining darts are combined into a single dart.
- Side zipper.

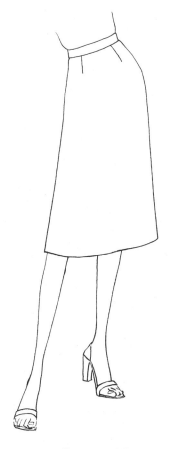

Illustration 4.18

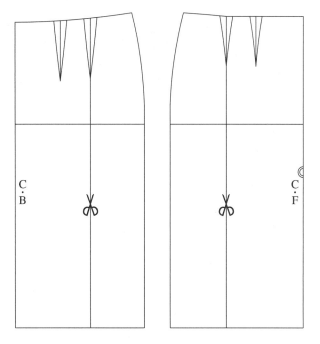

Drawing 4.40

Drawing 4.40. Back and front.

- Trace the skirt sloper.
- Draw the slash lines parallel to the center back and front, from the darts closest to the side seam to the hem.

Drawing 4.41. Back and front.

- Cut along the slash line to, but not through, the dart point.
- Close the dart until the slash line spreads open 2″ at the hem.

- Combine the remaining dart intakes and center the dart on the waistline.
- Lengthen each dart $^3/_8$″ to $^3/_4$″.
- Reshape the hem.

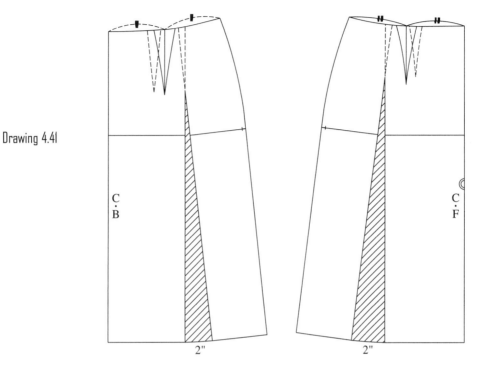

Drawing 4.41

Drawing 4.42. Finished patterns.

- Label the pattern pieces and mark the notches and grain lines, as shown.

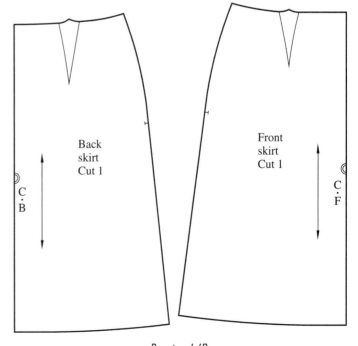

Drawing 4.42

FLARED YOKE SKIRT

The yoke style line runs from the side seam at the abdomen to the front and back, following the distinctive W-shaped lines, as shown.

Pattern Analysis
- There are front and back yokes with distinctive style lines.
- Waist darts are closed.
- Slash and spread is used to add flare.

Illustration 4.19

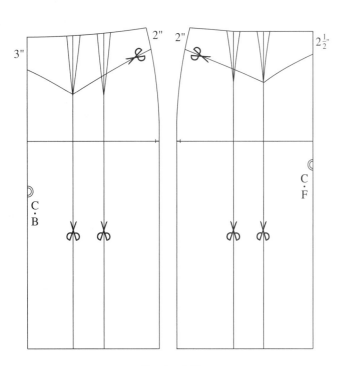

Drawing 4.43

Drawing 4.43. Back and front.

- Trace the skirt sloper.
- Draw the desired yoke style line.
- Draw two slash lines parallel to the center back and front, from the dart point to the hem.

Drawing 4.44. **Back and front yoke.**

- Separate the yoke.
- Close the darts and reshape the yoke.

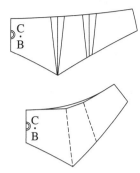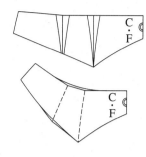

Drawing 4.44

Drawing 4.45. **Back and front skirt.**

- Cut along the slash lines to, but not through, the top.
- Spread the slash lines open 2″ at the hem.
- * **Note:** The amount of flare is equal on each side for a balanced flare.
- Reshape the hem.

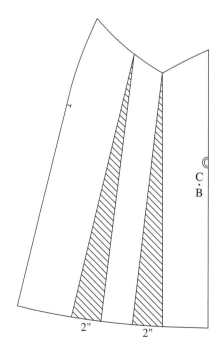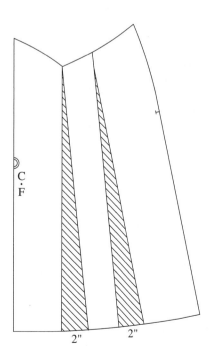

Drawing 4.45

• Label the pattern pieces and mark the notches and
  grain lines, as shown.

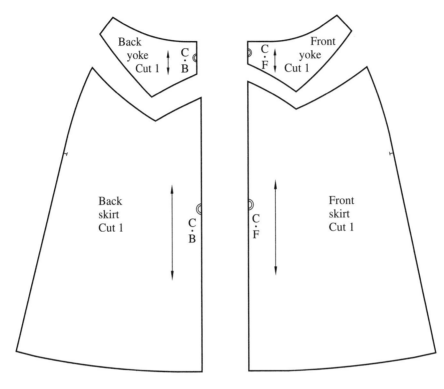

Drawing 4.46

GORED SKIRT

The gored skirt has individual gores, or panels, that collectively fit around the waist and gradually flare to the hemline. The number of panels for a gored skirt starts at four. The fullness is added at the hem then connected at or below the hipline. By varying the connection point, a trumpet shape or A-line may be created.

1. Four-Gore Skirt

This skirt features four panels, with no side seams.

Pattern Analysis
- The hip circumference is divided into four parts.
- Waist darts are combined and centered on the gore lines, then converted to gore lines.
- Fullness is added from the hip line to the hem of each side panel to achieve the A-line silhouette.
- Front and back side seams are combined to form a dart.

Illustration 4.20

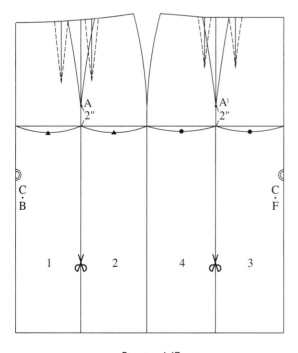

Drawing 4.47

Drawing 4.47. Back and front.

- Trace the skirt sloper.
- Mark the hip line midpoint on both slopers.
- Draw the gore lines parallel to the center back and front, from the waistline to the hem, passing through the midpoint.
- Measure up 2″ from the hip line on the gore lines, labeling A and A′ as shown.
- Combine the two darts into one dart.
- Center the new dart on the gore line, using A and A′ as the new dart points.

Drawing 4.48. Back and front.

- Cut along the gore line, eliminating the dart.
- Trace each panel separately.
- Measure out $^3/_8''$ from each gore line at the hem, excluding the center back and front, and mark.
- Redraw the gore lines and side seams, connecting points A and A′ to the marks, as shown.

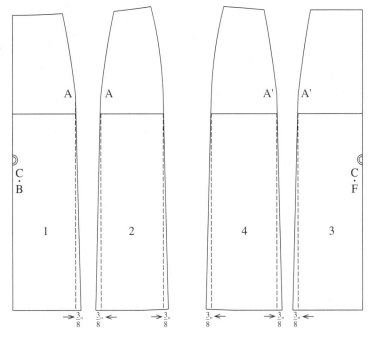

Drawing 4.48

Drawing 4.49. Finished patterns.

- Attach the back and front patterns at the side seam.
- Label the pattern pieces and mark the notches and grain lines, as shown.

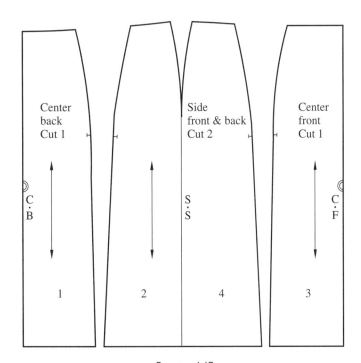

Drawing 4.49

Drawing 4.50.

- Fold the dart and reshape the waistline.

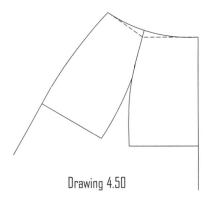

Drawing 4.50

2. Six-Gore Skirt

This skirt features six panels and an A-line silhouette.

Pattern Analysis
- The hip circumference is divided into six parts.
- Waist darts are combined and centered on the gore lines, then converted to gore lines.
- Fullness is added from the hip line to the hem of each side panel to achieve the A-line silhouette.

Illustration 4.21

Drawing 4.51. **Back and front.**

- Trace the skirt sloper.
- Divide the hip line into thirds.
- Draw a gore line parallel to the center back and front, passing through the first division, as shown.
- Combine the two darts into one, centered on the gore line.

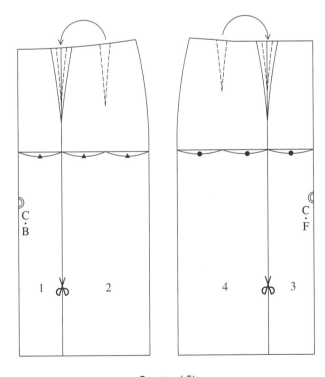

Drawing 4.51

Drawing 4.52.

- Cut along the gore lines, eliminating the darts.
- Trace each panel separately.

- Measure out $1\frac{1}{2}''$ from each gore line at the hem, excluding the center back and front, and mark.
- Draw the new gore line from the hip line to the mark at the hem.

Drawing 4.52

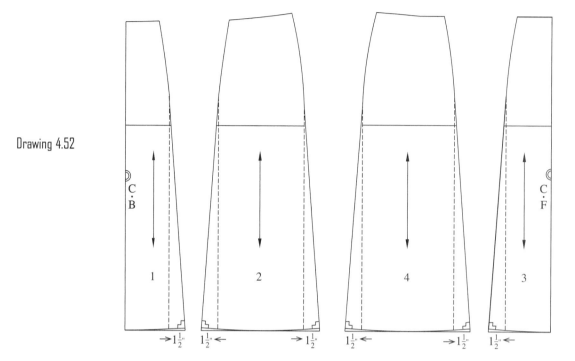

Drawing 4.53. Finished patterns.

- Label the pattern pieces and mark the notches and grain lines, as shown.

Drawing 4.53

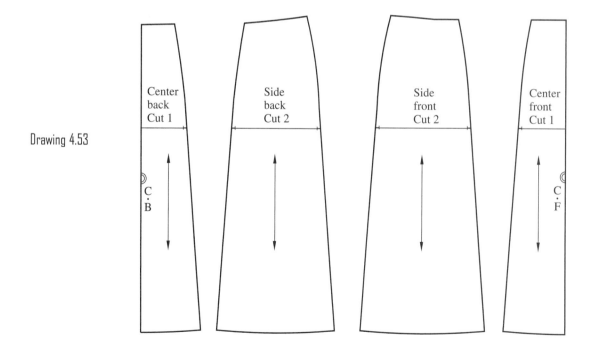

3. Ten-Gore Skirt

This skirt features ten panels and a trumpet silhouette.

Pattern Analysis
- The hip circumference is divided into ten parts.
- Waist darts are centered on the gore lines, then converted to gore lines.
- Flare is added from the knee to the hem of each side panel to achieve the trumpet silhouette.

Illustration 4.22

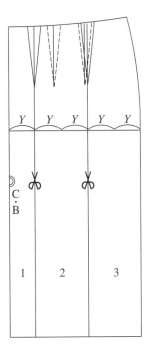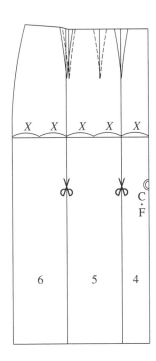

Drawing 4.54

Drawing 4.54. Back and front.

- Trace the skirt sloper.
- Divide the front hip line by five, and call this value X.
- Divide the back hip line by five, and call this value Y.
- Measure in X on the hip line, from the center front, and mark.
- Measure in Y on the hip line, from the center back, and mark.
- Measure in two times X from that mark, from the center front, and mark.
- Measure in two times Y from that mark, from the center back, and mark.
- Draw the gore lines parallel to the center back and front, passing through the marks.
- Center the darts on the gore lines.

Drawing 4.55. Back and front.

- Cut along the gore lines, converting the dart to a side seam.
- Draw a horizontal guideline.
- Trace each panel separately, matching the hip line to the guideline.
- Measure out 3″ from each gore line at the hem, excluding the center back and front, and mark.

* **Note:** The flare should be equal on each piece to keep balance.
- Draw the new gore line from the hip line to the mark at the hem.
* **Note:** The flare may blend from any point between the hip and knee, to the hem.
- Reshape the hem, ending square to each seam.

Drawing 4.55

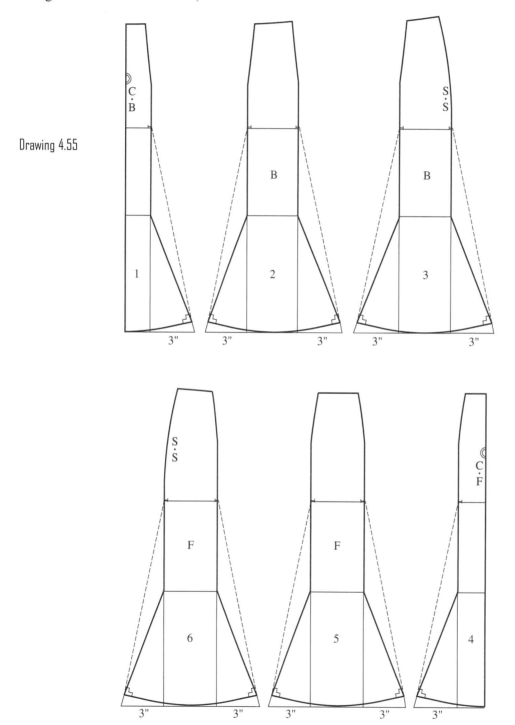

- Smooth the gore lines.
- Label the pattern pieces and mark the notches and
  grain lines, as shown.

Drawing 4.56

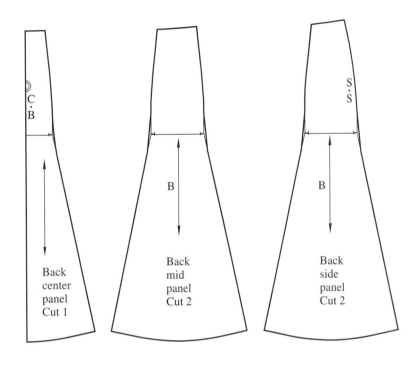

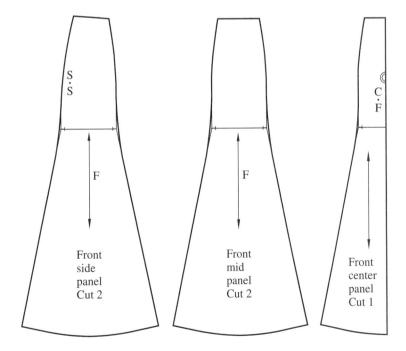

CIRCULAR SKIRT

The circular skirt has no darts at the waist and flares out from the waistline to a wide circumference at the hemline. Circular skirts fall into the following categorizes: quarter, half, three-quarter, and full. Various silhouettes can be created by varying the amount of fullness. This skirt will hang according to the direction of the grain line on the pattern pieces.

180°   270°   360°

Illustration 4.23

When creating patterns for 270° and 360° circular skirts, $1\frac{1}{2}''$ to $2''$ is generally subtracted from the target waist measurement to allow for the natural easing and stretching of fabric.

This difference between actual and calculated waist diameters necessitates a slight adjustment in the waistline of skirt patterns. The adjustments required for the pattern pieces of 270° and 360° skirts ranging from $24''$ to $40''$ have been calculated for the following tables, using this formula:

1. For waist sizes between $24''$ and $28''$, subtract $1\frac{1}{2}''$ and call the resulting value X. For waist sizes between $29''$ and $40''$, subtract $2''$ and call the resulting value X.

2. From the table, subtract the appropriate "Diameter" column value (Y) from X and call the resulting value Z.

3. If Z is a positive number, add it to the waistline of the skirt pattern. If Z is a negative number, subtract it from the waistline of the skirt pattern.

Example 1: $24''$ waistline

1. $X = 24'' - 1\frac{1}{2}'' = 22\frac{1}{2}''$
2. Y (from table) $= 22\frac{3}{4}''$
3. $Z = 22\frac{1}{2}'' - 22\frac{3}{4}'' = -\frac{1}{4}''$
4. $\frac{1}{4}''$ will be subtracted from the waistline on the skirt pattern.

Example 2: $40''$ waistline

1. $X = 40'' - 2'' = 38''$
2. Y (from table) $= 39\frac{1}{2}''$
3. $Z = 38'' - 39\frac{1}{2}'' = -1\frac{1}{2}''$
4. $1\frac{1}{2}''$ will be subtracted from the waistline on the skirt pattern.

360° Circular Skirt Radius Chart
Calculations for waists of 24″ through 40″ were made based on the observation that the waist radius equals one sixth of the waist measure minus $^3/_8″$ ($^w/_6 - ^3/_8″$).

Actual Waist Measurement	Adjusted Waist Measurement (X)	Calculated Radius ($^w/_6 - ^3/_8″$)	Diameter (Y)	Required Adjustment (Z) = Y − X
24	$22^1/_2″$	$3^5/_8″$	$22^3/_4″$	
25	$23^1/_2″$	$3^{13}/_{16}″$	$23^{13}/_{16}″$	
26	$24^1/_2″$	$3^{15}/_{16}″$	$24^7/_8″$	
27	$25^1/_2″$	$4^1/_8″$	$25^7/_8″$	
28	$26^1/_2″$	$4^5/_{16}″$	$26^{15}/_{16}″$	
29	$27″$	$4^7/_{16}″$	28	
30	$28″$	$4^5/_8″$	$29^1/_{16}″$	
31	$29″$	$4^{13}/_{16}″$	$30^1/_{16}″$	
32	$30″$	$4^{15}/_{16}″$	$31^1/_8″$	
33	$31″$	$5^1/_8″$	$32^3/_{16}″$	
34	$32″$	$5^5/_{16}″$	$33^1/_4″$	
35	$33″$	$5^7/_{16}″$	$34^1/_4″$	
36	$34″$	$5^5/_8″$	$35^5/_{16}″$	
37	$35″$	$5^{13}/_{16}″$	$36^3/_8″$	
38	$36″$	$5^{15}/_{16}″$	$37^7/_{16}″$	
39	$37″$	$6^1/_8″$	$38^7/_{16}″$	
40	$38″$	$6^5/_{16}″$	$39^1/_2″$	

270° Circular Skirt Radius Chart
Calculations for waists of 24″ through 40″ were
made based on the observation that the waist radius
equals the waist measure divided by 4.86 ($^w/_{4.86}$).

Actual Waist Measurement	Adjusted Waist Measurement (X)	Calculated Radius ($^w/_{4.86}$″)	Diameter (Y)	Required Adjustment (Z) = Y − X
24	23″	$4^{15}/_{16}$″	$23^1/_4$″	
25	24″	$5^1/_8$″	$24^1/_4$″	
26	25″	$5^3/_8$″	$25^3/_{16}$″	
27	26″	$5^9/_{16}$″	$26^3/_{16}$″	
28	27″	$5^3/_4$″	$27^1/_8$″	
29	$27^1/_2$″	$5^{15}/_{16}$″	$28^1/_8$″	
30	$28^1/_2$″	$6^3/_{16}$″	$29^1/_{16}$″	
31	$29^1/_2$″	$6^3/_8$″	$30^1/_{16}$″	
32	$30^1/_2$″	$6^3/_{16}$″	31″	
33	$31^1/_2$″	$6^{13}/_{16}$″	32″	
34	$32^1/_2$″	7″	$32^{15}/_{16}$″	
35	$33^1/_2$″	$7^3/_{16}$″	$33^{15}/_{16}$″	
36	$34^1/_2$″	$7^7/_{16}$″	$34^7/_8$″	
37	$35^1/_2$″	$7^5/_8$″	$35^7/_8$″	
38	$36^1/_2$″	$7^{13}/_{16}$″	$36^{13}/_{16}$″	
39	$37^1/_2$″	8″	$37^{13}/_{16}$″	
40	$38^1/_2$″	$8^1/_4$″	$38^3/_4$″	

1. 360° Circular Skirt

Drawing 4.57. Back and front.

- Prepare a 30″ by 60″ piece of paper.
- Fold the paper in half.
- Draw a line perpendicular to the fold line, leaving a 1″ seam allowance above the line.
- XY = Calculated radius from chart ($^w/_6 - {^3/_8}''$).
- XY′ = XY.

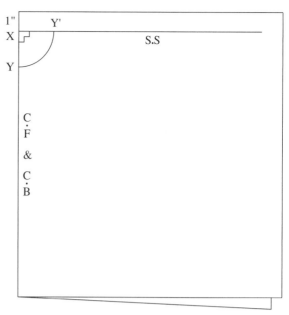

Drawing 4.57

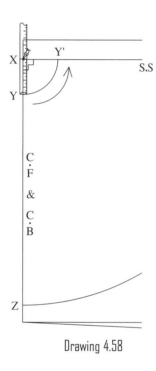

Drawing 4.58

Drawing 4.58.

- Place the tape measure on line XY, match the metal tip to point Y, and secure the tape measure with a pushpin at point X.
- Rotate the metal tip of the tape measure up, with a pencil, from point Y to Y′.
  Example: If XY = 6″, then secure the tape measure with a pushpin at 6″ on point X and rotate the metal tip of the tape, with a pencil, from Y to Y′.

Drawing 4.59.

- YZ = Skirt length.
- Y′Z′ = YZ.
- Place the tape measure on line XZ, matching the metal tip to point Z.
- Secure the tape measure with a pushpin at point X.
- Rotate the metal tip of the tape measure up, with a pencil, connecting point Z to Z′.
- Label the center front and center back along YZ. Label the side seam along Y′Z′.

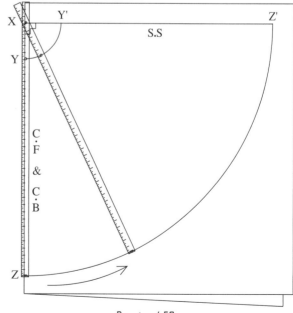

Drawing 4.59

Drawing 4.60.

- Cut out the pattern and unfold the paper.
- Trace the pattern to a new piece of paper and label each pattern, as shown.

Waistline and hem adjustment:
- Measure the waistline on the pattern. If this measurement is not $1^{1}/_{2}''$ to $2''$ smaller than the actual measurement, adjust the waistline, referring to the 360° circular skirt radius chart, earlier.
- Measure up $^{1}/_{4}''$ from the center front at the waistline and blend to the side seam.
- Measure down $^{1}/_{4}''$ from the center back at the waistline and blend to the side seam.
- Reshape the hemline by measuring up $^{1}/_{2}''$ between the side seam and the center back and front.

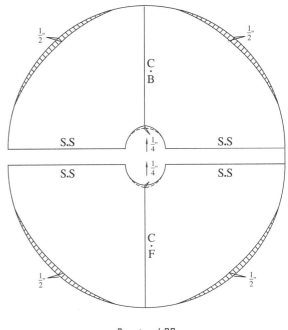

Drawing 4.60

Drawing 4.61. Finished patterns.

- The pattern can be cut into two or four pieces.
- Label the pattern pieces and mark the grain lines, as shown.

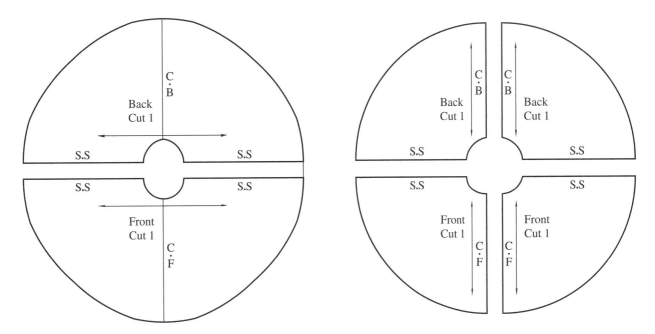

Drawing 4.61

Drawing 4.62. Grain line.

The skirt will hang differently according to the placement of the grain line on the pattern pieces. To achieve different drapes, the grain line can be placed parallel to the side seam, parallel to the center back and front, down the middle of the pattern piece, or on the bias.

- Figure 1: The grain line is placed parallel to the center front. The skirt will flare at both sides.
- Figure 2: The grain line is placed on the midpoint of center front and the side seam. The skirt will flare evenly.
- Figure 3: The grain line is placed parallel to the side seam. The skirt will flare at center front.
- Figure 4: The grain line is placed on the bias. The skirt will drape smoothly and evenly.

Illustration 4.24

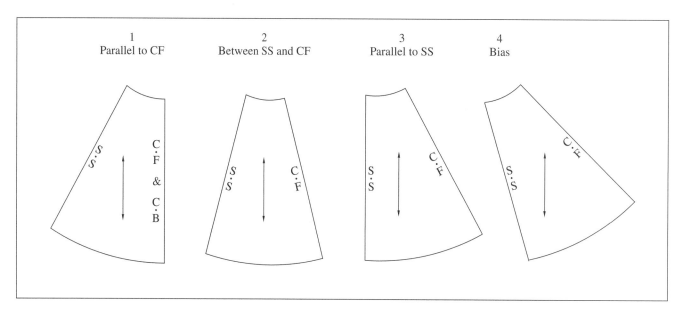

Drawing 4.62

2. 270° Circular Skirt

Drawing 4.63. Back and front.

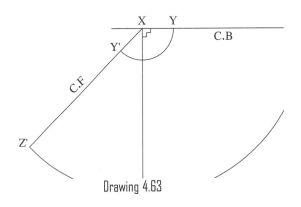

Drawing 4.63

- Draw a horizontal guideline.
- Draw a line perpendicular to the guideline and label X where it intersects the guideline.
- XY = Calculated radius from the earlier chart (^{W}/4.86).
- Draw a line at a 45° angle to the line drawn perpendicular to the guideline.
- XY′ = XY.
- Place the tape measure on line XY, match the metal tip to point Y, and secure the tape measure with a pushpin at point X.
- Rotate the metal tip of the tape measure up, with a pencil, from point Y to Y′.
- YZ = Skirt length.
- Y′Z′ = YZ.
- Place the tape measure on line XZ, matching the metal tip to point Z.
- Secure the tape measure with a pushpin at point X.
- Rotate the metal tip of the tape measure up, with a pencil, connecting point Z to Z′.
- Label the center back along XZ.
- Label the center front along XZ′.

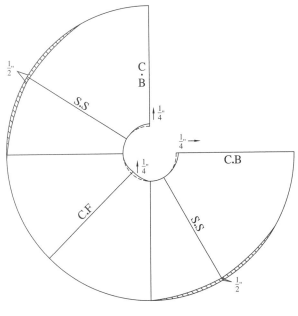

Drawing 4.64

Drawing 4.64.

- Cut out the pattern and unfold the paper.
- Trace the pattern to a new piece of paper, then label each segment, as shown.

Waistline and hem adjustment:
- Measure the waistline on the pattern. If this measurement is not 1$\frac{1}{2}$″ to 2″ smaller than the actual measurement, adjust the waistline, referring to the earlier 270° circular skirt radius chart.
- Measure up $\frac{1}{4}$″ from the center front at the waistline and blend to the side seam.
- Measure down $\frac{1}{4}$″ from the center back at the waistline and blend to the side seam.
- Reshape the hemline by measuring up $\frac{1}{2}$″ between the side seam and the center back and front.

- The pattern can be cut into two or four pieces.
- Label the pattern pieces and mark the notches and grain lines, as shown.

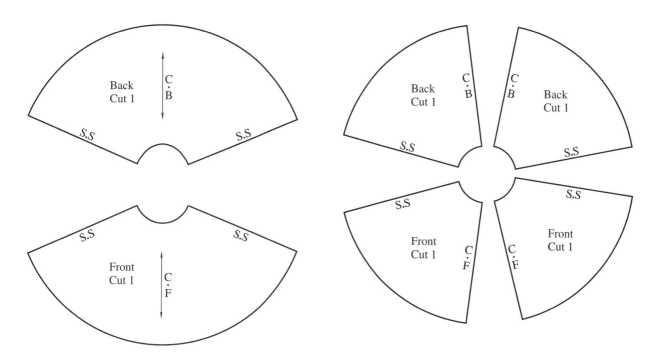

Drawing 4.65

3. 180° Circular Skirt

Because the 180° skirt is only a half circle, precise adjustment by formula is not necessary, as with the 270° and 360° skirts. Instead, a skirt sloper can be used and then adjusted by the slash and spread method.

Drawing 4.66.

- Trace the skirt sloper.
- Transfer the waist darts to the hem.

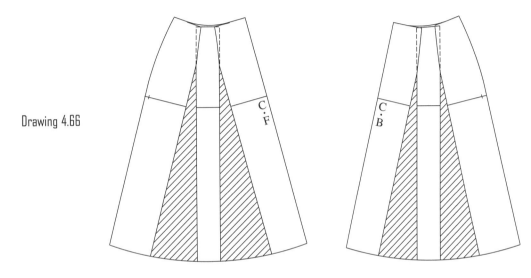

Drawing 4.66

Drawing 4.67.

- Balance the front and back hem circumferences, referring to Drawing 4.13.

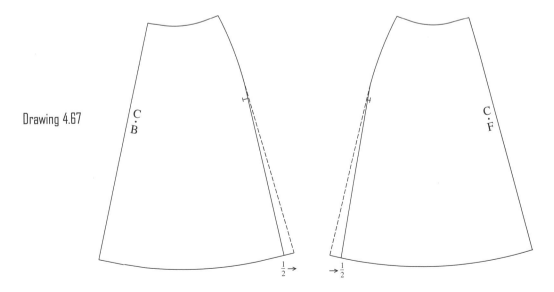

Drawing 4.67

Drawing 4.68. Back and front.

- On the back skirt pattern, divide the waist and hem-lines into three equal parts and mark.
- Draw the slash lines, connecting the marks as shown.
- Repeat for the front.

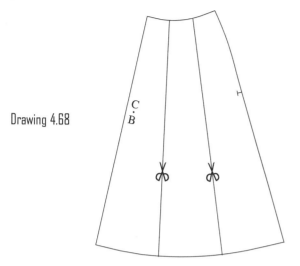

Drawing 4.68

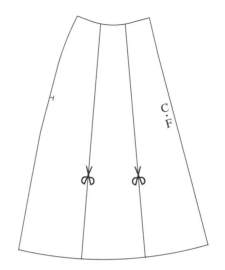

Drawing 4.69. Back and front.

- Slash the lines.
- Fold a 40″ square sheet of paper in half, forming a 45° angle at its top left corner.
- Place the pattern on the paper, positioning it so that its center back is flush to the folded edge of the paper.

- Spread the slash lines as necessary so that the side seam is flush to the edge.
- Retrace the waistline and hemline with a smooth curve.
- Flip the paper over and trace the pattern through to the other side.
- Repeat for the front.

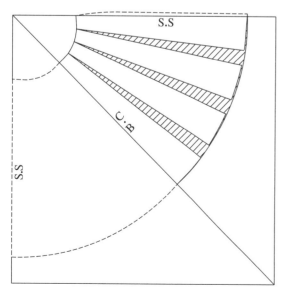

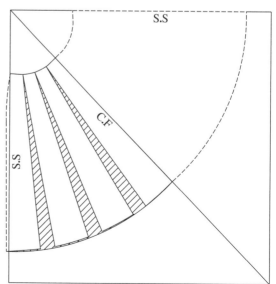

Drawing 4.69

- Unfold the paper for the completed back skirt pattern.
- Follow the same procedure to complete the skirt front.
- Label the pattern pieces and mark the notches and grain lines as shown.

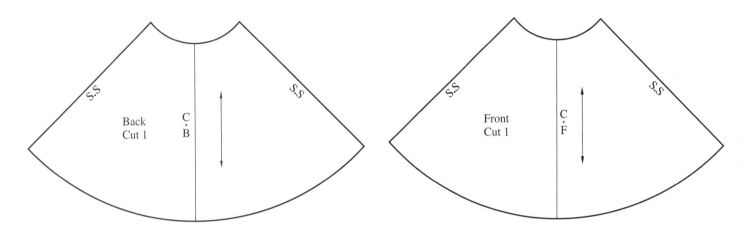

Drawing 4.70

GATHERED SKIRT

*T*he gathered skirt is made from a rectangular panel with shirring at the waistline. The A-line and flared skirts can be modified with additional fullness to create a gathered skirt.

Pattern Analysis
- The waist darts are converted to shirring.
- The center front and back are extended to provide for additional shirring.
- The hem is extended at the side seam to create the A-line silhouette.

Illustration 4.25

Drawing 4.71. **Back and front.**

- Trace the skirt sloper, but do not trace the waist darts.
- Add a 4″ to 6″ extension to the center back and center front for shirring.

- Measure out 1″ to 2″ from the side seams at the hem.
- Redraw the side seam and the hem.
- Mark the shirring placement 1″ to 2″ in from the side seam and ½″ below the waistline.

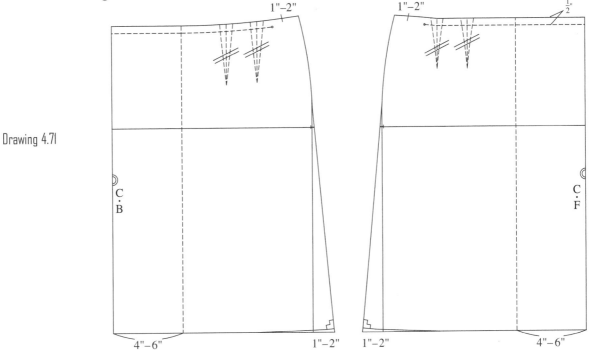

Drawing 4.71

Drawing 4.72. **Finished patterns.**

- Label the pattern pieces and mark the notches and grain lines, as shown.

Drawing 4.72

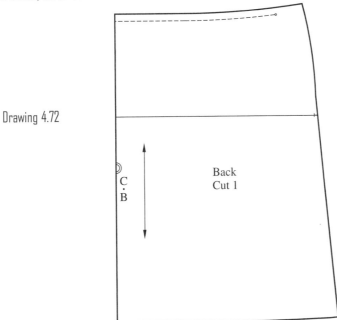

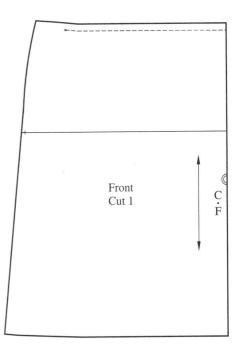

*P*leats are open folds sewn into the fabric of a garment for various purposes, such as providing shape and fullness. While useful in creating details, such as cuffs and collars, in various kinds of garments, pleats are particularly useful in providing for variation in skirts. There are five types of pleats: knife, inverted, box, accordion, and sunburst.

Drawing 4.73. **Knife pleat.**

- The knife pleat is folded in one direction. The intake of a knife pleat consists of two parts: the pleat width (A1) and the pleat intake (1B).
- When the pleat is folded, line 1 is folded over to meet on line B. The intake (1B) may be exactly two times the size of the pleat width or it may be smaller. If the intake is equal to the space, the pleats will match up exactly. If the intake is smaller than the space, the pleat will not match up.
- The fold line (2) is marked at the center of the pleat intake (1B).

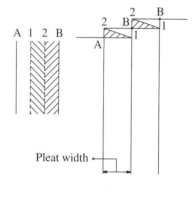

Drawing 4.73

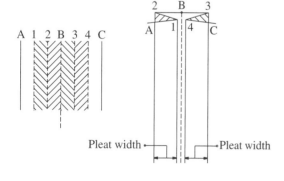

Drawing 4.74

Drawing 4.74. **Inverted pleat.**

- The inverted pleat is folded in two directions, with the folds meeting at the center of the pleat (B). The intake consists of two parts: 1B and 4B. A1 and C4 make up the pleat space and 1B and 4B make up the pleat intake.
- The fold lines (2) and (3) are marked at the center of the pleat intake 1B and 4B. BC is divided the same as AB.
- When the pleat is folded, lines 1 and 4 are folded over to meet on line B.

Drawing 4.75. Box pleat.

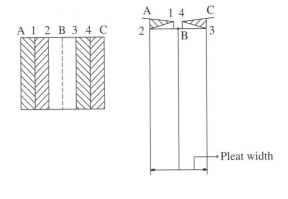

Drawing 4.75

- The box pleat is constructed the same as the inverted pleat.
- The box pleat is folded with the intake on the outside of the garment, matching line 2 to A and line 3 to C.

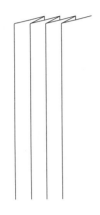

Drawing 4.76

Drawing 4.76. Accordion pleat.

- The accordion pleat is similar to the knife pleat. Each pleat is narrow and the width is equal from waist to hem.
- Making accordion pleats is easier with a special machine.

Drawing 4.77. Sunburst pleat.

- The sunburst pleat is similar to the accordion pleat, except that each pleat is narrow at the waist and wider at the hem.
- Making sunburst pleats requires a special machine.

Drawing 4.77

INVERTED PLEAT SKIRT

*T*here is an inverted pleat at the center front of the A-line skirt that is stitched from the waistline to the hip line.

Pattern Analysis
- The A-line skirt is used as a foundation.
- A 4″-pleat intake is added to the center front.

Drawing 4.78. Back and front.

- Trace the A-line skirt pattern.

Front:
- Add a 4″ extension to the center front.
- Draw a fold line in the center of the 4″ extension.
- * **Note:** Topstitching may be used along the center seam line to secure the top opening of the pleat.
- Label the pattern pieces and mark the notches and grain lines, as shown.

Illustration 4.26

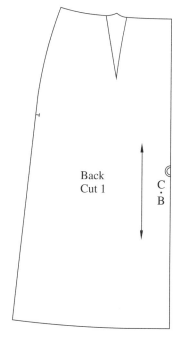

Drawing 4.78

Back
Cut 1

C
.
B

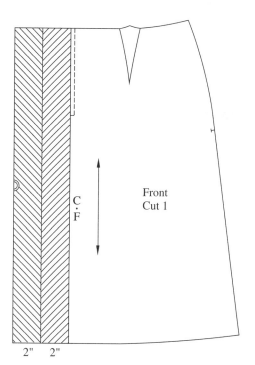

C
.
F

Front
Cut 1

2″   2″

SIDE PLEAT SKIRT

 he side pleat skirt has two knife pleats on each side, open toward the sides of the skirt.

Illustration 4.27

Pattern Analysis
- Waist darts are centered on the pleat lines.
- Flare is added from the hip to the hem of each side panel so the pleats will hang naturally.
- Darts are converted to pleat lines.
- The intake of each pleat is 4″ at the hip line and 3¼″ at the hemline.

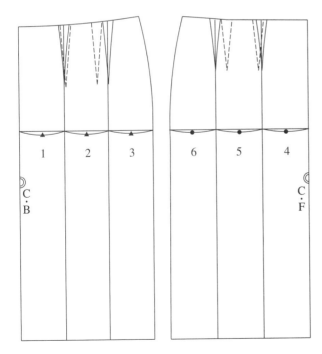

Drawing 4.79

Drawing 4.79. Back and front.

- Trace the skirt sloper.
- Divide the hip line into thirds and mark.
- Draw the pleat lines, parallel to the center back and front, and passing through the marks.
- Center the darts on the pleat lines.
- Number each section.

Drawing 4.80. Back and front.

- Cut along the pleat lines, eliminating the waist darts.
- Trace each section separately.
- Measure out $^3/_8''$ from each pleat line at the hem, excluding the center back and front, and mark.
- Draw the new pleat lines from the hip line to the marks at the hem.

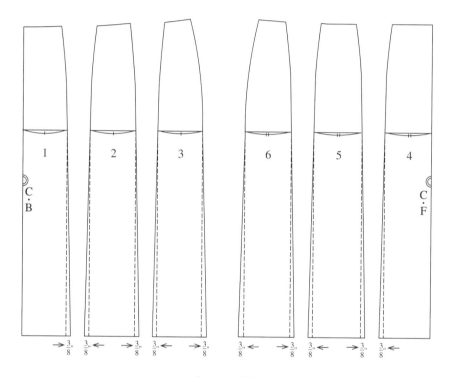

Drawing 4.80

Drawing 4.81. **Back and front.**

- Draw horizontal guidelines, as shown.
- Place the first pattern piece, matching the hip line to the guideline.
- Trace the first pattern piece.
- Measure out 4″ from the hip line, on the guideline, and mark.
- Measure out 3¼″ from the hemline of the first pattern piece and mark.
- Place the second pattern piece on the guideline, matching to the marks. Ensure that the hip line is aligned with the guideline.

- Trace the second pattern piece.
- Measure out 4″ from the hip line, on the guideline, and mark.
- Measure out 3¼″ from the hemline of the second pattern piece and mark.
- Place the third pattern piece on the guideline, matching to the marks. Ensure that the hip line is aligned with the guideline.
- Draw the new waistline and hemline to connect the three pattern pieces together.
- Draw the fold lines at the center of each pleat.

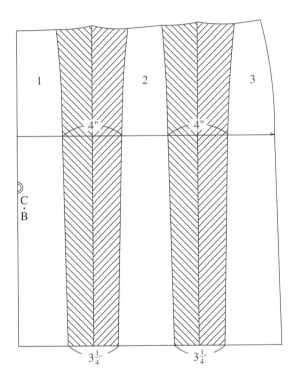
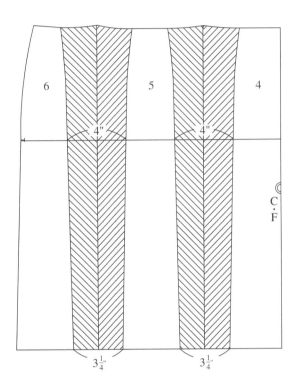

Drawing 4.81

- Cut away the dart areas.
- Label the pattern pieces and mark the notches and grain lines, as shown.

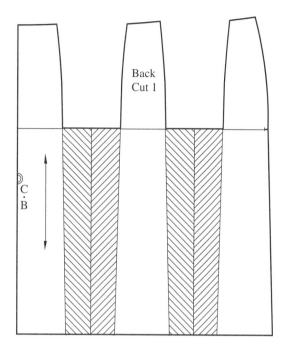
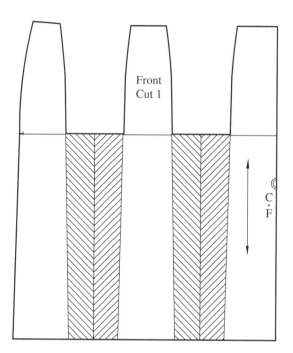

Drawing 4.82

BOX PLEAT SKIRT

$\mathcal{T}$here are box pleats all the way around the skirt, with 4″ pleat widths and intakes.

Pattern Analysis
- The number of pleats is dictated by the hip measurement and the size of the pleat space.
- The hip measurement is divided by the pleat width, which gives the number of pleats.
- The following measurements are used to complete the pattern:

     Hip measurement: 38″ + 2″ (ease).
     Pleat space: 4″.
     Number of pleats: 10 p.
     Waist measurement: $29^1/_2$″

Illustration 4.29

Drawing 4.83.

- Draw a vertical guideline the length of the skirt, labeling A and A′ at the end points, as shown.
- Measure down the hip depth from A and label X.
- Square out horizontal lines from A, X, and A′, then label each as the waist, hip, and hemlines, respectively.

Create the first pleat as follows:
- Measure in 2″ from A and label 2 for the first pleat intake.
- Square a line down from point 2 to the hem.
- **Note:** The intake of the first pleat has been halved because it will ultimately be combined with the intake of the last pleat.
- Mark a fold line in the center of the pleat intake and label 1.
- Measure in 4″ from point 2 for the pleat space and label 3.
- Square a line down from 3 to the hem.
- Measure in 2″ from point 3 for the pleat intake and label C.
- Square a line down from C to the hem.

- Mark a fold line in the center of the pleat intake and label 4.

Create the remaining pleats:
- Repeat the previous steps to create a total of ten pleats.

Shape the first pleat as follows:
- **Note:** Upon completion of the pleats, the waist should measure 30″ and the hip 40″. Each pleat will remove 1″ from the waist, evenly distributed on each side of the pleat space.

Example:
- Waistline pleat width = 3″ (W + ½″)/10.
- Hip line pleat width = 4″ (H + 2″)/10.
- Remove the difference from each pleat = 1″.
- Distributed as ½″ on each side of the pleat.
- Measure in ½″ from points 2 and 3 on the waistline, and mark.
- Connect the marks to the hipline, blending down from the waistline with a slightly curved line.

Shape the remaining pleats:
- Repeat the preceding steps to adjust all ten pleats.

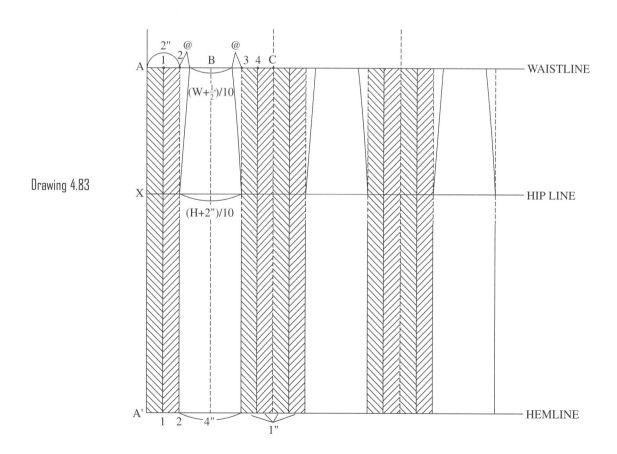

Drawing 4.83

TIERED SKIRT

A tiered skirt is essentially a straight skirt with a series of flounces connected to it. The flounces are generally cut longer as they progress down the skirt, each being one and one-half times, or more, wider than the preceding one. The tiers can be gathered or flared, attached or separate, to vary the silhouette.

Pattern Analysis
• Darts are converted to shirring.
• Each of three successive flounce panels is proportionally longer and wider than the last.

Illustration 4.29

Drawing 4.84. Back and front.

- Trace the skirt sloper, but do not trace the waist darts.
- Extend the full skirt length as desired.
- Divide the skirt length into three sections, gradually increasing the depth of each section.
- Expand the width of the tiers for the desired amount of fullness on each section.
- **Note:** Each section may be as much as one and one-half times as wide as the proceeding section, for fullness, according to the following formula:

  Tier A = One fourth of the waist measurement × 1.5.

  Tier B = A × 1.5.

  Tier C = B × 1.5.

  Waist measurement: 24″.

  Example: Tier A = 6″ × 1.5 = 9″.

  Tier B = 9″ × 1.5 = 13½″.

  Tier C = 13½″ × 1.5 = 20¼″.

Reshaping the side seams:

- Measure out ⅝″ from the bottom of the top tier at the side seam and mark.
- Measure up ¾″ from the top of the top tier at the side seam and mark.
- Connect the marks.
- Reshape the top edge of the tier, blending as shown.
- Reshape the bottom tier, blending from a right angle at the side seam, as shown.
- Repeat for the second and third tiers, measuring up ⅜″ from the top of the top of each tier, as shown.

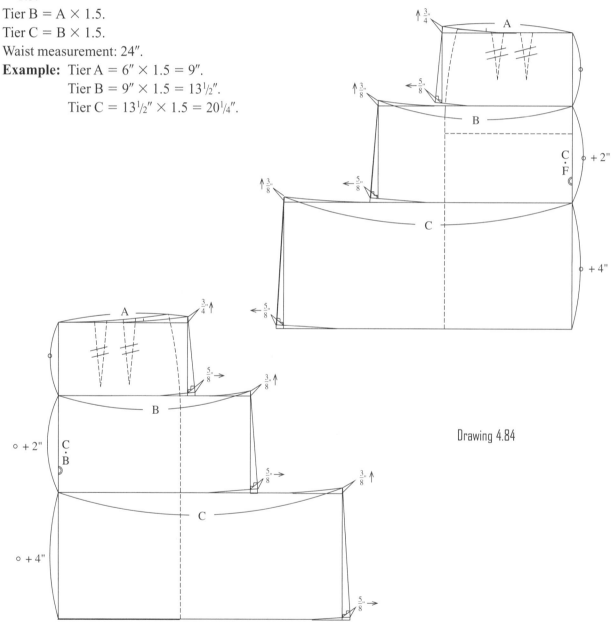

Drawing 4.84

Drawing 4.85. Finished patterns.

- Label the pattern pieces and mark the grain lines, as shown.
- * **Note:** Depending on the width of the fabric being used, some pieces may have to be cut from multiple pieces and then sewn together.

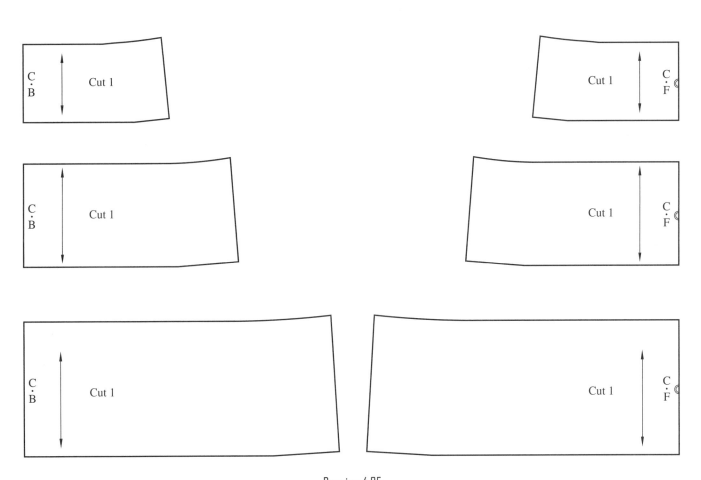

Drawing 4.85

WRAP SKIRT

$\mathcal{T}$he wrap skirt is open from the waist to the hem, wrapping around the body. It can be secured by buttons or ties, and generally overlaps at the front.

Pattern Analysis
* The A-line skirt is used as a foundation.
* To accommodate wrapping, an extension is added at the center front, 4″ at the waist, and 5″ at the hemline.

Illustration 4.30

Drawing 4.86. Back and front.

* Trace the A-line skirt.

Front:
* Add an extension to the center front by measuring out 4″ at the waistline and 5″ at the hem, as shown.
* **Note:** The extension is 1″ wider at the hem to prevent the skirt from flapping open.

* Redraw the center front and the extension edge with dashed fold lines, as shown.
* Add a 2″ facing to the extension edge.
* **Note:** The facing will be turned under the wrap extension.
* Label the pattern pieces and mark the grain lines, as shown.

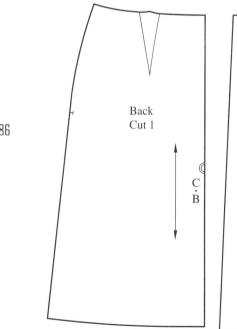

Drawing 4.86

Back
Cut 1

C
·
B

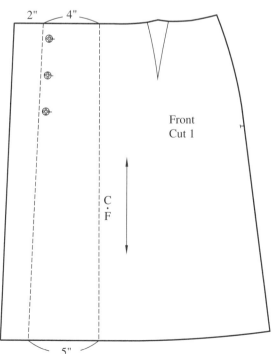

2″   4″

Front
Cut 1

C
·
F

5″

- Draw the waistband the length of the waist measurements plus the wrap extension.
- Mark the button and buttonhole placements, as shown.

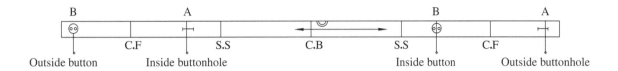

B	A		B	A
Outside button	C.F S.S	C.B	Inside button S.S	C.F Outside buttonhole

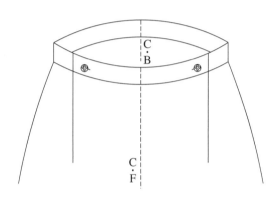

Drawing 4.87

PEGGED SKIRT

 he pegged skirt is tapered from the hip so that
the hem circumference is less than the hip circumference. The hips may be accentuated with additional
pleats or shirring at the waistline.

✲

Pattern Analysis
- The side seam is tapered from the hip line.
- Darts are converted to a portion of the tucks.
- Fullness is added at the waist by slashing and
  spreading diagonally, from the waistline to the side
  seam and hem.

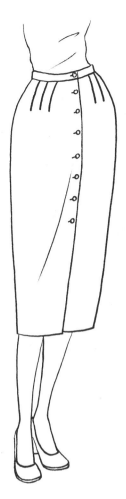

Illustration 4.31

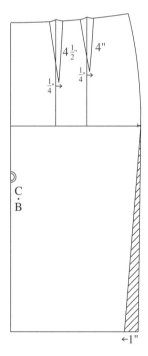

Drawing 4.88

Drawing 4.88. Back.

- Trace the back skirt sloper.
- Redraw the dart closest to the center back $4\frac{1}{2}''$
  long, then redraw the other dart $4''$ long.
- Move the dart points $\frac{1}{4}''$ toward the side seam.
- Measure in $1''$ from the side seam at the hem, then
  taper the side seam from the hip to the hem.

Drawing 4.89. Front.

- Trace the front skirt sloper.
- Divide the waistline into fourths, labeling the marks A, B, and C, as shown.
- Add a 1″ extension to the center front.
- Measure down 3″ from the hip line on the side seam and mark.
- Connect C to the mark.
- Draw slash lines from points A and B to the hem, as shown.
- Divide the two darts into three parts.
- Center the darts along each slash line, as shown.

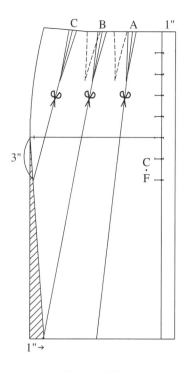

Drawing 4.89

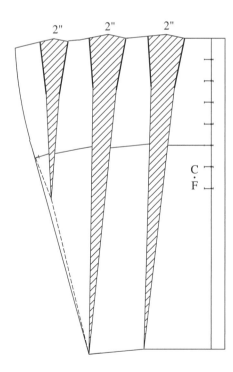

Drawing 4.90

Drawing 4.90.

- Cut along the slash lines from the waistline to, but not through, the side seam and the hem.
- Spread each section 2″ at the waistline.
- * **Note:** Fullness on each section can be equal or different, depending on the desired pegged effect.
- Cut out the pattern piece, leaving 1″ of space above the waistline.
- At the waistline, fold the pleats away from the center front, so that the pleat intakes fall toward the center front.
- Redraw the waistline.
- Mark each tuck opening 2″ down from the waistline, as shown.

- Label the pattern pieces and mark the notches and grain lines, as shown.

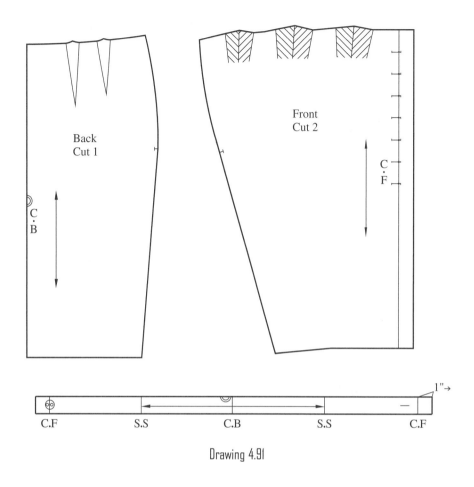

Drawing 4.91

DRAPED SKIRT

his skirt is tapered from the hip to the hem and draped at the side seam.

※

Pattern Analysis
• The side seam is tapered from the hip line.
• The left side waist darts are converted to a portion of the drape.
• Fullness is added at the side seam by slashing and spreading diagonally, from the left side seam to the right side seam.

Illustration 4.32

Drawing 4.92. Back.

- Trace the back skirt sloper.
- Redraw the dart closest to the center back 4½″ long, then redraw the other dart 4″ long.
- Move the dart points ¼″ toward the side seam.
- Measure in ⅝″ from the side seam at the hem, then taper the side seam from the hip to the hem.

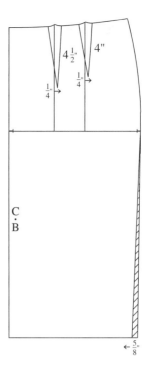

Drawing 4.92

Drawing 4.93.

- Trace the entire front skirt sloper.
- Measure in ⅝″ from the side seam at the hem, then taper the side seam from the hip to the hem.
- Draw the slash lines, as shown.

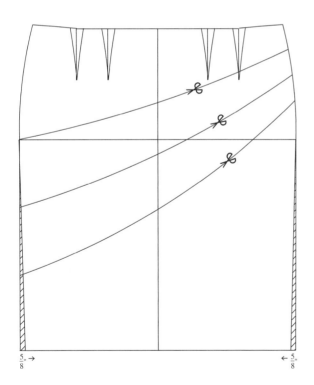

Drawing 4.93

Drawing 4.94.

- Cut along the slash lines from the right side seam to, but not through, the left side seam.
- Spread each slash line 3″ at the side seam.
- Close the two darts on the right side of the pattern.
- Fold each spread section up toward the waistline, then redraw the right side seam with a curved line.
- Draw the left side seam with a straight line.

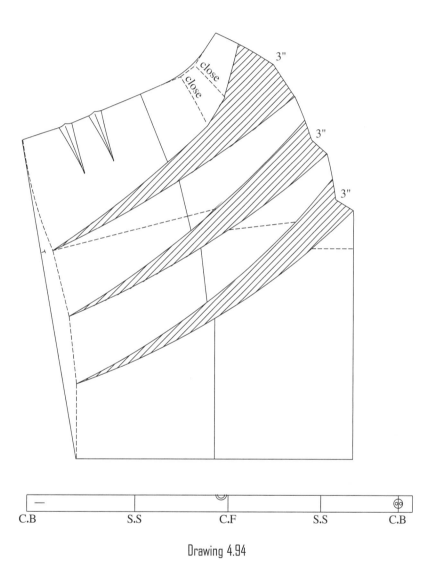

Drawing 4.94

Drawing 4.95. Finished patterns.

- Label the pattern pieces and mark the notches and grain lines, as shown.

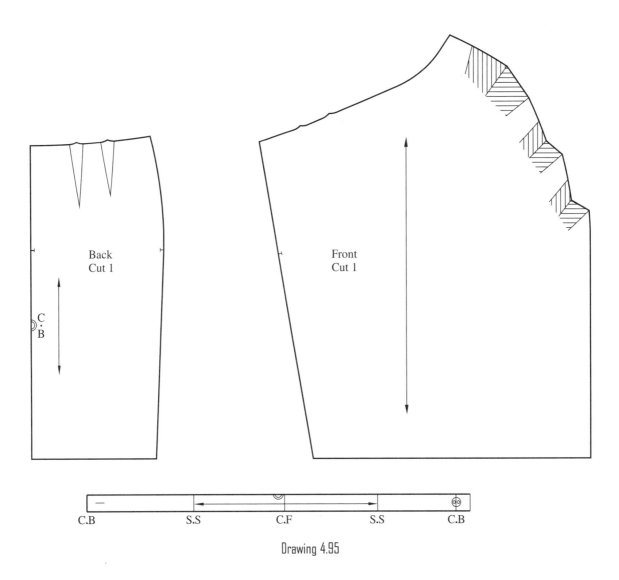

Drawing 4.95

BALLOON SKIRT

$\mathcal{T}$he balloon skirt is shirred to a small waistline, which "balloons" out and then tapers back down to a narrow hem. The lower hem is attached to an A-line underskirt in order to generate the balloon shape.

Pattern Analysis
- The A-line skirt is used as the underskirt pattern.
- The underskirt is traced for the over skirt, then it is lengthened at the hem to create a puff.
- Fullness for the balloon silhouette is added by slashing and spreading the over skirt from the waist to the hem.

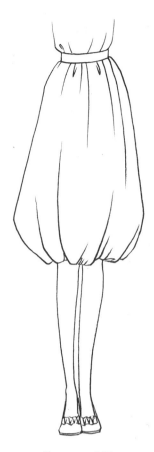

Illustration 4.33

Drawing 4.96. Back and front underskirt.

- Trace the front and back A-line skirt but do not trace the waist darts.
- Extend up from the hip line at the side seam, following the line of the side seam, as shown.
- Reshape the waistline.

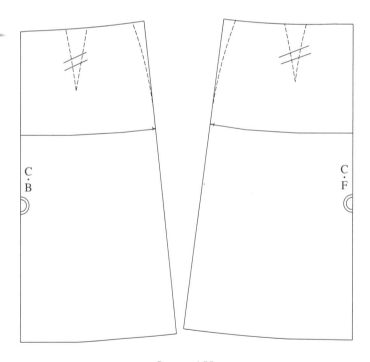

Drawing 4.96

Drawing 4.97. **Back and front over skirt.**

- Trace the front and back underskirt.
- Extend the skirt 5″ at the hem.
- Measure up 2½″ from the new hem and mark the fold line.
- **Note:** The hem extension may vary. The fold line is always placed halfway down the extension.
- Divide the waistline and hemline into thirds.
- Draw slash lines from the hemline to the waistline, passing through the marks.
- Number each section, as shown.

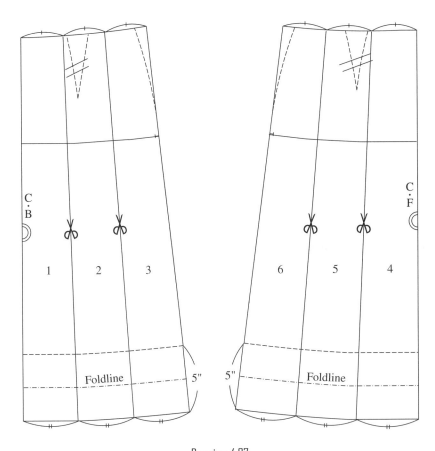

Drawing 4.97

- Cut along the slash lines.
- Spread each section as desired for fullness.
* **Note:** The more space there is between the sections, the fuller the shape.
- Reshape the waistline and hem.

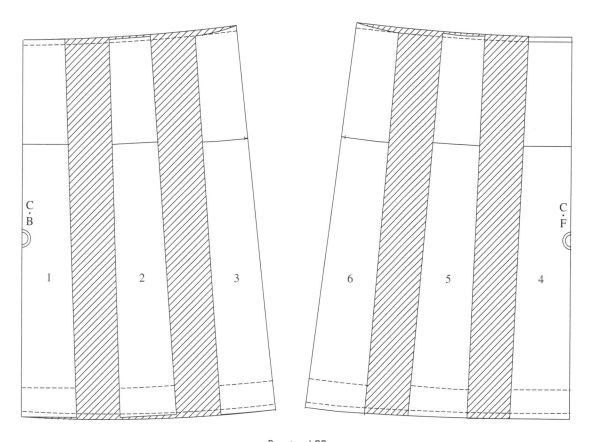

Drawing 4.98

Drawing 4.99. Finished patterns.

• Label the pattern pieces and mark the notches and
grain lines, as shown.

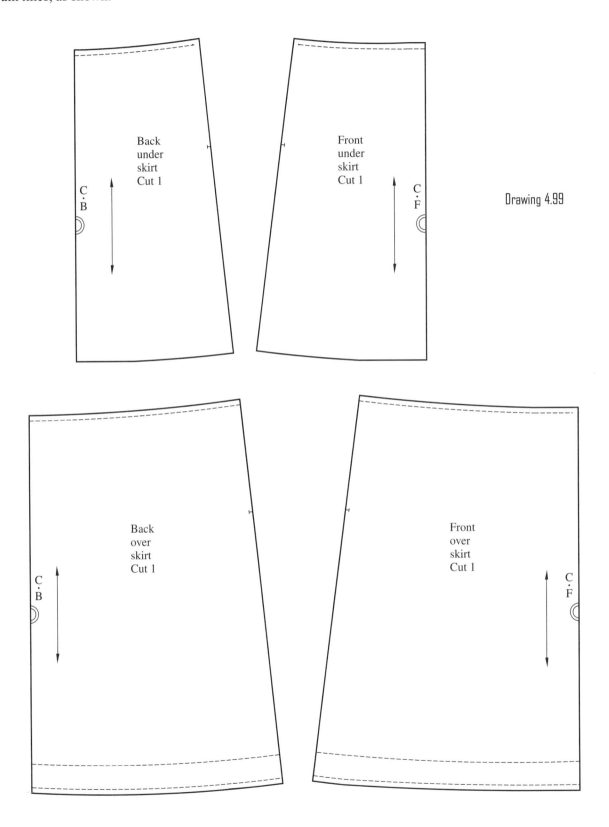

Back
under
skirt
Cut 1

C
·
B

Front
under
skirt
Cut 1

C
·
F

Drawing 4.99

Back
over
skirt
Cut 1

C
·
B

Front
over
skirt
Cut 1

C
·
F

CULOTTE SKIRT

he culotte skirt has a crotch seam, which divides it into two sections. Often categorized as a style of pant, these garments feature pleats and flare, and may be of varying lengths.

❖

Pattern Analysis
- The skirt sloper is used as a foundation.
- Crotch depth and curve are developed, using the hip measurement.
- The back crotch curve is deeper than that of the front.

Drawing 4.100.

- Trace the front and back skirt sloper.

Front:
- AB = Crotch depth plus $3/8''$ to $1 1/4''$ for ease.
- BC = One third of the hip line plus $1/2''$.
- Square out from B and label C.
- Square down from C to the hem and label D.
- BE = BC. Label E.
- Connect point E to C.
- Draw a line from B, perpendicular to EC, and label X.
- Mark the midpoint of line BX.
- Draw a crotch curve from E to C, passing through the midpoint of BX, ending square to C.

Back:
- FG = Length of line AB (from Front).
- F′ = Measure down $3/8''$ from F, to allow for back curvature.
- GH = One half of the hip line plus $1/2''$.
- Square out from point G and label H.
- Square down from point H to the hem and label I.
- GJ = GH. Label J.
- Connect point J to H.
- Draw a line from G, perpendicular to JH, and label Y.
- Mark the midpoint of line GY.
- Draw a crotch curve from J to H, passing through the midpoint of GY, ending square to H.

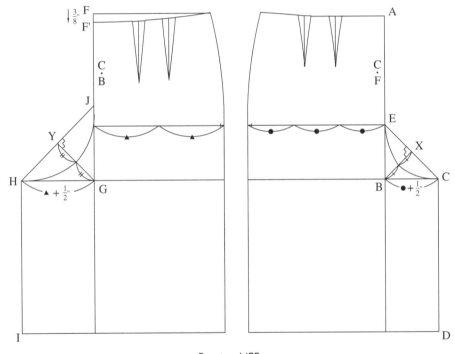

Drawing 4.100

- Label the pattern pieces and mark the notches and grain lines, as shown.

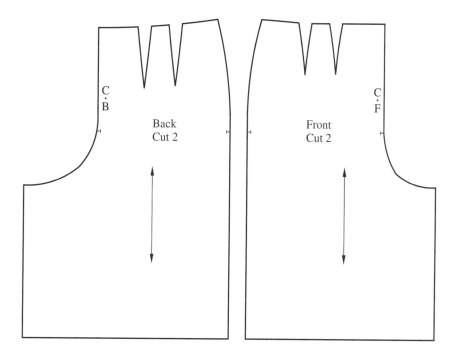

Drawing 4.101

A-LINE CULOTTE SKIRT

Pattern Analysis
- Portions of the front and back waist darts are transferred to the hem to spread it 2″.
- The remaining darts are combined into a single dart.

Drawing 4.102. Front and back.

- Trace the culotte skirt pattern.
- Measure out ¼″ from the inseam on the hem.
- Draw the new inseam.
- Draw a slash line, from the dart point closest to the side seam, perpendicular to the hem.

Illustration 4.35

Drawing 4.102

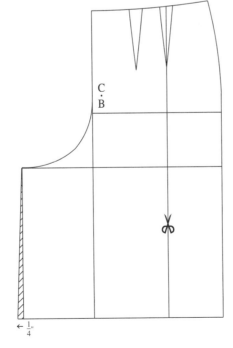

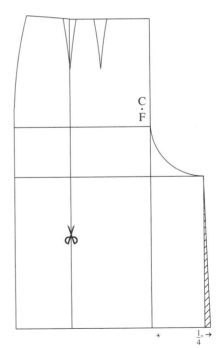

Drawing 4.103. **Front and back.**

- Cut along the slash line to, but not through, the dart point.
- Close the waist dart until the slash line spreads 2″ at the hem.
- Reshape the hemline.
- Combine the remaining darts into one dart.
- Center the dart on the waistline.

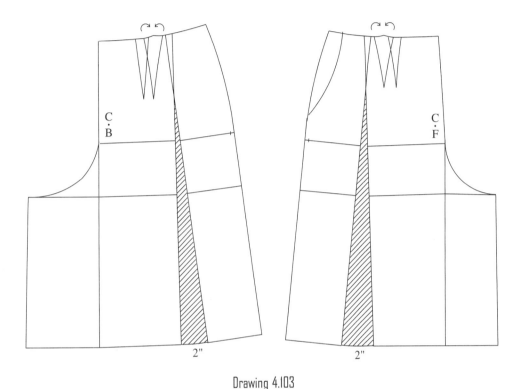

Drawing 4.103

Drawing 4.104. **Pocket.**

- Refer to the front hip pocket instructions from Drawing 7.76 in Chapter 7 (Details) to complete the pocket.

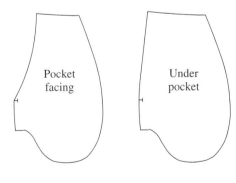

Drawing 4.104

- Label the pattern pieces and mark the notches and grain lines, as shown.

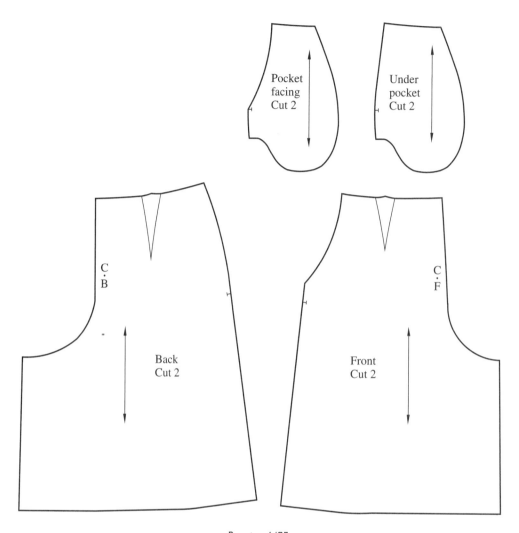

Drawing 4.105

INVERTED PLEAT CULOTTE SKIRT

Pattern Analysis
- An inverted pleat is added at the center front.

Drawing 4.106. Front and back.

- Trace the A-line culotte skirt pattern.

Front:
- Label A and B at the center front.
- Number each section, as shown.

Illustration 4.36

Drawing 4.106

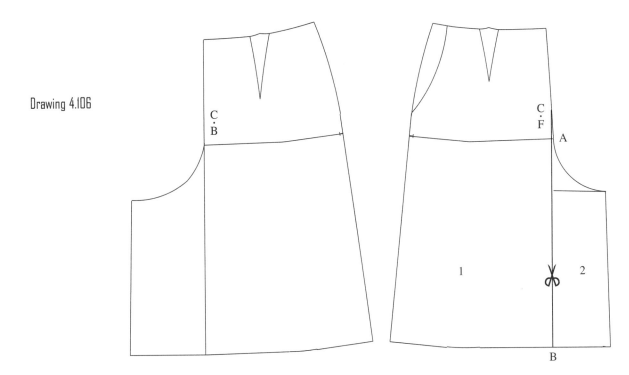

Drawing 4.107. Pocket

- Refer to the front hip pocket instructions from Drawing 7.76 in Chapter 7 (Details) to complete the pocket.

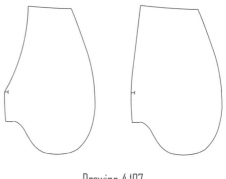

Drawing 4.107

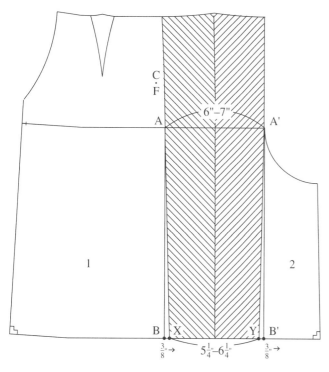

Drawing 4.108

Drawing 4.108. Front.

- Cut along line AB.
- Draw a horizontal guideline on a separate sheet of paper.
- Place the first pattern, matching the hip line to the guideline.
- Measure out $^3/_8''$ from point B and label X.
- Connect point A to X.
- Measure out $6''$ to $7''$ from A, on the hip line, and label A$'$.
- Measure out $5^1/_4''$ to $6^1/_4''$ from X, on the hem, and label Y.
- Connect point A$'$ to Y.
- Draw the pleat line, from A$'$ to the waistline.
- Mark the fold line in the center of the pleat intake.
- Measure out $^3/_8''$ from point Y, at the hem, and label B$'$.
- Connect point A$'$ to B$'$.
- Place the second pattern, matching A to A$'$ and B to B$'$.
- Retrace the pattern.

• Label the pattern pieces and mark the notches and grain lines, as shown.

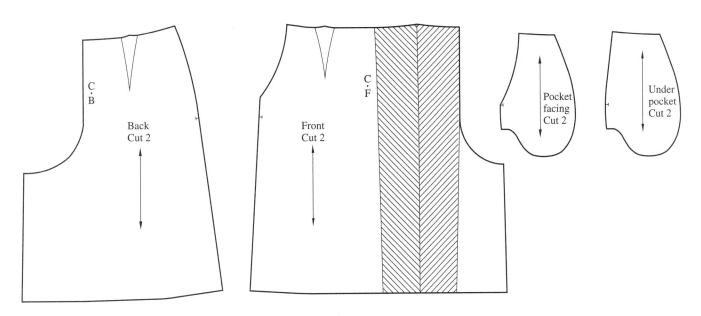

Drawing 4.109

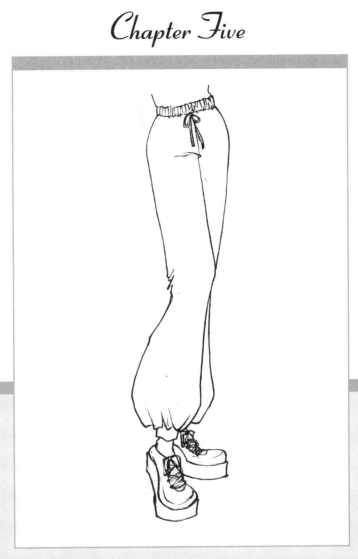

Chapter Five

THE PANT

INTRODUCTION TO THE PANT

amount of ease at the hip circumference, the crotch depth, and the crotch length.

*P*ants are garments worn on the lower torso. Unlike skirts, pants have tubes surrounding each leg. There is a wide variety of pant silhouettes, including fitted, slim, wide, tapered, straight, bell, and pegged. Depending on the style and fabric used, pants can be worn for recreation, business, or formal occasions. Numerous variations can be developed from the basic pants sloper, using methods that include dart manipulation; slash-and-spread; changing the waistline, adding pockets, and varying the pant length. Pant fit is altered primarily by changing three items: the

Drawing 5.1. Pant components.

A. Waistband.
B. Belt loop.
C. Pants fly.
D. Side seam.
E. Front pleats.
F. Crease.
G. Hip pocket.
H. Front pocket.
I. Cuff hem.

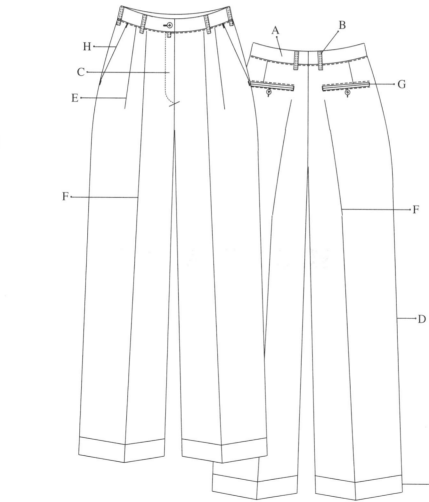

Drawing 5.1

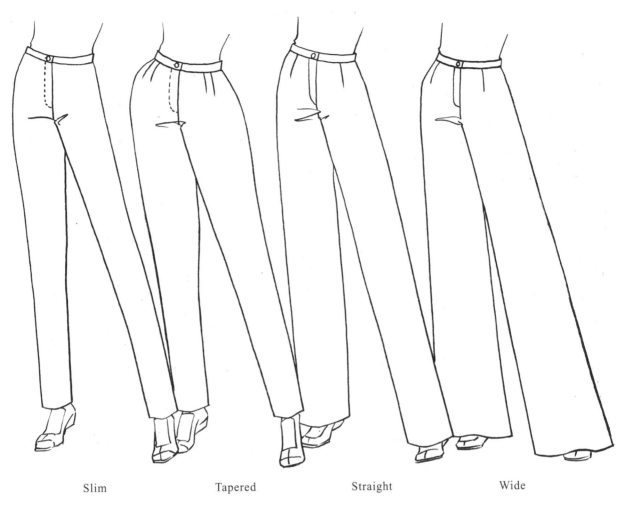

Slim   Tapered   Straight   Wide

Illustration 5.1

Slim
Also called stovepipe or cigarette pants, this style of pants is like the straight pant, only even narrower from hip to hem.

Tapered
A style of pants with pleats added to the front waist-line to give fullness in the hip area, before tapering to the hem.

Straight
A style of pants that falls straight from hip to hem without tapering.

Wide
A style of pants that flares out from hip to the hem, with a wider hem circumference.

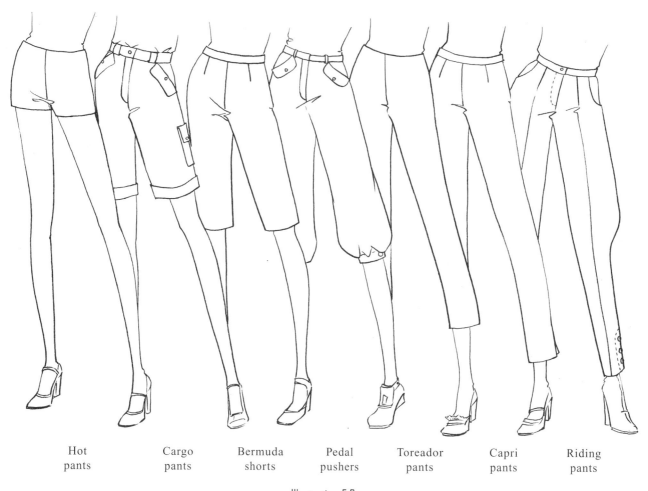

| Hot pants | Cargo pants | Bermuda shorts | Pedal pushers | Toreador pants | Capri pants | Riding pants |

Illustration 5.2

Hot Pants
These extremely short pants were popular in the early 1970s.

Cargo Pants
These are pants of varying lengths, featuring extra large side pockets at the mid-thigh with either button or Velcro closures.

Bermuda Shorts
These casual pants are cut to fit close to the leg.

Pedal Pushers
These short pants are often cuffed, so as to be comfortable while riding a bike.

Toreador Pants
These tight fitting, mid-calf–length pants are similar to those worn by a bullfighter, or toreador.

Capri Pants
These above-the-ankle pants typically feature a slit on the side.

Riding Pants
This style is full at the thigh and hip, but tight at the knee; also called hunt or show breeches.

- The following chart illustrates the names and typical lengths for various common pants.

Style	Length
Short shorts	Fall 1″ to 1½″ below crotch depth level.
Jamaica shorts	Fall at mid-thigh.
Bermuda shorts	Fall 2″ above the knee.
Knee-length shorts	Fall at the knee.
Pedal pushers	Fall 2″ below the knee.
Calf pants	Fall 4″ below the knee.
Capri pants	Fall just above the ankle.
Full-length	Fall anywhere below the ankle.

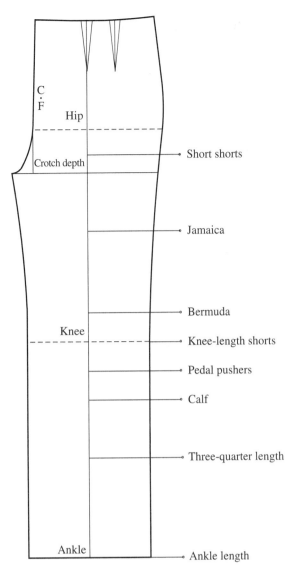

Drawing 5.2

STRAIGHT PANTS

his is a style of pants that falls straight from hip to hem.

✳

Pattern Analysis

- The pants pattern is developed from the sloper.
- Front hip pockets and back bound pockets are used.
- There is a fly front zipper.
- The lining pattern is developed form the pants pattern.
- Marker directions are provided for both garment and lining.

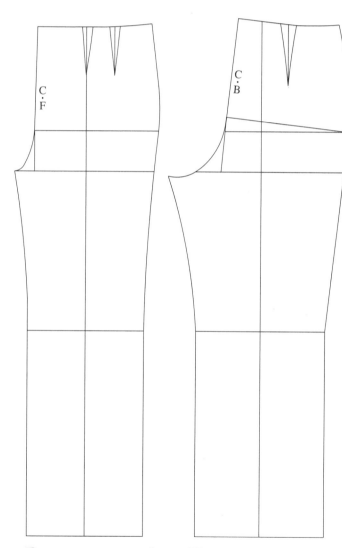

Drawing 5.3

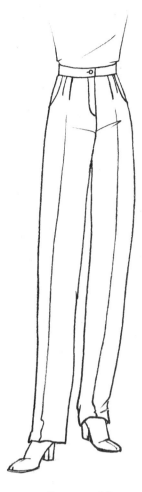

Illustration 5.3

Drawing 5.3. Front and back.

- Trace the pants sloper.

Drawing 5.4. Front hip pocket.

- Refer to the instructions given in the Front Hip Pocket section from Drawing 7.76 in Chapter 7 (Details) to complete the pocket, using the dimensions shown.

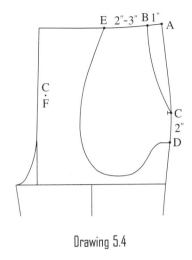

Drawing 5.4

E   A

Pocket facing

E   B

Under pocket

Drawing 5.5

Drawing 5.5. Pocket facing and under pocket.

- Trace the pocket facing separately; this includes the pocket shape to the side seam (A-C-D-E-A).
- Trace the under pocket separately (B-C-D-E-B).

Drawing 5.6. Garment.

- Remove section A-B-C-A.
- * **Note:** The garment includes the side seam up to and along the pocket style line (BC).

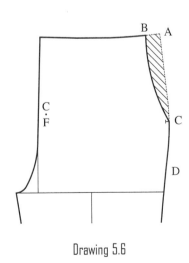

Drawing 5.6

Drawing 5.7. **Back bound pocket.**

- Draw the bound pocket and under pockets, using the dimensions shown.
- Mark the pocket placement $1^3/4''$ in from the center back and $2''$ below the waistline.
- **Note:** The pocket will not be constructed until after the dart is sewn.
- Trace the under pocket separately.

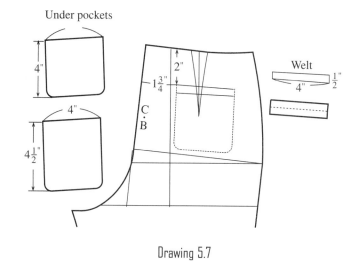

Drawing 5.7

Drawing 5.8. **Front fly.**

Left side:
- Draw the left fly facing $2^1/2''$ wide and $7''$ to $8''$ long.
- Mark the fold line at the center of the fly facing.

Right side:
- Add an extension $1^1/4''$ wide and $7''$ to $8''$ long, to the right side of the pant at the center front.

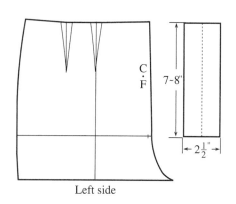

Left side

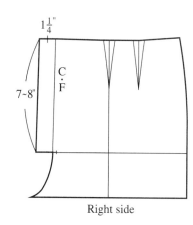

Right side

Drawing 5.8

Drawing 5.9. **Waistband.**

- Draw the waistband, using the following dimensions:
    Length: Waist measurement plus $1/2''$.
    Height: $1^1/4''$.
    Button extension: $1''$.

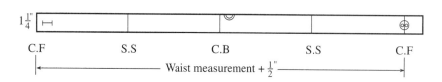

Drawing 5.9

Drawing 5.10. Finished patterns.

- Add the seam allowances:

    Waistline, waistband, pocket, and center back and front = $^3/_8''$.

    Side seam = $^5/_8''$.

    Front fly facing = $^3/_8''$ at the top and bottom, and $^5/_8''$ at the side.

    Hem = $1^1/_2''$.

- Label the pattern pieces and mark the notches and grain lines, as shown.

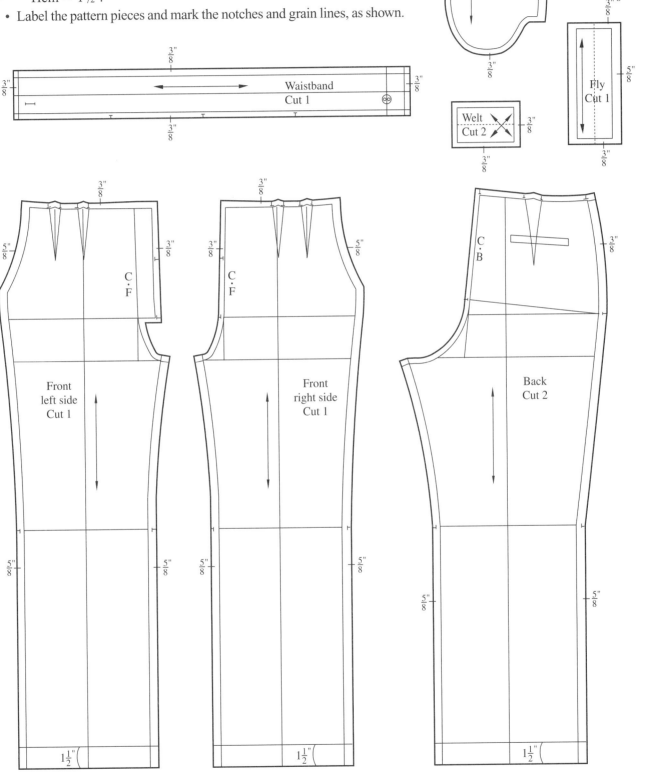

Drawing 5.10

Drawing 5.11. Lining.

* **Note:** Lining patterns are drawn with dashed lines.
- Trace the front and back pant patterns.
- Add ⅛″ to the side seam, crotch, inseam, center front, and center back.
- Raise the hem ³/₄″.

Drawing 5.12. Left side front.

- Measure in 1¼″ at the center front on the waistline.
- Square down 7″ from this point.
- Remove this section.

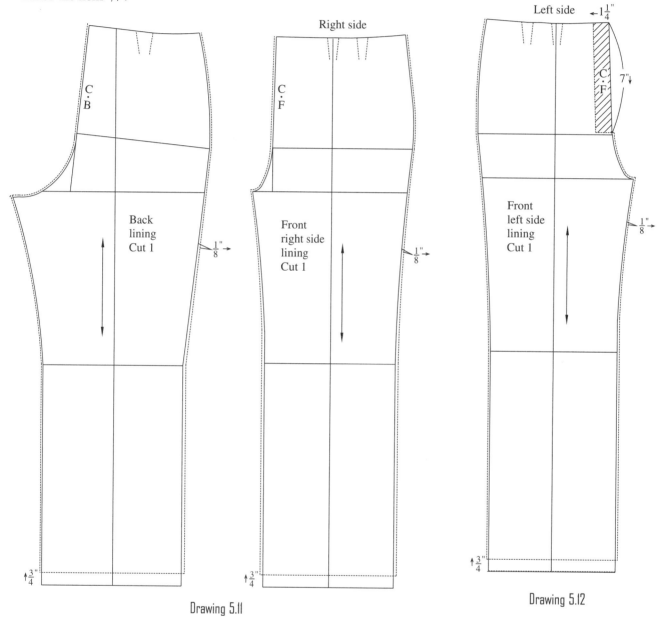

Drawing 5.11

Drawing 5.12

Drawing 5.13. Pocket.

- Copy the under pocket pattern for the pocket lining from Drawing 5.5 and Drawing 5.7.

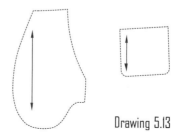

Drawing 5.13

Drawing 5.14. **Lining.**

- Add the seam allowances:
    Waistline, pocket, and center back and front = $^3/_8''$.
    Side seam = $^5/_8''$.
    Hem = $1^1/_4''$.
- Label the pattern pieces and mark the notches and grain lines.

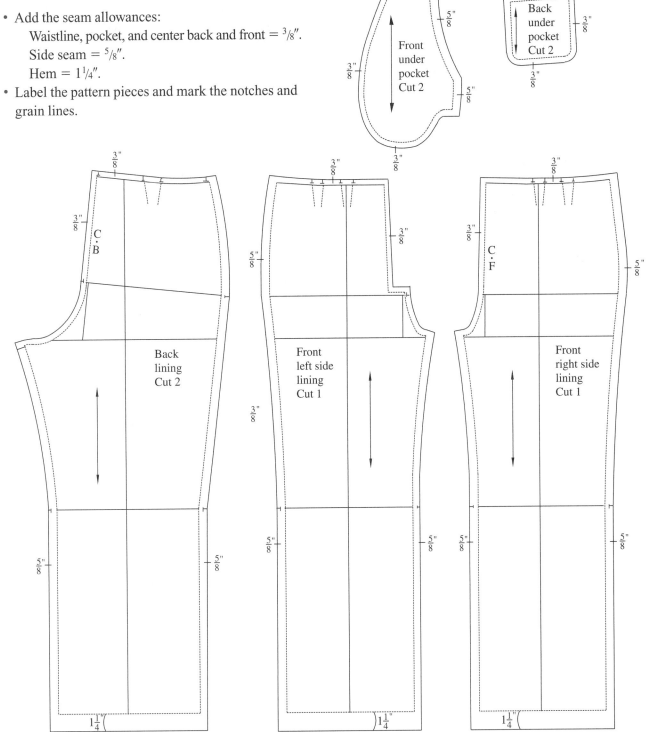

Drawing 5.14

Drawing 5.15. Garment marker.

- The garment marker is produced by laying out all of the pattern pieces on the fabric. The pattern pieces should be placed so that their grain lines match the straight grain of the fabric. The width of the fabric and sizes of the pattern pieces will dictate how the pieces are laid. Much of this process is handled by computers in industry, but it is still important to be familiar with the relationship between fabric and pattern.

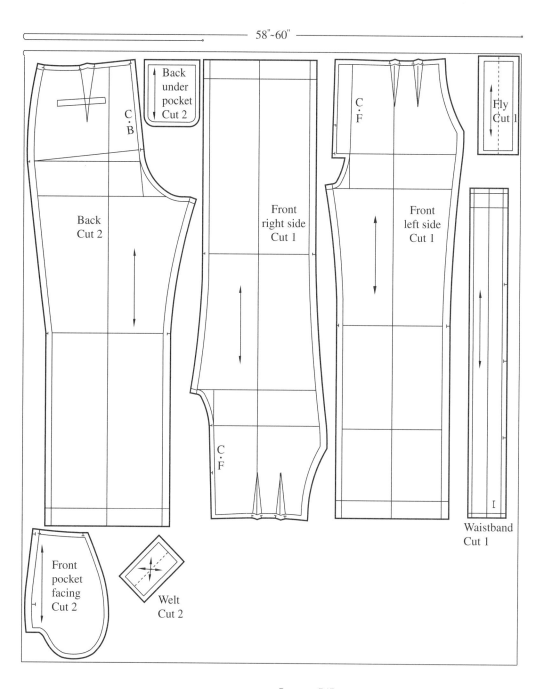

Drawing 5.15

Drawing 5.16. Lining marker.

- As with the garment marker, the lining marker is produced by laying out all of the pattern pieces on the fabric. The pattern pieces should be placed so that their grain lines match the straight grain of the fabric. The width of the fabric and sizes of the pattern pieces will dictate how the pieces are laid. Again, much of this process is handled by computers in industry, but it is still important to be familiar with the relationship between fabric and pattern.

Drawing 5.16

45"

C·B

Back lining Cut 1

Back lining Cut 1

C·F

Front right side lining Cut 1

C·B

Front left side lining Cut 1

Front under pocket

Front under pocket

Back under pocket

Back under pocket

Drawing 5.17. **Preparation.**

• Attach the interfacing to the wrong side of the fabric on the pocket opening, fly extension, waistband, and pocket welt.

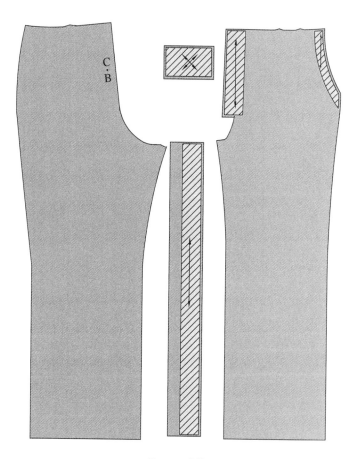

Drawing 5.17

- Serge or zigzag all seam allowances, except for the waist and pocket openings.
- Fold the fly panel in half, then serge or zigzag the seam allowances along the side and bottom.

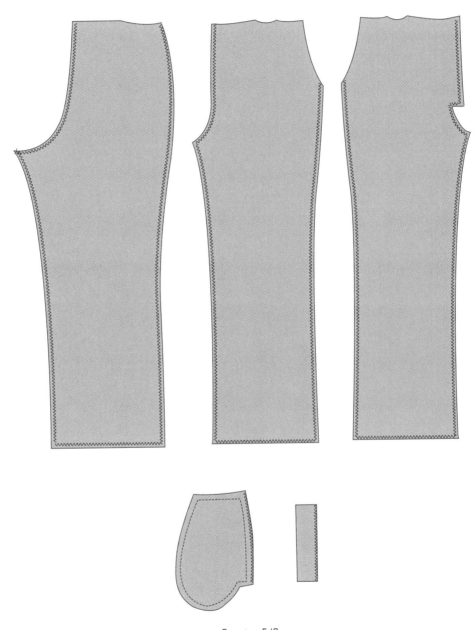

Drawing 5.18

- Sew the front and back darts, then press toward the center back and front.
- Attach the front side pocket.

Side pocket attachment:
- Place the pocket lining against the right side of the garment fabric, then stitch at the pocket opening.
- Trim the seam allowance of the lining to $1/4''$.
- Fold back the pocket lining, then press.
- Topstitch along the pocket opening edge.
- Place the pocket back under the front panel of the garment, matching the waist and side seam.
- Stitch the pocket lining and side seam to hold the pocket in place.
- Flip the garment over, then stitch the pocket lining and pocket back together.

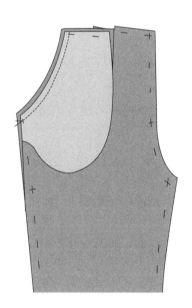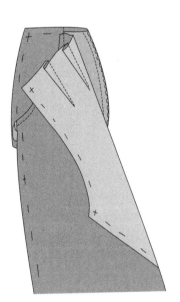

Drawing 5.19

Drawing 5.20. One-piece bound pocket construction.

- Fold the welt in half, wrong sides together, then press.
- Baste the welt onto the pocket placement line, making certain that the folded edge of the welt is facing the bottom of the garment.
- Place the pocket lining (cut from the lining fabric) over the welt, then stitch the lining, welt, and garment together, $\frac{1}{4}''$ from the edge.
- Place the pocket lining (cut from the garment fabric) opposite the other pocket, then stitch the pocket and garment in place, $\frac{1}{4}''$ from the edge.

- On the wrong side of the fabric, cut carefully between the two stitch lines for the pocket opening, making certain to leave $\frac{3}{8}''$ to $\frac{1}{2}''$ at the sides.
- Cut the corners diagonally.
- Push the pocket linings toward the inside of the pant.
- Shape the welt, then press.
- Stitch the two pocket linings together, including the triangular pieces of fabric.
- Topstitch along the sides and upper edge of the pocket opening, if desired.

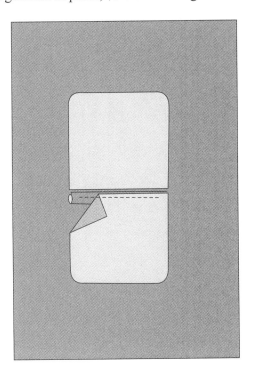

Drawing 5.20

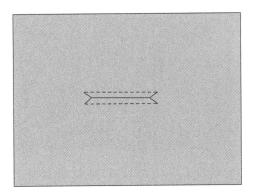

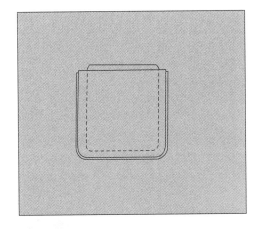

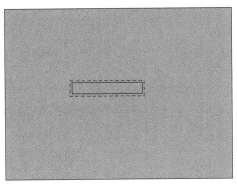

- Place the right side of the front pant panels together, then stitch between the notches on the crotch curve (approximately 2″).
- Press the seam open.
- Fold the fly in half, with the wrong sides together.
- Place the zipper face down on the unfolded edge of the fly, and sew.
- On the left pant panel, fold ⅛″ in from the center front and press.
- **Note:** The seam allowance is now ½″.
- On the right pant panel, fold the fly extension under the center front and press.

- Attach the zipper and fly to the left front panel of the pants, with the teeth aligned on the fold.
- Close the zipper, covering it with the right side of the pants.
- Baste the zipper and fly together in place, from the underside. Baste only the zipper and fly—do not catch the garment in the basting stitches.
- Topstitch the right side of the pants, catching the right side of the zipper in the stitches, making certain not to catch the under fly while topstitching.
- Tack the lower portion of the zipper by backstitching multiple times, making certain to catch the bottom portion of the under fly in the tack stitches.

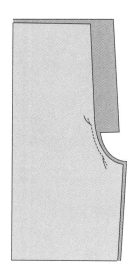

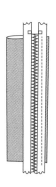

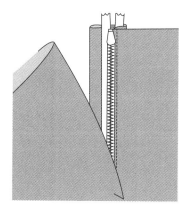
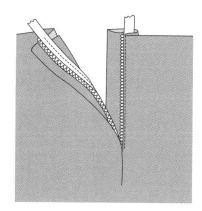
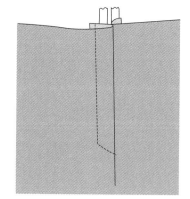

Drawing 5.21

Drawing 5.22.

- Place the front and back panels together, with the
  right sides of the fabric next to each other, then
  stitch the side seams and inner leg seams.

Drawing 5.22

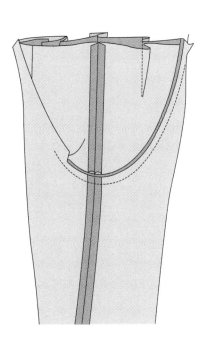

Drawing 5.23

Drawing 5.23.

- Open the seams and press.
- Turn one leg of the pants into the other, with the
  wrong side of the fabric facing out.
- Stitch the crotch seam once and then again $\frac{1}{8}''$
  above the previous stitch line for reinforcement.

Drawing 5.24. Lining construction.

- Sew the darts as tucks.
- Stitch the side seams and the inner leg seams.
- Serge or zigzag the seam allowances.
- Press all seam allowances toward the back.
- Sew the crotch curve from the center back at the waist to the zipper opening.
- Fold the hem of the lining up $^3/_8''$, then again $^3/_4''$, and stitch.
- Baste the linings around the zipper and fly at the center front, making certain that the seam allowances are folded toward the wrong side of the pants fabric.

Lining attachment:
- **Note:** Refer to the instructions given in the tapered Skirt Construction from Drawing 4.33 in Chapter 4.
- Place the wrong side of the lining and pants fabric together.
- Match the notches, side seams, darts, and tucks, then baste the waistline $^1/_8''$ above the stitch line.
- Attach the waistband to the pants.

Finishing:
- Press the hem, then catch stitch it in place.
- Chain stitch the lining to the pants at the side seams and inseams.
- Finish the closure on the waistband with a button and buttonhole.

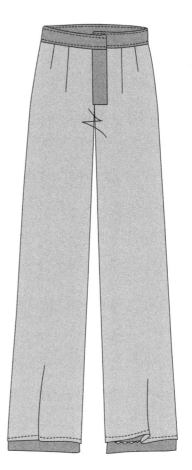

Drawing 5.24

JEAN PANTS

 his is a style of ankle-length pants, featuring two front hip pockets, two back pockets, a V-shaped yoke at the back, and double topstitching and rivets for reinforcement at stress points. Originally worn as work pants by laborers and farm workers, jeans were first made from indigo denim but are now made from a variety of fabrics.

✺

Pattern Analysis
• Waist darts are eliminated.
• The crotch depth is shortened.
• The legs are narrowed for a slim fit.
• There are two front hip pockets and two back pockets.
• The waistband is developed as part of the pants pattern.
• The yoke style line is featured in back.

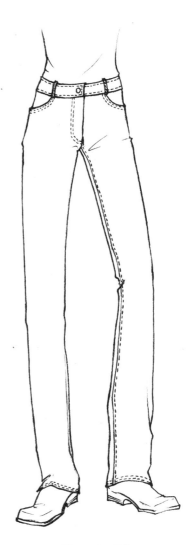

Illustration 5.4

Drawing 5.25. **Front.**

- Trace the front pants sloper, but do not trace the waist dart.
- Measure in $3/4''$ from the center front at the waist and label A.
- Measure one fourth of the waist measurement plus $1/4''$ from A and label A′.
- Reshape the waistline.
- Label B at the center front on the hip line.
- Measure one fourth of the hip measurement from B and label B′.
- Connect point A to B.
- Connect point A′ to B′ with a curved line.
- Raise the crotch line $1/2''$.
- Reshape the crotch curve.
- Measure in $5/8''$ on each side of the knee.
- Measure in $1''$ on each side of the hem.
- Draw the new inseam and out seam, using the measurements shown.

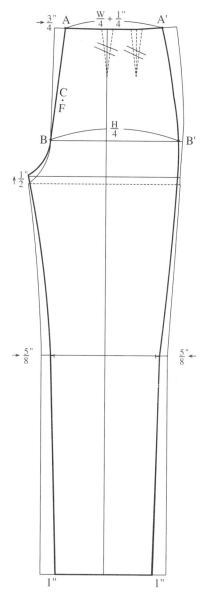

Drawing 5.25

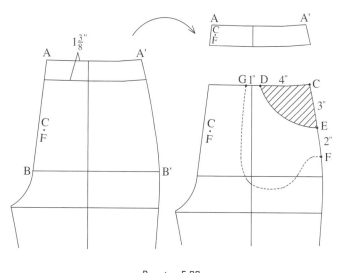

Drawing 5.26

Drawing 5.26. **Waistband and front pocket.**

- Measure down $1^3/8''$ from the waistline and draw a line parallel to the waistline.
- Separate the band.

Pocket:
- Refer to the instructions given in the Front Hip Pocket section from Drawing 7.76 in Chapter 7 (Details) to complete the pocket, using the dimensions shown.

Drawing 5.27.

- Trace the garment, pocket, and waistband separately.

Drawing 5.27

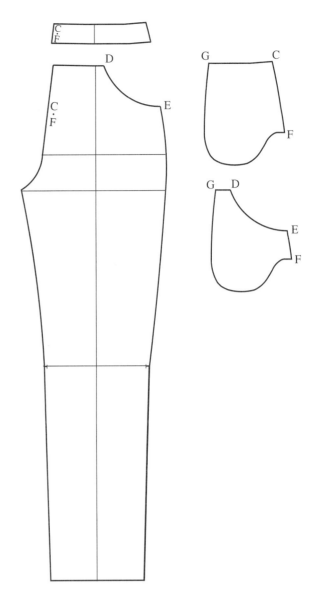

Drawing 5.28. Back.

- Trace the back pants sloper, but do not trace the waist dart.
- Measure in $3/4''$ and up $1/2''$ from the center back at the waist and label D.
- Measure one fourth of the waist measurement plus $1/4''$ from D to the waistline and label D$'$.
- Reshape the waistline.
- Label E at the center back of the hip line.
- Measure one fourth of the hip measurement from E and label E$'$.
- Measure up $1/2''$ and in $5/8''$ from the crotch point.
- Reshape the center back and crotch curve.
- Measure in $5/8''$ on each side of the knee.
- Measure in $1''$ on each side of the hem.
- Draw the new inseam and out seam, according to these measurements.

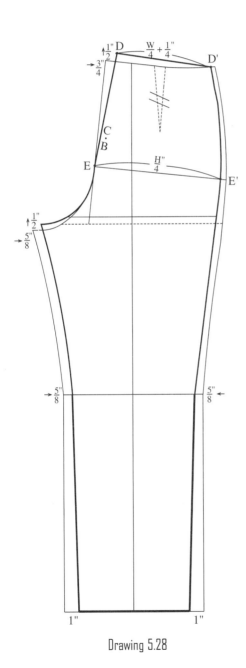

Drawing 5.28

Drawing 5.29. Back waistband and yoke.

- Measure down $1\frac{3}{8}''$ from the waistline and draw a line parallel to the waistline.
- Draw the yoke line from $1\frac{1}{4}''$ down the side seam to $2\frac{3}{8}''$ down the center back.
- Separate the band and yoke.

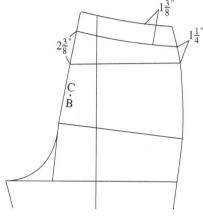
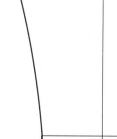

Drawing 5.29

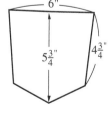

Drawing 5.30

Drawing 5.30. Back patch pocket.

- Draw the pocket, using the dimensions shown.
- Mark the pocket placement on the back pattern, as shown in Drawing 5.29.

Drawing 5.31. **Waistband.**

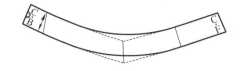

Drawing 5.31

- Flip the back piece over, then connect the front and back waistbands at the side seams.
- Trace as one continuous piece.

Drawing 5.32. **Finished patterns.**

- Mark the notches and grain lines, as shown.

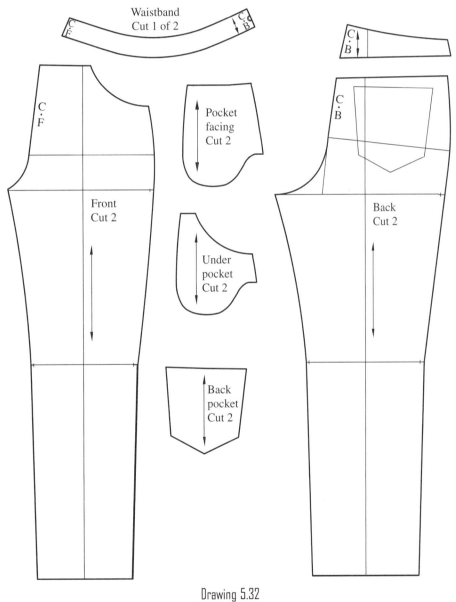

Drawing 5.32

HIP HUGGERS

$\mathcal{A}$lso called hipbone pants or hipsters, this style of pants rests on the hips or below the natural waistline. Any style of pant can be modified to be a hip hugger.

Pattern Analysis
- The jean pants patterns from Drawings 5.25 and 5.28 are used to develop the close-fitting silhouette.
- The waistline is lowered.

Drawing 5.33

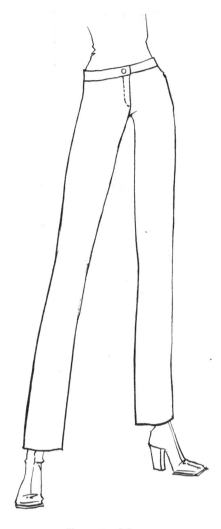

Illustration 5.5

Drawing 5.33. Front and back.

- Trace the jean pattern, using Drawing 5.25 for the front and Drawing 5.28 for the back.
- Lower the waistline 1¹⁄₄″.
- Remove this section.

Drawing 5.34. **Waistband.**

- Measure down 1″ from the new waistline and draw
  a line parallel to the waistline.

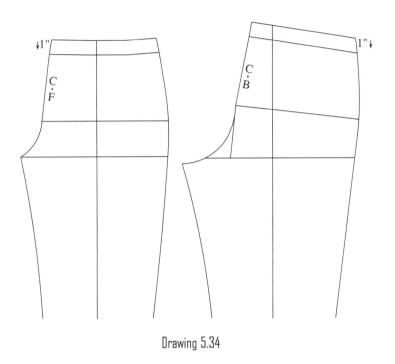

Drawing 5.34

Drawing 5.35.

- Separate the waistband.
- Flip the back piece over and connect the front and
  back waistbands at the side seams.
- Trace the waistband as one continuous piece.

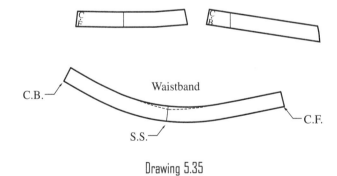

Drawing 5.35

• Mark the grain lines, as shown.

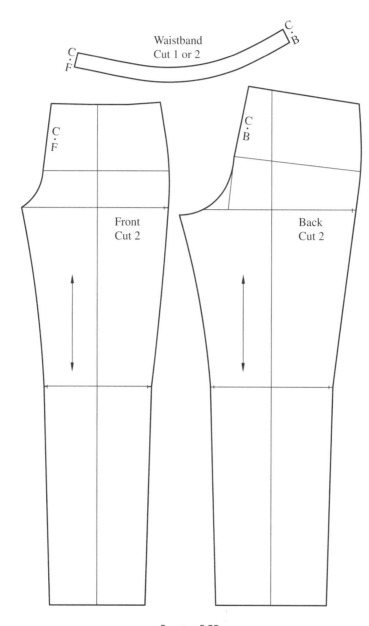

Drawing 5.36

BELL BOTTOMS

his style features a close fit at the knee that flares out to form a bell-shaped silhouette at the hem. This effect is created by adding fullness to both the inner and outer seams at the hem.

✵

Pattern Analysis
- The legs are tapered at the knee and flared out at the hem.
- There is a facing waistband.

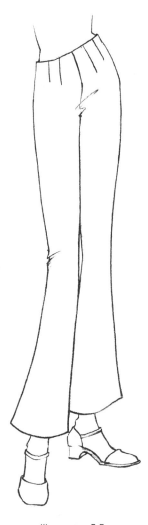

Illustration 5.6

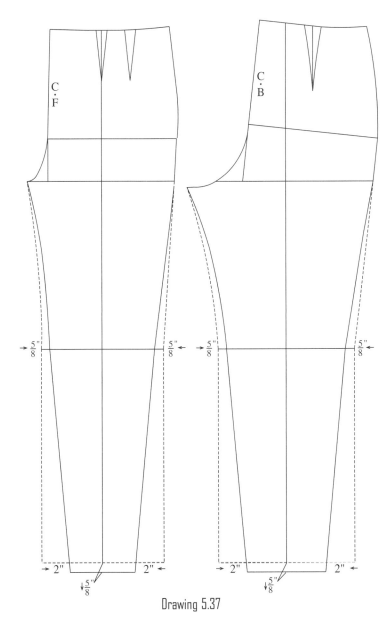

Drawing 5.37

Drawing 5.37. Front and back.

- Trace the pants sloper.
- Measure in $5/8''$ at knee level.
- Measure in $2''$ at the hem.
- Lower the hem $5/8''$.
- Reshape the inseam and out seam.

Drawing 5.38.

- Measure down 2″ from the waistline and draw a line parallel to the waistline.
- Trace the facing separately.
- Add 2″ of flare to each side of the hem.

- Reshape the inseam and out seam, blending from the knee to the new hem.
* **Note:** The flare may blend from the knee or below, depending on the desired style line.
- Reshape the hem with a slight curve, ending square at the inseam and out seam.

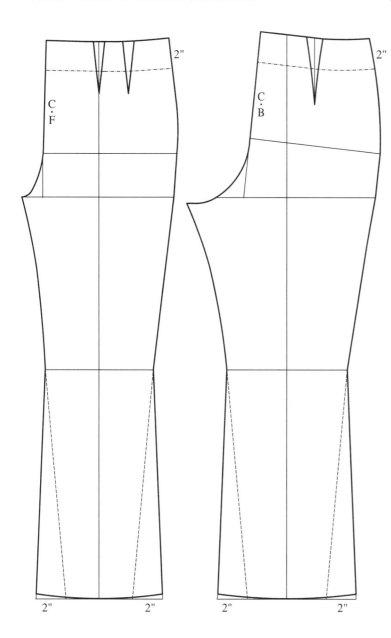

Drawing 5.38

Drawing 5.39. Facing.

- Close the darts, then reshape the facing.

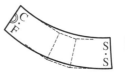

Drawing 5.39

• Mark the notches and grain lines, as shown.

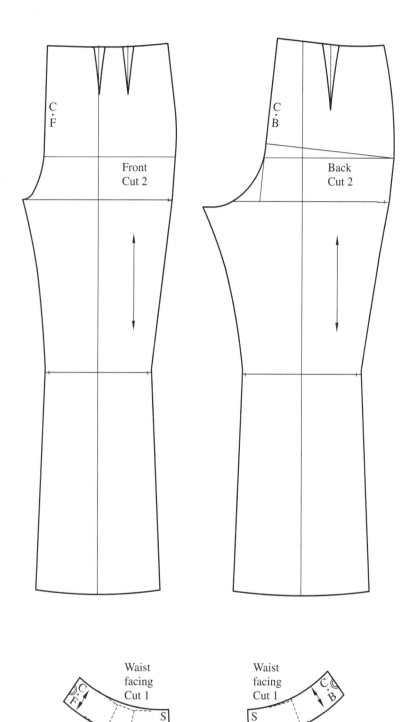

Drawing 5.40

WIDE LEG PANTS

his is a style of pants that increases in width with a straight, nonflared shape as they fall from the hip to the hem.

✳

Pattern Analysis
- Portions of the front and back waist darts are transferred to the hem to spread it 2″.
- The remaining darts are combined into a single dart.
- Inseams and side seams fall straight to the hem.

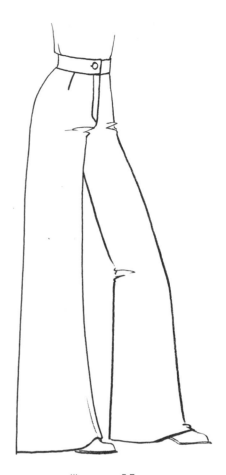

Illustration 5.7

Drawing 5.41. **Front and back.**

- Trace the pants sloper.
- Draw the out seam from the hip line to the hem, perpendicular to the hem.
- Measure the distance from the center line to the new out seam, at the knee.
- Measure out the same distance from the center line toward the inseam, at the knee.

- Measure the distance from the center line to the new out seam, at the hem.
- Measure out the same distance from the center line toward the inseam, at the hem.
- Draw the new inseams to these measurements.

Back:
- Reposition the dart over the center line.

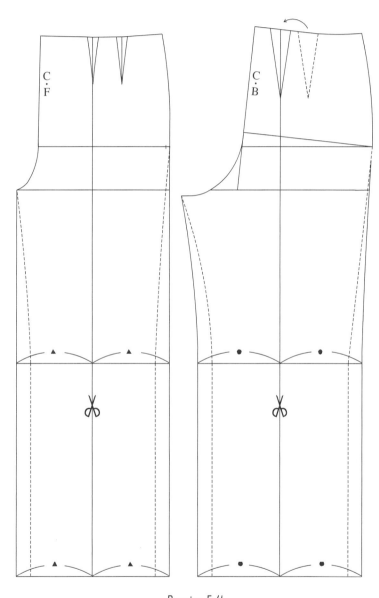

Drawing 5.41

- Slash the center line to, but not through, the dart point.
- Close the dart until the slash line spreads open 3″ at the hem.
- Reshape the hem.
- Reposition the remaining darts at the center line.

- Slash the center line to, but not through, the dart point.
- Close the dart until the slash line spreads open 3″ at the hem.
- Reshape the hem.
- Reposition the remaining darts at the waistline midpoint.

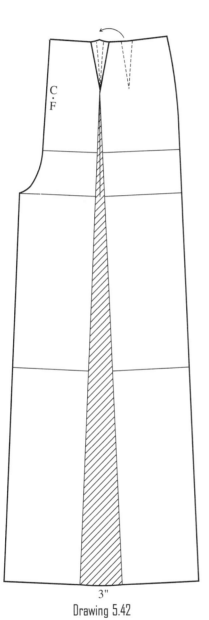

3″

Drawing 5.42

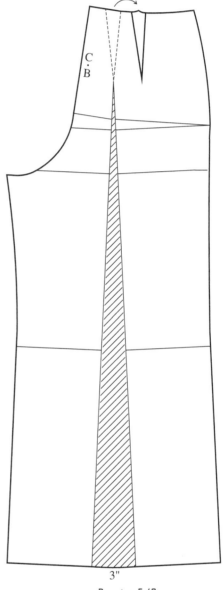

3″

Drawing 5.43

Drawing 5.44. **Wasitband.**

- Draw the waistband, using the following dimensions.
  Length = Waist measurement plus $\frac{1}{2}''$.
  Height = $1\frac{1}{4}''$.
  Button extension = 1″.

Waist measurement $\frac{1}{2}''$

Drawing 5.44

Drawing 5.45. **Finished patterns.**

- Mark the notches and grain lines, as shown.

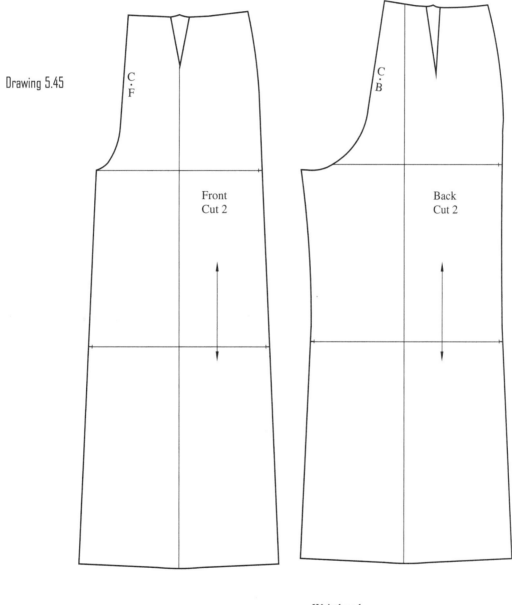

Drawing 5.45

C
·
F

C
·
B

Front
Cut 2

Back
Cut 2

Waistband
Cut 1

TWO-PLEAT PANTS

$\mathcal{I}$n this style of pants, pleats are added to the front waistline to create fullness, which then tapers to the hem.

❖

Pattern Analysis

- Crotch depth is lengthened for a loose fit.
- Pleat intake is added at the waistline.

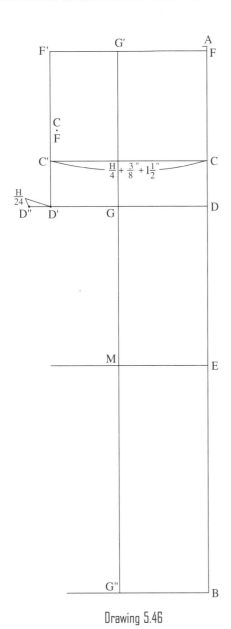

Drawing 5.46

Illustration 5.8

Drawing 5.46. Front pants foundation.

- AB = Pant length.
- AC = Hip depth.
- AD = Crotch depth plus $^3/_8''$ to $^3/_4''$ for ease.
- AE = Knee length. One half of line DB minus 2''.
- Measure down $^3/_8''$ from A for waistband height, and label F.
- CC′ = One fourth of the hip measurement plus $^3/_8''$ for ease and $1^1/_2''$ for pleats.
- FF′ = CC′.
- DD′ = CC′.
- Square up from C′ to F′ at the waistline.
- Square down from C′ to D′ at the crotch line.
- D′D″ = One twenty-fourth of the hip measurement.
- G = The midpoint of line DD″.
- Square up and down from point G.
- Label G′ at the waistline and G″ at the hem.
- Label M at the knee level on G′G″.

Drawing 5.47. Crotch curve.

- H = Measure in $3/8''$ from F′.
- I = One third of D′F′.
- Connect H to I.
- Connect I to D″.
- Draw a line from D′, perpendicular to ID″, and label X.
- Mark a point on D′X two thirds of its length from D′.
- Draw a crotch curve from I to D″, passing through the two-thirds mark.

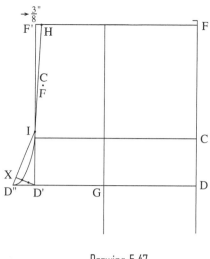

Drawing 5.47

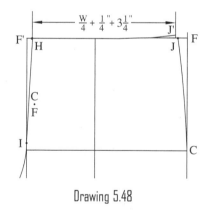

Drawing 5.48

Drawing 5.48. Waistline and pleats.

- HJ = One fourth of the waist measurement plus $1/4''$ for ease and $3 1/4''$ for pleats.
- Measure up $1/4''$ from J and label J′.
- Blend J′ to the midpoint of the waistline with a slightly curved line.
- Blend J′ to C with a curved line.

Drawing 5.49. Inseam and side seam.

- K = The midpoint of D′D″.
- L = Measure out 5″ from G″.
- Connect K to L with a straight line.
- Label N at the knee level on KL.
- Connect D″ to N with a curved line, blending into line NL.
- G″L′ = G″L.
- MN′ = MN.
- Connect N′ to L′ with a straight line.
- Connect C to N′ with a slightly curved line, blending into line N′L′.

Drawing 5.50. Pleats placement.

- Y = Measure out $^3/_8$″ from point G′.
- Connect Y to G″ with a dashed line.
- Y′ = Measure over 2″ from Y, as shown.
- Connect from Y′ to G″ with a dashed line.
- Mark 2″-long pleat lines from Y and Y′, following the dashed line.
- Z = Measure out $1^1/_2$″ from Y′.
- Z′ = Measure out $1^1/_4$″ from Z.
- Square a line down from the midpoint of ZZ′ to CC′ (hip line) and label X.
- Connect point X to points Z and Z′ with a dashed line.
- Mark 2″-long pleat lines from Z and Z′, following the dashed line.

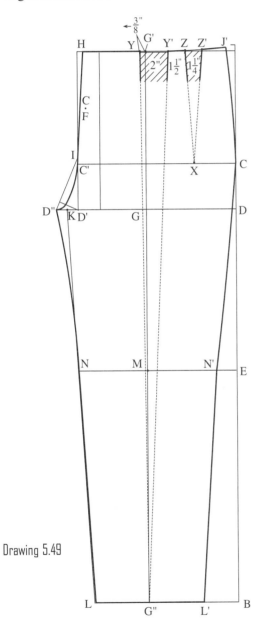

Drawing 5.49

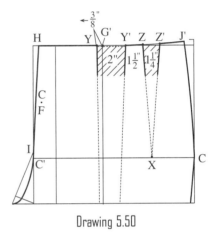

Drawing 5.50

Drawing 5.51. **Back.**

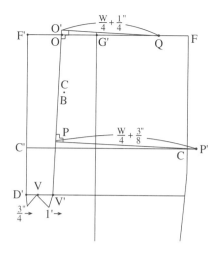

Drawing 5.51

- Draw the pants foundation, following the instructions for Drawing 5.46.
- Measure in $3/4''$ from D$'$ and label V.
- Measure in $1''$ from V and label V$'$.
- O = The midpoint of F$'$G$'$.
- Connect V$'$ to O, extending through the waistline.
- Extend C$'$C (hip line) from point C.
- P$'$ = One fourth of the hip measurement plus $3/8''$ from OV$'$ on the hip line (C$'$C).
- Draw a line from P$'$ perpendicular to OV$'$, then label P at the intersection of this line and OV$'$.
- Q = One fourth of the waist measurement plus $1/8''$ from OV$'$ on the waistline (F$'$F).
- Draw a line from Q perpendicular to OV$'$, then label O$'$ at the intersection of this line and OV$'$.

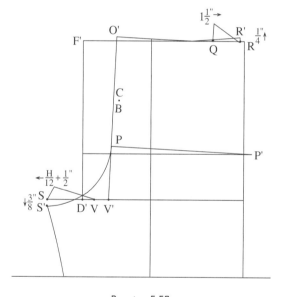

Drawing 5.52

Drawing 5.52. **Waistline and crotch curve.**

- R = Measure out $1\frac{1}{2}''$ from Q for dart intake.
- R$'$ = Square up $1/4''$ from R.
- Blend R$'$ to the waistline (O$'$Q) with a slightly curved line.
- Measure out from V one twelfth of the hip measurement plus $1/2''$ and label S.
- Measure down $3/8''$ from S and label S$'$.
- Draw a $1''$ line from S$'$ toward D$'$, running parallel to D$'$S.
- Draw the back crotch curve from P to the parallel line at S$'$, as shown.

Drawing 5.53. **Dart placement, inseam, and side seam.**

- Measure in 3″ from point O′ and label 1.
- Measure in 3/4″ from point 1 and label 2.
- Square a line 5″ down from the midpoint of points 1 and 2, and label 3.
- Draw the dart legs by connecting point 3 to points 1 and 2.
- Measure over 1½″ toward the side seam, then draw the second dart using points 4, 5, and 6.
- Draw a hip curve connecting point R′ to P′.
- MT = The length of MN (from front) plus ½″.
- MT′ = MT.
- G″U = The length of G″L plus ½″.
- G″U′ = G″U.
- Connect T′ to U′ with a straight line.
- Connect P′ to T′ with a slightly curved line, blending into line T′U′.
- Connect T to U with a straight line.
- Connect S′ to T with a slightly curved line, blending into line TU.

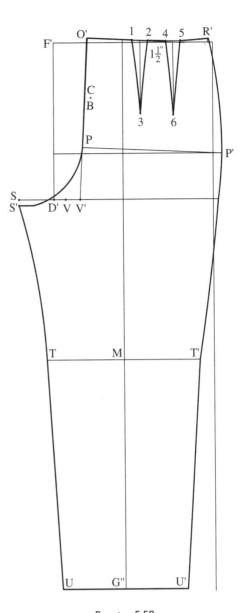

Drawing 5.53

- Mark the notches and grain lines, as shown.

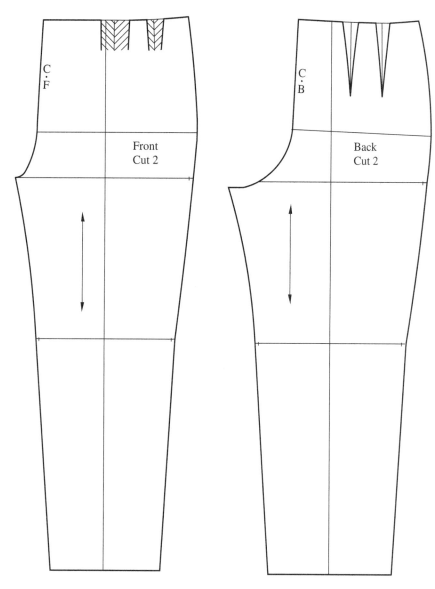

Drawing 5.54

LEGGINGS WITH ELASTIC BAND

his is a style of pants made of a stretch fabric for a close fit, generally conforming to the shape of the leg.

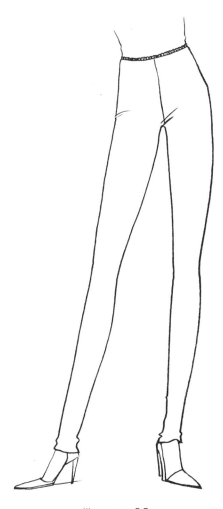

Pattern Analysis

- The crotch depth and length are shortened.
- Waist darts are eliminated.
- The legs are narrowed for a tight fit that conforms to the shape of the leg.
- The center back seam is raised at the waistline to compensate for the shortening of the crotch.
- The waistband is continued from the pants pattern as a fold-over casing to contain an elastic band.
- Front and back side seams are connected, eliminating the side seam.

Illustration 5.9

Drawing 5.55. Front.

- Trace the front pants sloper, but do not trace the waist darts.
- Raise the hem 1″.
- Measure in 1¼″ from the center front at the waist and label A.
- Measure over one fourth of the waist measurement from A and label A′.
- Reshape the waistline.
- Measure in ³/₈″ from the center front at the hip line and label B.
- Connect point A to B with a straight line.
- Raise the crotch line ⁵/₈″.
- Measure in ³/₈″ at the crotch point and mark.
- Reshape the crotch curve, connecting point B to the mark.
- Measure over one fourth of the hip measurement minus ½″ from B and label B′.
- Draw a hip line curve connecting point A′ to B′.
- Measure out 2³/₄″ from the center line on each side of the knee.
- Measure out 1³/₄″ from the center line on each side of the hem.
- **Note:** The pant width may be varied.
- Reshape the inseam and out seam.

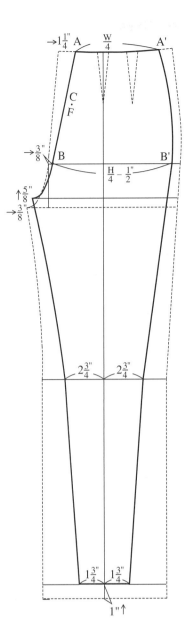

Drawing 5.55

Drawing 5.56. **Back.**

- Trace the front legging pattern.
- Extend the center back 1½″ from A at the waist and label D.
- Measure one fourth of the waist measurement from D to line AA′ and label D′.
- Reshape the waistline.
- Draw a hip line curve connecting point D′ to B′.
- Extend the crotch line 1½″ at the crotch point.
- Reshape the back crotch curve.
- Measure out 3¼″ from the center line on each side of the knee.
- Measure out 2¼″ from the center line on each side of the hem.
- Reshape the inseam and out seam.

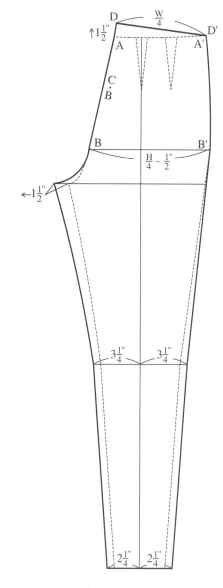

Drawing 5.56

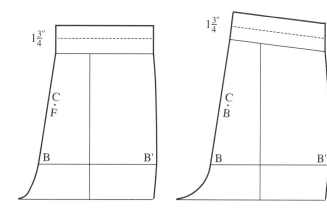

Drawing 5.57

Drawing 5.57. **Elastic waistband.**

- Draw a casing line 1³/₄″ up from and parallel to the waistline.
- Extend the center front and center back lines to the casing line.
- Extend the hip lines to the casing line.
- Mark the fold line at the center of the casing.

182 *Apparel Making in Fashion Design*

Drawing 5.58. Leggings with waistband.

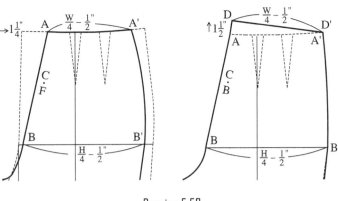

Drawing 5.58

- Follow the steps used to create the leggings with elastic band, only the length of AA′ will be equal to one fourth of the waist measurement minus ½″.
- Draw the waistband.

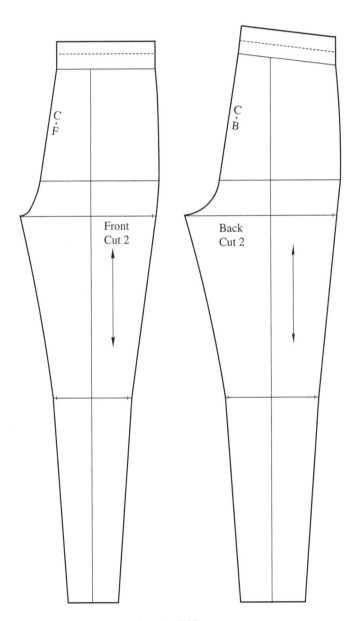

Drawing 5.59

Drawing 5.59. Finished patterns.

- Mark the notches and grain lines, as shown.

Drawing 5.60. Leggings without side seam.

- Trace the front legging pattern.
- Label B′ at the hip line on the side seam.
- Draw a horizontal guideline from B′.
- Draw a vertical guideline through B′.
- Align the back legging pattern, matching the hip line to point B′ at the side seam, then trace it.
- At the center front on the waist, mark in an amount equal to the distance from the front side seam to the vertical guideline.
- At the center back on the waist, mark in an amount equal to the distance from the back side seam to the vertical guideline.
- Reshape the front and back side seams, passing through the marks.
- On the front inseam at both the knee and hem, mark in an amount equal to the distance from the front side seam to the vertical guideline.
- On the back inseam at both the knee and hem, mark in an amount equal to the distance from the back side seam to the vertical guideline.
- Reshape the front and back inseams, from the crotch point to the hem, passing through the marks.
- Reshape the waistline with a smooth, continuous line.
- Draw a parallel line 1½″ above the waistline to create the casing for the elastic band.
- Mark the fold line ³⁄₄″ below the casing line.

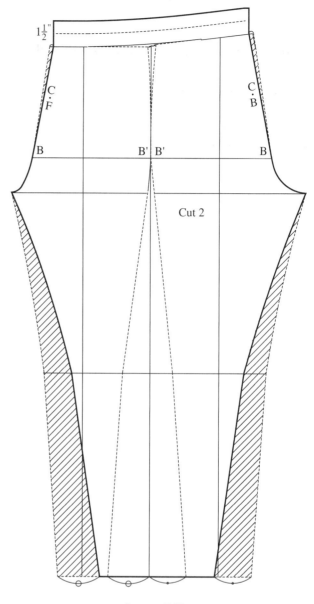

Drawing 5.60

BAGGY PANTS

his is a unisex style of pants that are pulled on and secured with a drawstring at the waist.

❁

Pattern Analysis
- Darts become part of the shirring.
- Additional fullness is added between the front and back side seams and inseams.
- The crotch depth is lengthened for a loose fit.
- Waistband is continued from the pants pattern as a fold-over casing to contain a drawstring.

Illustration 5.10

Drawing 5.61. Front and back.

- Trace the front pants sloper.
- Draw a horizontal guideline, passing through the front crotch line, as shown.
- On the horizontal guideline, measure in 2″ from the side seam and draw a vertical guideline.
- From there, measure over another 2″ in the same direction and mark.
- Align the back sloper, matching the side seam to the mark, then trace it.

- Lower the crotch line $5/8$″.
- Extend the front and back crotch curves out $5/8$″.
- Reshape the crotch curves.
- Square up from the hip lines, extending the center front line 3″ above the waistline.
- Draw the casing for the string perpendicular to the center front, connecting to the center back.
- Mark the fold line $1\frac{1}{2}$″ below the casing line.
- Extend the hem $1\frac{1}{2}$″.
- Square down from the new crotch line, to the new hemline.

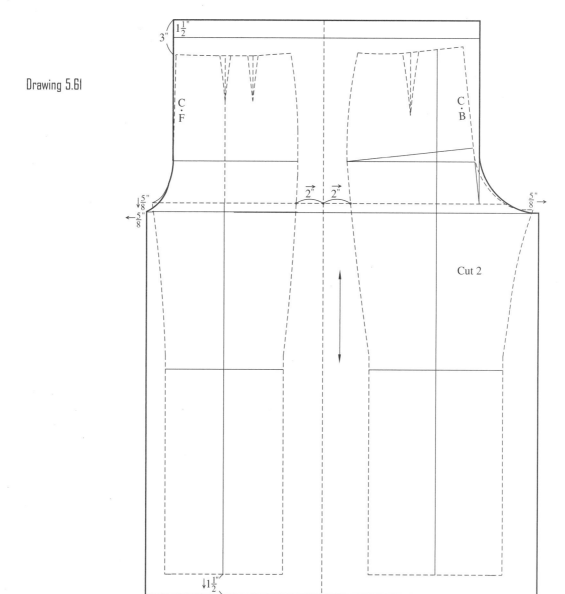

Drawing 5.61

Drawing 5.62. Cuff.

- Draw the cuff, using the dimensions shown.

Drawing 5.62

SHORT PANTS

n this style of pants pleats are added to the front waistline for fullness. The pants length falls between mid-thigh and knee level.

Illustration 5.11

Pattern Analysis

- The pattern is developed from the pants sloper, with a shortened length.
- Waist darts become part of the pleats.
- An additional pleat intake is created by slashing from the waistline to, but not through, the hem, and then spreading at the waistline.
- There is a cuffed hem.

• Trace the front and back pants slopers.

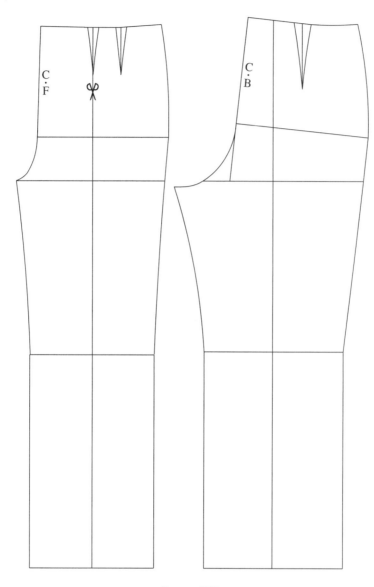

Drawing 5.63

Drawing 5.64. Front.

- Cut along the center line to, but not through, the hem.
- Spread the slash line open 1½″ at the waistline.

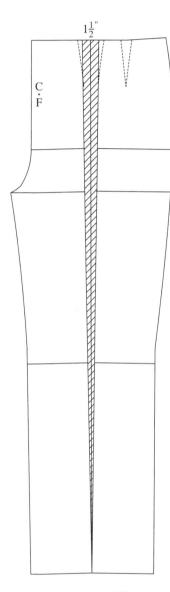

Drawing 5.64

Drawing 5.65. Front pleats and pocket.

- * **Note:** The total pleat intake consists of both darts plus a 1½″ spread.
- The first pleat is 2″ wide and is centered over the center line.
- The width of the second pleat is equal to the remainder of the total pleat intake (*n*) and is placed 1½″ over from the first pleat.
  Example: If the total intake of both darts and the 1½″ spread equals 3″, make the first pleat 2″ wide (centered over the center line), and make the second pleat 1″.
- Draw the pocket style line 6″ to 7″ long.

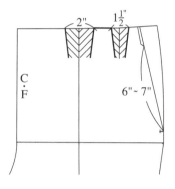

Drawing 5.65

Drawing 5.66. Pocket.

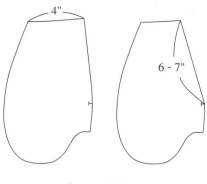

Drawing 5.66

- Refer to the front hip pocket instructions from Drawing 7.76 in Chapter 7 to complete the pocket, using the dimensions shown.

Drawing 5.67. Front and back.

- Decide the pants length from the crotch line.
- Measure in $1/4''$ on both sides of the hem.
- **Note:** The measurement on each side of the center line, at the hem, is equal.
- Reshape the inseams and out seams.

Rolled-up cuffs:
- Measure down $3^1/4''$ from the hem for the cuff.
- Add a $1^1/4''$ hem.
- Mark the fold lines at the center of the cuff and at the hem.
- Fold along the fold lines and redraw the inseam and out seam.

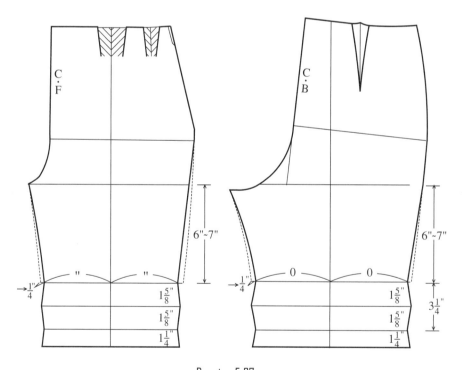

Drawing 5.67

• Label the pattern pieces and mark the notches and
  grain lines, as shown.

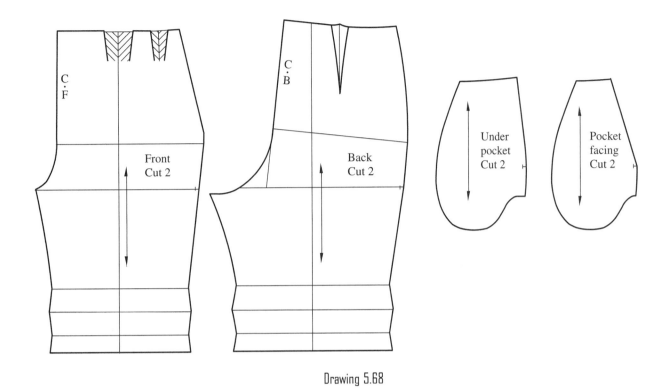

Drawing 5.68

Chapter Six

THE DART

INTRODUCTION TO THE DART

$\mathcal{D}$arts are used to control the excess fabric between the bust and waist circumferences, between the top and bottom of the shoulder blade of top garments, and between the waist and hip circumferences of bottom garments. Placed at the fullest areas of the body, darts are essential for creating garments that fit individual body contours accurately. The top front dart coincides with the bust point, whereas the bottom dart coincides with the hip and abdomen measurements. These dart points are always in the same position and cannot be relocated to another area of the pattern (bodice—bust point; skirt—hip or abdomen). However, the darts themselves can be transferred to another position on the pattern, so long as they still end at the original dart point.

✺

Illustration 6.1

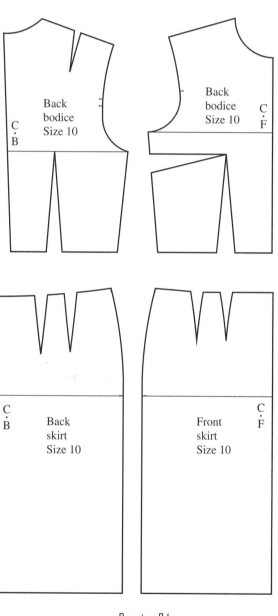

Drawing 6.1

Dart Point

The dart point is the end point of the dart. Its position may vary with bust size, but it is always positioned in an area where the body's contour is at its fullest, generally ¹/₂" to 2" away from the bust point. This generates a smoother, more naturally rounded look in the finished garment.

Dart Intake

The dart intake is the amount of excess fabric that is taken in to control the fit of the garment. This intake is positioned between the dart legs and is removed from the garment when the dart is sewn. The dart intake may be decorative as well as functional and may be sewn as a dart, tuck, or gather, depending on the design.

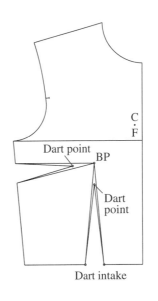
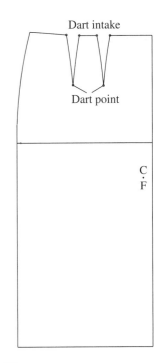

Drawing 6.2

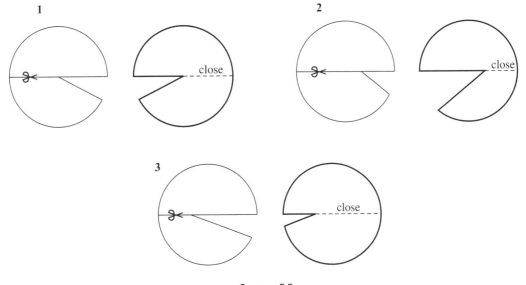

Drawing 6.3

Drawing 6.3. **Dart intake amount.**

1. If the existing dart length equals the length of the slash line, the new dart will thus be the same as the original dart.
2. If the new dart length is longer than the original dart length, the dart intake will be larger than the original dart intake.
3. If the new dart length is shorter than the original dart length, the dart intake will be smaller than the original dart intake.

Dart Placement

Darts can be transferred to any of the positions indicated by the lines below, or even to positions between the lines.

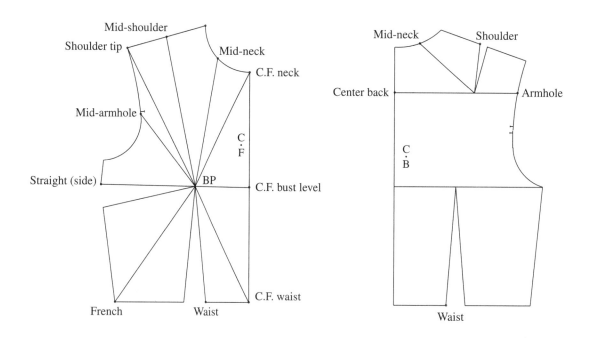

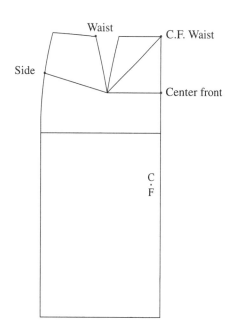

Drawing 6.4

Dart Equivalent

The darts can be converted into tucks, pleats, or shirring, depending on the desired style, to create a different appearance, as follows:

Converting Skirt Darts

- A dart is sewn from the seam line to the dart point.
- A pleat is precisely folded and sewn only at the seam line.
- Shirring, as a more random distribution of the excess fabric, is also sewn only at the seam line.
- A tuck dart is sewn only from the seam line to a certain point along the dart.

Illustration 6.2

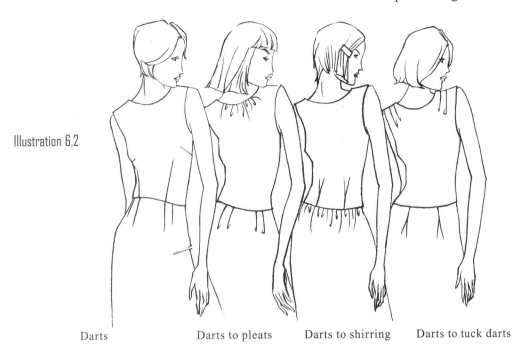

Darts   Darts to pleats   Darts to shirring   Darts to tuck darts

Drawing 6.5.

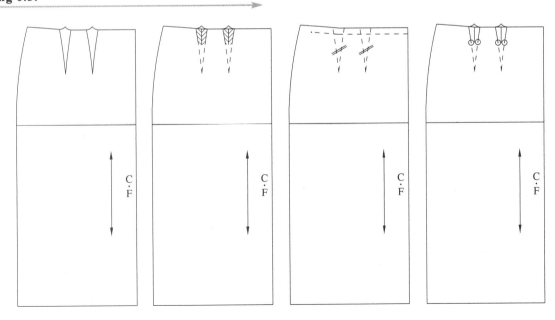

Drawing 6.5

Dart Manipulation

Dart manipulation is the process of transferring a dart from one position to another. There are two different methods for dart transfer: slash and close, and pivot. Both methods are relatively effective as a means of manipulating the darts, but as slash and close is more straightforward visually, this text focuses exclusively on that method. By transferring darts, various style lines or design details can be created; however, this will not change the fit.

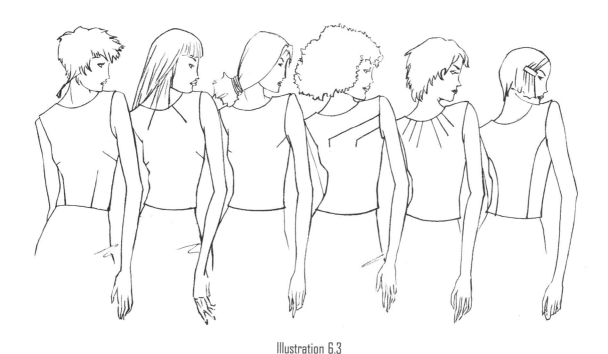

Illustration 6.3

Slash and Close versus Pivot Methods

The slash and close and pivot methods of dart transfer offer different approaches to achieving the same net result. Although this text focuses on the use of slash and close, it is still important to understand both methods. The following brief overview compares and contrasts each of these processes. This comparison is made in the context of the specific application of both methods to create both side and neck darts.

Design Feature
• The waist dart is transferred to the neckline.
• The side and neck darts are sewn.

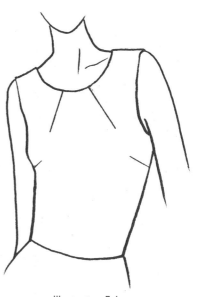

Illustration 6.4

Drawing 6.6. Slash and close method.

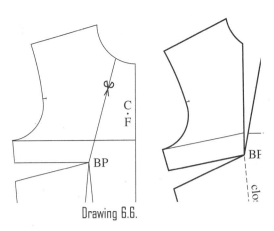

Drawing 6.6.

- To transfer the dart to the desired position, draw a new dart from the desired position to the bust point (BP).
- Slash this line to the bust point, and close the existing dart.
- Reposition the new dart to the slash line.
- Retrace the pattern on another piece of paper.

Drawing 6.7. Pivot method: Instead of slashing the new dart line, the pattern is pivoted around when the dart is closed.

- Draw the position of the new dart from the bust point to the mid-neckline on the front bodice.
- Label points A, B, and X.
- Place a pushpin at the bust point.

- Trace the pattern piece from A, around center front, to point X.
- Close the waist dart by pivoting and matching point B to A. The new dart leg will pivot to the placement of the second dart leg at the neck.
- Trace the remainder of the pattern piece from point X to point B.

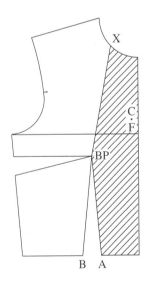 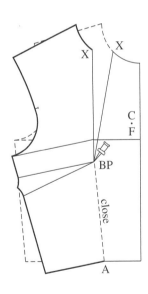 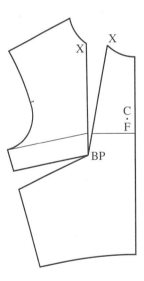

Drawing 6.7

DART 1. ONE-POSITION DART

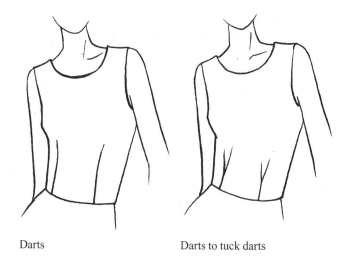

Darts   Darts to tuck darts

Illustration 6.5

he single dart can be placed on any seam line of the garment.

❋

Design Feature 1: Waist Dart
- The side dart is transferred to the waist dart.
- The waist dart can be sewn as darts or as tuck darts.

Drawing 6.8.

- Trace the front bodice sloper.
- Close the side dart.
- *** Note:** the side dart is transferred to the waist.
- Mark the center of the waist dart.
- Reposition the dart point 1" from the bust point, as shown.
- Redraw the dart legs.
- True the side seam with a straight line.

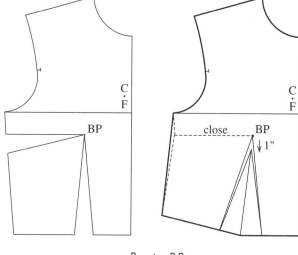

Drawing 6.8

Drawing 6.9. Converting a dart to a tuck dart.

- Measure up 2" from the waistline on each dart leg and mark with a circle, as shown.
- Mark the fold line, centered between the dart legs.

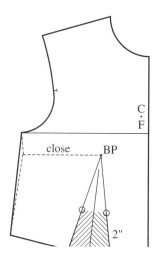

Drawing 6.9

Design Feature 2: Neck Dart

- The side and waist darts are transferred to the neck.
- The neck dart starts anywhere on the neckline.
- The neck darts can be sewn as darts or as shirring.

Darts   Darts to Shirring

Illustration 6.6

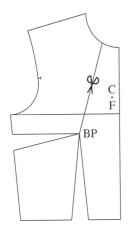 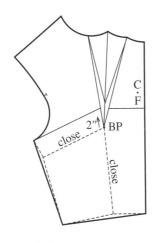

Drawing 6.10

Drawing 6.10. **Finished pattern.**

- Trace the front bodice sloper.
- Draw a slash line from the bust point to a point on the neckline.
- Cut along the slash line to, but not through, the bust point.
- Close the waist and side darts and the slash line will spread open.
- * **Note:** This creates the mid-neck dart.
- Mark the center of the new dart.
- Reposition the dart point 2" above the bust point, as shown.
- Redraw the dart legs.
- True the waistline and side seam.

Drawing 6.11. **Converting darts to shirring.**

- Add 1" to the neckline and then reshape the neckline with a smooth curve.

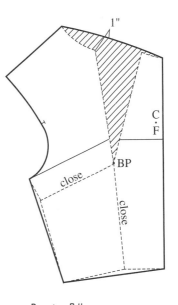

Drawing 6.11

Design Feature 3: Center Front Dart

- The side and waist darts are transferred to the center front.
- The seam lines vary, depending on which part of center front is placed on the fold, as follows:
  1. When the top portion of the center front is placed on the fold, the seam line is from the center front dart down to the waistline.
  2. When the lower portion of the center front is placed on the fold, the seam line is from the center front dart up to the neckline.
  3. When the pattern is cut as two pieces, the seam line is down the entire center front of the bodice.

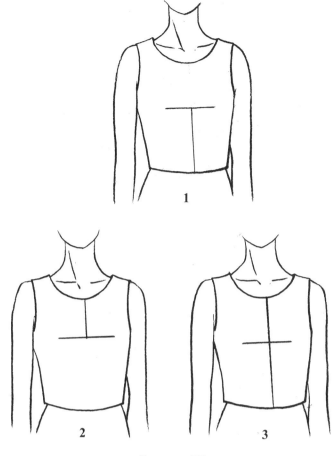

Illustration 6.7

Drawing 6.12. **Finished pattern.**

- Trace the front bodice sloper.
- Draw a slash line perpendicular to the center front from the bust point.
- Cut along the slash line to the bust point.
- Close the waist and side darts and the slash line will spread down.
- **Note:** This creates the center front dart.
- Mark the center of the new dart.
- Reposition the dart point $1/2$" from the bust point, as shown.
- Redraw the dart legs.
- True the waistline and side seam.

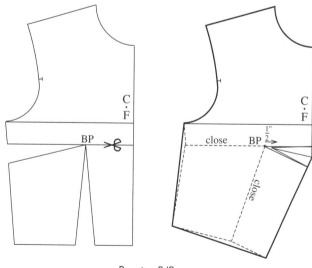

Drawing 6.12

DART 2. TWO-POSITION DART

$\mathcal{T}$he two darts are each placed on different seam lines to create a smoother fit in the finished garment. When starting with a one-dart pattern, transfer half of the existing dart to the first dart placement and the other half to the second dart placement. By dividing the dart's angle in this way, the fullness at each dart end point is lessened, thus achieving a smoother fit.

Design Feature 1: Shoulder Tip and Waist Darts

- Two darts are used—one at the waist and one at the shoulder tip.
- The side dart is transferred to the shoulder tip.

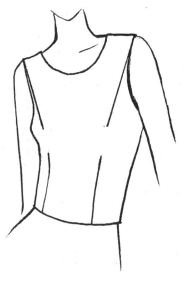

Illustration 6.8

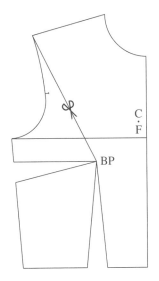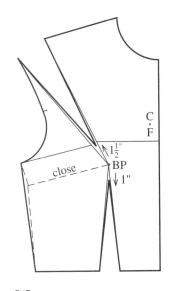

Drawing 6.13

Drawing 6.13. **Finished pattern.**

- Trace the front bodice sloper.
- Draw a slash line from the shoulder tip to the bust point.
- Cut along the slash line to the bust point.
- Close the side dart and the slash line will spread open.
- *** Note:** This creates the shoulder tip dart.
- Mark the darts at their centers.
- Reposition the dart points $1^1/_2$" from the bust point, as shown.
- Redraw the dart legs and true the side seam.

Design Feature 2: Armhole and Waist Darts

- Two darts are used—one at the waist and one at the armhole.
- The side dart is transferred to mid-armhole.

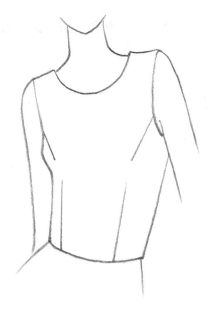

Illustration 6.9

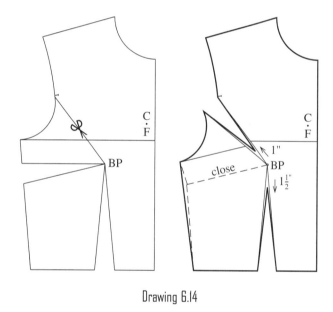

Drawing 6.14

Drawing 6.14. Finished pattern.

- Trace the front bodice sloper.
- Draw a slash line from a point at mid-armhole to the bust point.
- Cut along the slash line to the bust point.
- Close the side dart and the slash line will spread open.
- * **Note:** This creates the mid-armhole dart.
- Mark the darts at their centers.
- Reposition the dart point of the mid-armhole dart 1" from the bust point, as shown.
- Reposition the dart point of the waist dart $1\frac{1}{2}$" from the bust point, as shown.
- Redraw the dart legs and true the side seam.

DART 3. MULTIPLE DARTS

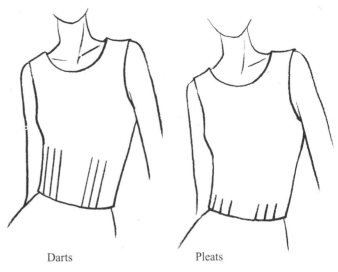

hen the total dart excess is split among multiple darts, the result is a smoother fitting garment. This is achieved by first combining the two existing darts into one, then dividing the dart into multiple darts.

Darts   Pleats

Illustration 6.10

❋

Design Feature 1: Waist Dart
- The side dart is transferred to the waist, combined with the waist dart, and then split into multiple darts.
- The darts can be sewn as darts or pleats.

Drawing 6.15.

- Trace the front bodice sloper.
- Draw slash lines 1" from each side of the waist dart, connecting to the bust point with diagonal lines.

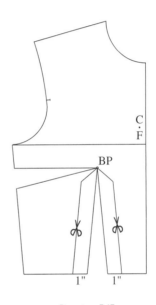

Drawing 6.15

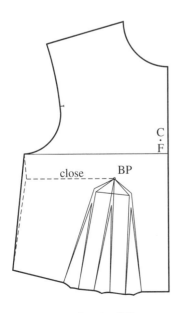

Drawing 6.16

Drawing 6.16. Finished pattern.

- Cut along the slash lines to the bust point.
- Close the side dart.
- Spread each slash line an equal amount apart, including the waist dart.
- Reposition the dart points away from the bust point, then draw the new dart legs.
- **Note:** Each dart may be the same length or vary.
- True the side seam.

Drawing 6.17. Converting darts to pleats.

- Draw the pleat lines 2" up from the waist on the dart legs.

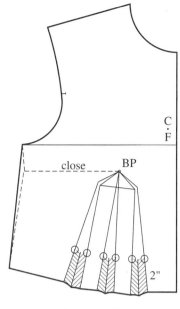

Drawing 6.17

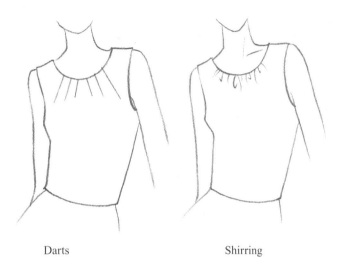

Darts   Shirring

Illustration 6.11

Design Feature 2: Neckline Dart
- The side and waist darts are transferred to the neck, and then split into multiple darts.
- The darts can be sewn as darts or shirring.

Drawing 6.18.

- Trace the front bodice sloper.
- Draw a guideline from the mid-neck point to the bust point.
- Draw three slash lines from the guidelines, 1" apart and connecting diagonally to the bust point.

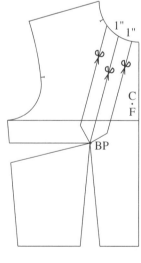

Drawing 6.18

Drawing 6.19. Finished pattern.

- Cut along the slash lines to the bust point.
- Close the side and waist darts.
- Spread each slash line an equal amount apart.
- Draw the new dart legs, repositioning the dart points away from the bust point.
- * **Note:** Each dart may be the same length or vary.
- True the side seam and waistline.

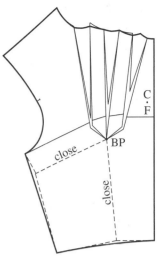

Drawing 6.19

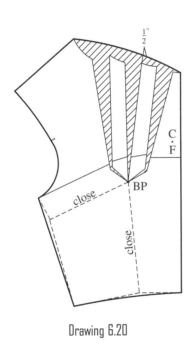

Drawing 6.20

Drawing 6.20. Converting darts to shirring.

- Add ¹/₂" from the slash line at the neck.
- Reshape the neckline with a smooth curve.

Style lines can be created by crossing over or away from the bust point. They absorb dart intake within seam lines while providing the same control over fit. The dart will be completely cut away, after which the bodice pattern is separated into multiple pieces, then sewn back together. Shifting the waist darts can enhance the natural quality of the style line.

Classic Princess Lines

A princess line is created by combining the side and waist darts into a seam line. Princess lines can be created at the original waist dart position, or by shifting it toward or away from the center front and center back. Princess style lines start from a point on the armhole or shoulder line, then continue over the dart point to the waistline. This style line is most commonly used in blouses, dresses, jackets, and coats.

Design Feature 1: Princess Line from Shoulder
• The side dart is transferred to mid-shoulder, and the waist and shoulder darts are converted to the princess style line.

Illustration 6.12

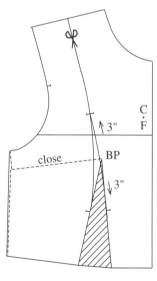

Drawing 6.21

Drawing 6.21.

• Trace the front bodice sloper.
• Transfer the side dart to the waist dart.
* **Note:** Refer to the one-position dart instructions from Drawing 6.8.
• Draw a princess style line from mid-shoulder, blending with the waist dart.
• Measure down 3" from the bust point on each waist dart leg and mark a notch.
• Measure up 3" from the bust point on each shoulder dart leg and mark a notch.

Drawing 6.22. **Finished pattern.**

- Separate the pattern pieces, eliminating the waist dart.
- Smooth the princess line.

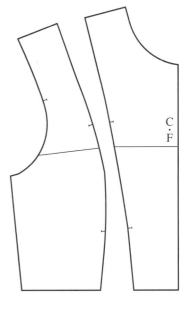

Drawing 6.22

Illustration 6.13

Design Feature 2: Princess Line from Armhole
- The side dart is transferred to the waist dart.
- The princess line starts mid-armhole and blends to the waist dart.
- The waist dart is converted to the princess style line.

Drawing 6.23.

- Trace the front bodice sloper.
- Transfer the side dart to the waist dart.
- Reposition the waist dart to accommodate the desired style line placement, as shown.
- Draw a princess style line from the middle of the armhole, blending with the waist dart.
- Measure down 3" from the bust point on each waist dart leg and mark a notch.
- Measure up 1" from the bust point and mark a notch.

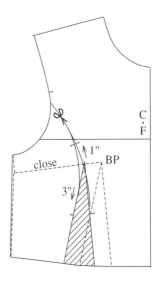

Drawing 6.23

Drawing 6.24. Finished pattern.

- Cut along the princess style line, eliminating the waist dart.

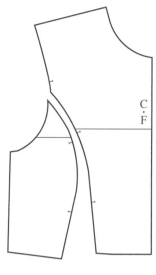

Drawing 6.24

Illustration 6.14

Drawing 6.25.

- Trace front bodice sloper.
- Draw a slash line from the neck to the bust point.
- Mark the notches.
- Transfer the side dart to the neck.
- True the side seam.

Style Line Variations

The darts are converted to the style line, which will now provide the same control over fit. The resulting style line will start from the shoulder tip, the mid-shoulder, or somewhere on the neckline or armhole, pass through the bust point, and continue on to the waistline.

Design Feature 1
- The side dart is transferred to the neck.
- The neck and waist darts are converted to the style line.

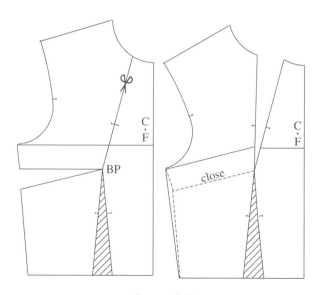

Drawing 6.25

Drawing 6.26. Finished pattern.

- Separate the pattern pieces, eliminating the waist dart.
- Smooth the style line.

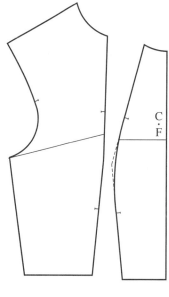

Drawing 6.26

Illustration 6.15

Design Feature 2
- The side dart is transferred to mid-shoulder, and the waist dart is transferred to the center front at the waist.
- The shoulder and center front darts are converted to the style line.

Drawing 6.27.

Trace the front bodice sloper.
- Draw a slash line from the midpoint of the shoulder to the bust point.
- Draw a slash line from the center front at the waist to the bust point.
- Measure up 3" from the bust point and mark a notch.
- Measure down 3" from the bust point and mark a notch.

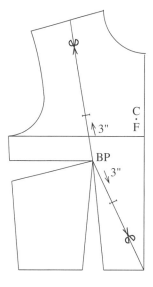

Drawing 6.27

Drawing 6.28. Finished pattern.

- Cut along the slash lines to, but not through, the bust point.
- Close the waist and side darts and the slash lines will open.
- True the waistline and the side seam.
- Separate the pattern pieces.
- Smooth the style line.

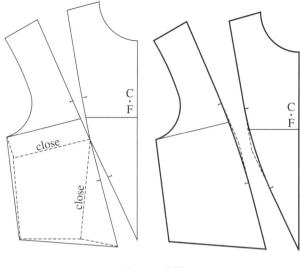

Drawing 6.28

Illustration 6.16

Design Feature 3
- The side dart is transferred to the waist dart.
- The style line starts mid-armhole, passes through the bust point, and continues on to the waist dart.
- The waist dart is converted to the style line.

Drawing 6.29.

- Trace the front bodice sloper.
- Transfer the side dart to the waist dart.
- Draw a style line from the middle of the armhole to the bust point.
- True the side dart.

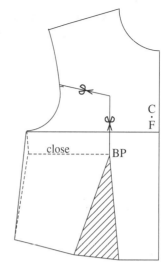

Drawing 6.29

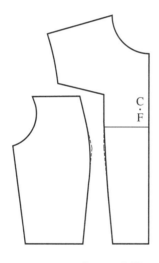

Drawing 6.30

Drawing 6.30. Finished pattern.

- Cut along the style line, through the bust point as shown, eliminating the waist dart.
- Smooth the style line.

DART 5. ADDITIONAL SLASH AND SPREAD

arts may be combined with additional fullness in various ways, such as gathers, pleats, or tucks.

❋

Design Feature 1
- The waist and side darts become part of the fullness, which may be shirred or left open in a flared silhouette.
- Additional fullness is provided using the one-side slash and spread method.

Shirring

Flare

Illustration 6.17

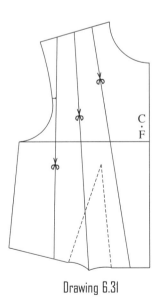

Drawing 6.31

Drawing 6.31.

- Trace the front bodice sloper.
- Transfer the side dart to the waist.
- * **Note:** Refer to the one-position dart instructions from Drawing 6.8.
- Draw the desired number of slash lines from the waistline to the shoulder line.

Drawing 6.32. Finished pattern.

- Cut along the slash lines from the waistline to, but not through, the shoulder line.
- Spread the slash lines as desired for fullness.
- Measure down at least 1" from the slash lines and draw the new hemline for the added fullness and a smooth shape.
- Reshape the shoulder line.

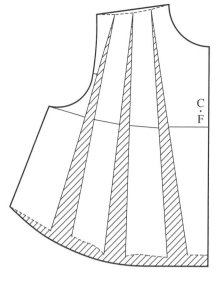

Drawing 6.32

Illustration 6.18

Design Feature 2
- The waist dart is sewn, and the neck dart is converted to shirring with added fullness.

Drawing 6.33.

- Trace the front bodice sloper.
- Transfer the waist dart to the neck.
- **Note:** Refer to the instructions given in the one-position dart section from Drawing 6.10.
- Draw a slash line from any point on the neckline to the waist for additional fullness.
- Mark a notch ½" over from the slash line, as shown, for the shirring position.

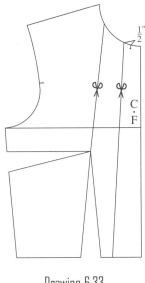

Drawing 6.33

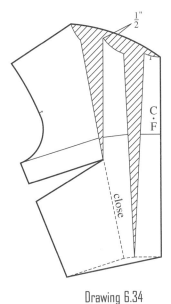

Drawing 6.34

Drawing 6.34. Finished pattern.

- Cut along the slash line to, but not through, the waistline.
- Close the waist dart.
- Spread the slash line as desired for fullness.
- Measure up ½" from the slash lines and draw the new neckline with a smooth curve.
- True the waistline.

DART 6. YOKE STYLE LINE WITH FULLNESS

$\mathscr{A}$ yoke can be added to the upper part of a garment as a style variation. On shirts, dresses, and jackets, it is placed above the bust line in the front and above the shoulder blades in the back. Yokes are generally decorative and intended only to add interest to the garment, but they can also serve as reinforcement devices.

Design Feature 1

- The yoke style line starts from the shoulder, then follows the neckline curve.
- The side and waist darts are transferred to the yoke style line, then shirred.

Illustration 6.19

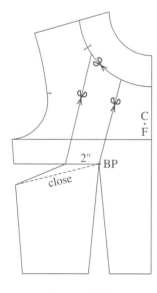

Drawing 6.35

Drawing 6.35.

- Trace the front bodice sloper.
- Draw the yoke style line.
- Reposition the side dart 2" away from the bust point, as shown.
- Draw the slash line from a point on the neckline to the bust point.
- Draw the slash line from a point on the neckline to the side dart point.
- Mark a notch $1/2$" over from the slash line, as shown, for the shirring position.

Drawing 6.36. Finished pattern.

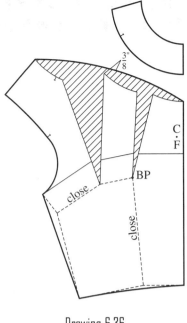

Drawing 6.36

- Separate the yoke piece.
- Cut along the slash lines to, but not through, the dart points.
- Close the waist and side darts and the slash lines will open.
- Measure up ³/₈" (or more) from the slash lines and draw the new neckline with a smooth curve.
- True the side seam and waistline.

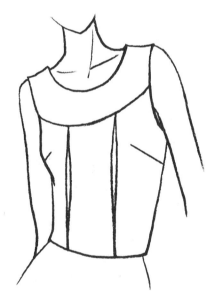

Illustration 6.20

Design Feature 2
- The yoke style line starts at the armhole, then curves toward the center front.
- The waist dart becomes part of the pleat, and the side dart is sewn as a dart.

Drawing 6.37.

- Trace the front bodice sloper but do not trace the waist dart.
- Draw the yoke style line from the armhole to the center front, as shown.
- Reposition the side dart point 1" from the bust point.

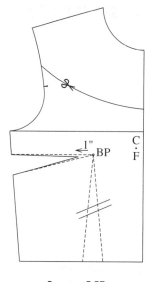

Drawing 6.37

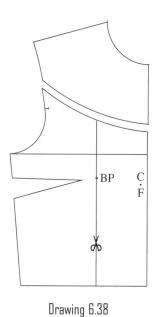

Drawing 6.38

Drawing 6.38.

- Separate the yoke piece.
- Draw a slash line from the desired position for the pleats, then cut along the slash line.

Drawing 6.39. Finished pattern.

- Retrace the pattern pieces, placing them 4" apart for the inverted pleats.
- Mark the fold lines on the pleat.
- Fold the pleat lines and reshape the yoke line on the bodice.

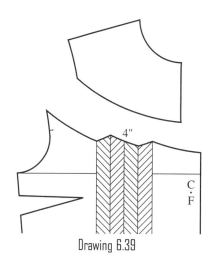

Drawing 6.39

DART 7. STYLIZED DART

Stylized darts can be transferred to any seam line on the garment and are often used to create unusual lines and shapes, such as asymmetric and angled lines. To accomplish this, transfer the darts away from the stylized area to a temporary position.

Asymmetric Dart Variations

Asymmetric darts cross the center front of the garment. To create an asymmetric dart, begin with the entire front bodice sloper.

Design Feature 1
- Both darts start at any angle from the right side armhole to each bust point.
- The first dart crosses the center front, and the second dart is parallel to the first dart.

Illustration 6.21

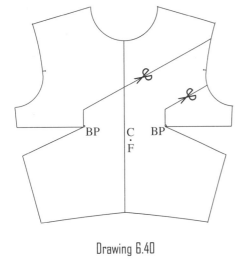

Drawing 6.40

Drawing 6.40.

- Transfer the waist dart to the side dart.
- **Note:** Refer to the one-position dart instructions from Drawing 6.8.
- Trace the entire front bodice sloper.
- Draw the new dart lines at any angle, from the right armhole, ending square to each bust point.

Drawing 6.41.

- Cut along the new dart lines to the bust points.
- Close both side darts and the new dart lines will spread open.

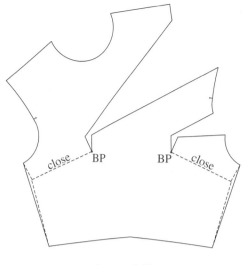

Drawing 6.41

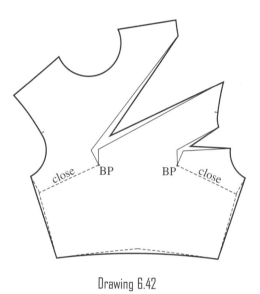

Drawing 6.42

Drawing 6.42. Finished pattern.

- Reposition the dart points.
- True the side seams and waistline.

Illustration 6.22

Design Feature 2

- Two darts run parallel to each other.
- One dart runs from the waistline, across the center front, to a bust point.
- The second dart runs from the shoulder, across the center front, to the other bust point. This dart also helps to form the V-neck shape.

Drawing 6.43.

- Transfer the waist dart to the side dart.
- **Note:** Refer to the one-position dart instructions from Drawing 6.8.
- Trace the entire front bodice sloper.
- Draw the new dart lines: one from the shoulder to the bust point, and the other from the waist to the bust point, as shown.
- Draw the V-neckline, as shown.

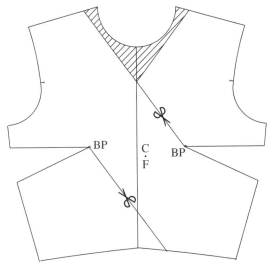

Drawing 6.43

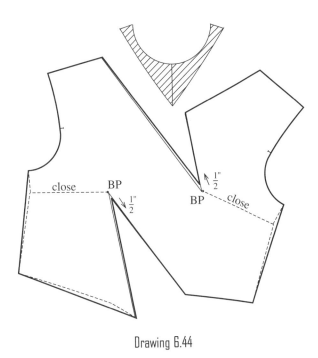

Drawing 6.44

Drawing 6.44. Finished pattern.

- Cut along the new dart lines to the bust points.
- Close both side darts and the new dart lines will spread open.
- Reposition the dart points ½" from the bust point.
- True the side seam and waistline.

Illustration 6.23

Asymmetric Dart with Additional Fullness

Design Feature
- There are darts from the shoulder and side seam, each running to a different bust point, and shirred for additional fullness.
- The neckline has a V shape.

Drawing 6.45.

- Transfer the waist dart to the side dart.
- Trace the entire front bodice sloper.
- Draw the dart lines: from shoulder to bust point, and from side seam to bust point, as shown.
- Mark notches at the desired location on the style line for the shirring.
- Draw three slash lines from the shoulder, intersecting the style line, as shown.
- Draw three slash lines from the side seam, intersecting the style line, as shown.

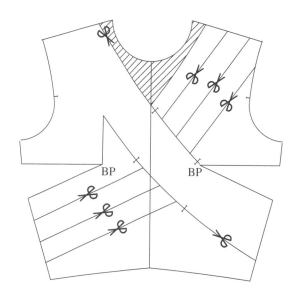

Drawing 6.45

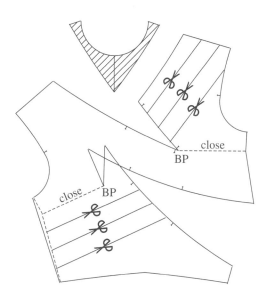

Drawing 6.46

Drawing 6.46.

- Cut along the dart lines to the bust points.
- Close both side darts and the dart lines will spread open.

Drawing 6.47. Finished pattern.

- Cut along the slash lines.
- Spread the slash lines as desired for fullness.
- Measure out $^3/_8$" from the slash lines and reshape the style lines for a contoured shape.
- True the side seam and waistline.

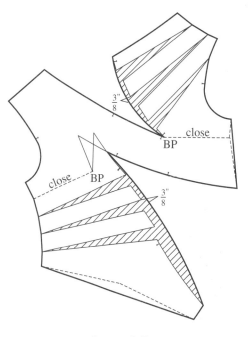

Drawing 6.47

Intersecting Dart Variations

The intersecting dart is similar to the asymmetric dart. It crosses the center front, intersecting a short dart.

Design Feature
- There are two darts, one from each bust point.
- The first dart crosses the center front and ends at the waistline.
- The second dart intersects the first dart line.

Illustration 6.24

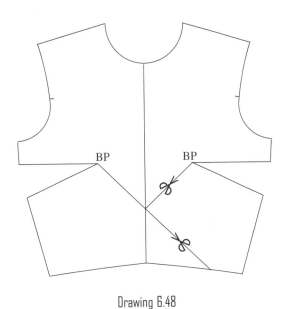

Drawing 6.48

Drawing 6.48.

- Transfer the waist dart to the side dart.
- Trace the entire front bodice sloper.
- Draw the new dart line, from the bust point at any angle, crossing at center front and ending at the waistline.
- Draw a second dart line, from the other bust point at any angle, intersecting with the first dart line.

Drawing 6.49. Finished pattern.

- Cut along the first dart line to the bust point, closing the corresponding side dart.
- Cut along the second dart line to the bust point, closing the corresponding side dart.
- **Note:** This will create the intersecting darts.
- Reposition the dart points $^1/_2$" from the bust point, as shown.
- True the side seam and waistline.

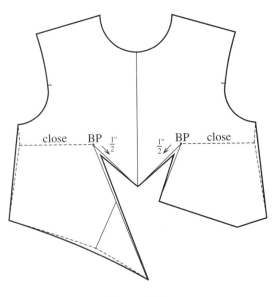

Drawing 6.49

DART 8. INTERSECTING DART CONVERTED TO FULLNESS

*T*his variation features two darts. One dart is transferred to another seam line as a new dart. The second dart is transferred so as to intersect the other dart line, where it is converted into shirring.

Design Feature 1

- The first dart crosses the center front and ends mid-armhole.
- The second dart intersects the first dart line and is then shirred.

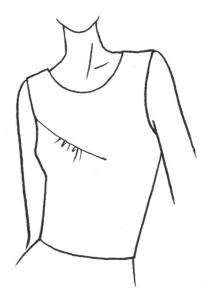

Illustration 6.25

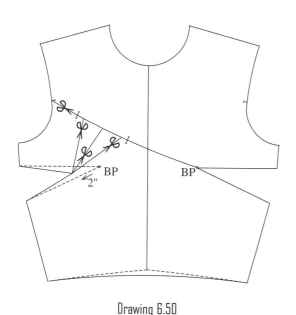

Drawing 6.50

Drawing 6.50.

- Transfer the waist dart to the side dart.
- Trace the entire front bodice sloper.
- Draw a style line from mid-armhole to the bust point, crossing at center front.
- Reposition the other side dart point 2" from the bust point.
- Draw three slash lines, at any angle from the new dart point and intersecting the style line. Mark notches ½" from the first and third slash lines.

Drawing 6.51.

- Cut along the style line from the armhole to the corresponding side dart.
- Close the side dart and the style line will spread open.

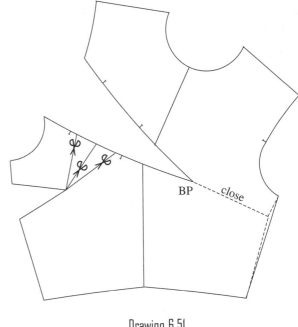

Drawing 6.51

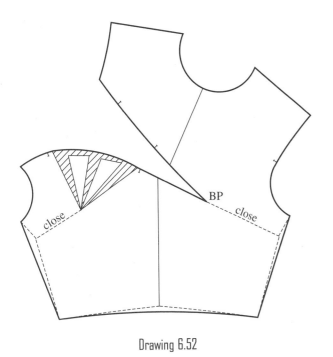

Drawing 6.52

Drawing 6.52. Finished pattern.

- Cut along the three slash lines to the corresponding side dart and close the side dart.
- Spread the slash lines an equal amount.
- Measure up $\frac{1}{2}$" from the slash lines, then reshape the style line for a smooth curve.
- True the side seam and waistline.

Design Feature 2

- A style line runs from the shoulder, following the neckline shape.
- The waistline is transferred to the style line.
- The side dart is transferred to intersect the style line and is then shirred.

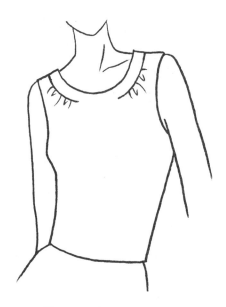

Illustration 6.26

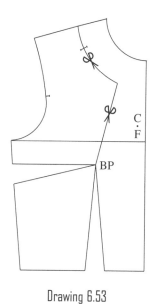

Drawing 6.53

Drawing 6.53.

- Trace the front bodice sloper.
- Draw a style line, starting on the shoulder and ending at the bust point, as shown.
- Mark notches at the desired location on the style line for the shirring.

Drawing 6.54.

- Cut along the style line to, but not through, the bust point.
- Close the waist dart and the style line will spread open.
- Draw two slash lines from the bust point, intersecting the style line as shown.

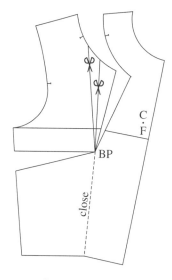

Drawing 6.54

Drawing 6.55. **Finished pattern.**

- Cut along both slash lines to, but not through, the bust point.
- Close the side dart and spread the slash lines an equal amount.
- Measure up $^3/_8$" (or more) from the slash lines, then reshape the style line for a smooth curve.
- True the side seam and waistline.

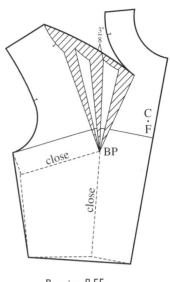

Drawing 6.55

Design Feature 3
- The style runs from the lower armhole to the waistline.
- Cutting along the style line creates two panels: the side panel and center panel.
- The side dart is closed within the side panel but left open in the center panel.
- The waist dart is transferred to the open portion of the side dart (in the center panel) and is then shirred.

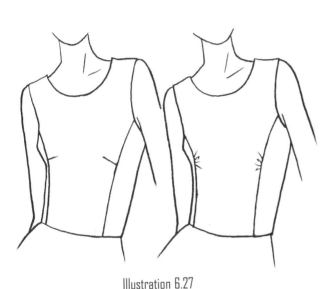

Illustration 6.27

Drawing 6.56.

- Trace the front bodice sloper
- Draw the style line from the armhole.
- Mark notches $^1/_2$" above and below the side dart legs.

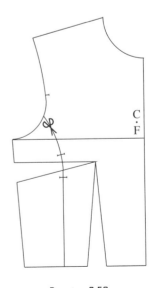

Drawing 6.56

Drawing 6.57. Finished pattern.

- Cut along the style line.
- Transfer the waist dart to the open portion of the side dart (in the center panel).
- Close the side dart on the side panel.
- True the side seam and waistline.

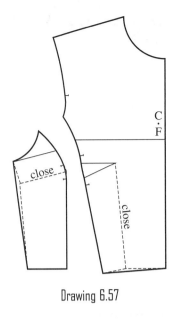

Drawing 6.57

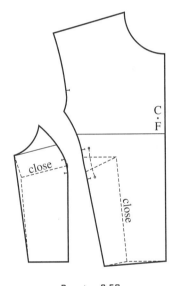

Drawing 6.58

Drawing 6.58. Converting darts to shirring.

- The side dart is converted to shirring.

DART 9. BACK DART

$\mathcal{T}$he back sloper features both a waist and a shoulder dart. The waist dart is generally not transferred, but it may be converted to pleats, gathers, shirring, or a style line, or even eliminated. The shoulder dart may be transferred to the neck, center back, armhole or waist dart, or eliminated by being eased out or taken out at the shoulder tip.

Eliminating the shoulder dart

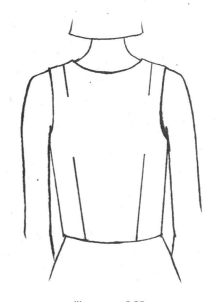

Illustration 6.28

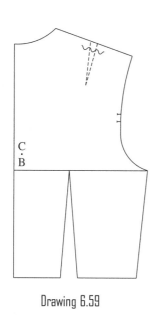

Drawing 6.59

Drawing 6.59. Easing in.

- The shoulder dart is eased in while sewing.

Drawing 6.60. Taking out.

- Measure in from the shoulder tip the amount of the shoulder dart intake.
- Reshape the armhole.

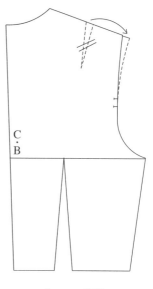

Drawing 6.60

Design Feature 2

- The shoulder dart is transferred to the neck.
- Both the shoulder and waist darts are sewn as darts.

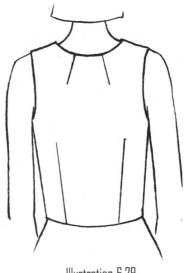

Illustration 6.29

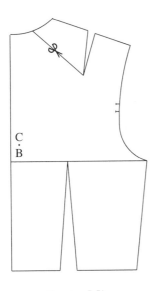

Drawing 6.61

Drawing 6.61.

- Trace the back bodice sloper.
- Draw a slash line from the neckline to the shoulder dart point.

Drawing 6.62. Finished pattern.

- Cut along the slash line to, but not through, the dart point.
- Close the shoulder dart and the slash line will spread open.
- * **Note:** This creates the neck dart.
- Measure in 3" from the center back and mark with a vertical guideline.
- Redraw the dart so that the dart point falls on the guideline.
- True the shoulder seam.

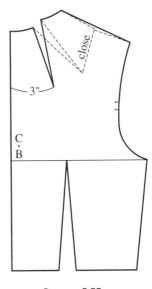

Drawing 6.62

Design Feature 3

- The shoulder dart is transferred to the center back.
- Both the center back and waist darts are sewn.

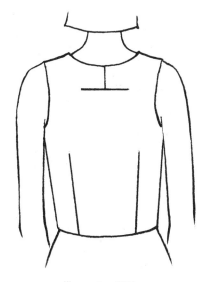

Illustration 6.30

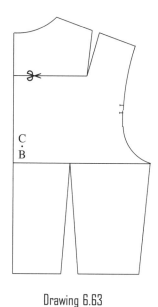

Drawing 6.63

Drawing 6.63.

- Trace the back bodice sloper.
- Draw a slash line from center back to the shoulder dart point.

Drawing 6.64. Finished pattern.

- Cut along the slash line to, but not through, the dart point.
- Close the shoulder dart and the slash line will spread open.
- * **Note:** This creates the center back dart.
- True the shoulder seam.

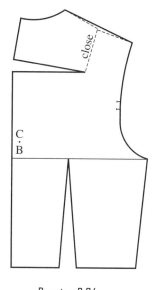

Drawing 6.64

Design Feature 4
• The shoulder dart is transferred to the armhole.
• Both the armhole and waist darts are sewn.

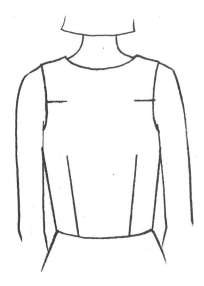

Illustration 6.31

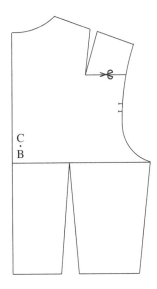

Drawing 6.65

Drawing 6.65.

• Trace the back bodice sloper.
• Draw a slash line from the armhole to the shoulder dart point.

Drawing 6.66. Finished pattern.

• Cut along the slash line to, but not through, the dart point.
• Close the shoulder dart and the slash line will spread open.
* **Note:** This creates the armhole dart.
• True the shoulder seam.

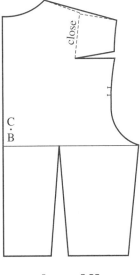

Drawing 6.66

DART 10. BACK YOKE STYLE LINE

Design Feature 1: With Shirring
- The yoke style line runs from the armhole to the center back.
- The shoulder dart is transferred to the yoke style line.
- The waist dart is left open for a looser fit.
- A pleat is added to the bodice at the yoke line, by extending the center back to create the pleat intake.

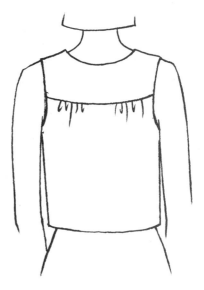

Illustration 6.32

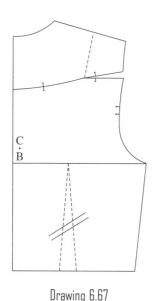

Drawing 6.67

Drawing 6.67.

- Trace the back bodice sloper, but do not trace the waist dart.
- Transfer the shoulder dart to the armhole, then draw the yoke style line from the dart point.
- Mark two notches: one 2" from the armhole, and one 2" from the center back.

Drawing 6.68.

- Draw two slash lines from the yoke line to the waist, between the notches.
- Separate the yoke.
- Cut along the slash lines to, but not through, the waistline.

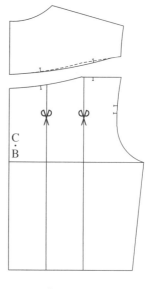

Drawing 6.68

Drawing 6.69 Finished pattern.

- Spread the slash lines as desired for fullness.
- Measure up ¹/₂″ from the slash lines and reshape the yoke line with a smooth curve.
- True the waistline.

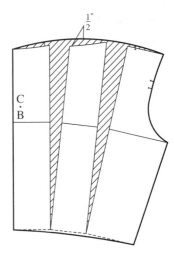

Drawing 6.69

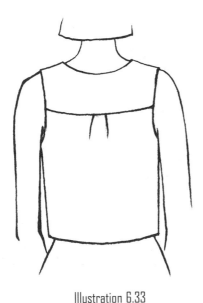

Illustration 6.33

Design Feature 2: Yoke with Pleats
- The yoke style line runs from the armhole to the center back.
- The shoulder dart is transferred to the yoke style line.
- The waist dart is left open for a looser fit.
- A box pleat is added to the bodice at the yoke line, by adding a 2" pleat intake at the center back.

Drawing 6.70 Finished pattern.

- Follow the instructions for the back yoke with shirring to the point just after the yoke has been separated.
- Add a 2" extension to center back for the pleat intake.
- Mark the center of the pleat.

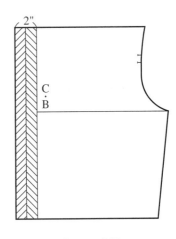

Drawing 6.70

DART 11. BACK PRINCESS STYLE LINE

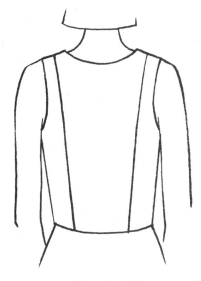

In this variation the waist and shoulder darts may be shifted to provide a smooth princess line from the shoulder seam.

Design Feature 1: Princess Line from Shoulder
- The shoulder and waist darts are converted to the princess style line.

Illustration 6.34

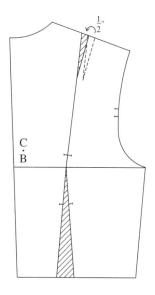

Drawing 6.71

Drawing 6.71.

- Trace the back bodice sloper.
- Reposition the shoulder dart $\frac{1}{2}$" toward the center back.
- Connect the dart points of the shoulder and waist darts with a straight line.
- Mark the notches.

Drawing 6.72. Finished pattern.

- Cut along the princess line, eliminating the shoulder and waist darts.
- Smooth the princess line.

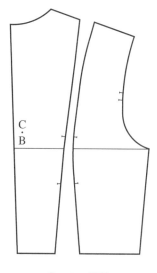

Drawing 6.72

Design Feature 2: Princess Line from Armhole

- The princess line starts mid-armhole and blends to the waist dart.
- The waist dart is converted to the princess style line.
- The shoulder dart is eliminated.

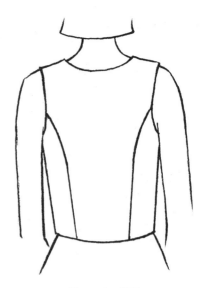

Illustration 6.35

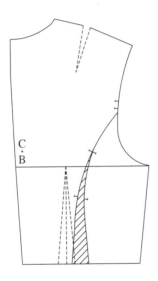

Drawing 6.73

Drawing 6.73.

- Trace the back bodice sloper.
- Reposition the waist dart to accommodate the desired style line placement, as shown.
- Draw a princess style line from the armhole, blending with the waist dart.
- Mark the notches on the princess line.

Drawing 6.74. Finished pattern.

- Cut along the princess style line, eliminating the waist dart.
- Smooth the princess line.
- Ease out the shoulder dart.

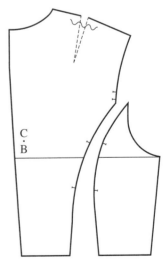

Drawing 6.74

Chapter Seven

D E T A I L S

BUTTONS

*A*lthough the main function of the button is to fasten, it can be used as a decorative element as well. There are two basic types of buttons: sew-through and shank. A sew-through button has two or four holes for attachment to the garment, whereas a shank button has a shank attached to the underside. When stitching a sew-through button to the garment, it is necessary to make a thread shank at the base of the button that is $1/16$″ long for thin fabric, and $1/8$″ long for thick fabric.

Drawing 7.1. Button shape variations.

Drawing 7.1

Sew through   Shank

Drawing 7.2. Button size variations.

Buttons vary in size from small to large and come in many shapes, including circular, rectangular, triangular, spherical, and almost limitless customized shapes. Button diameter is generally described in units of inches, centimeters, or line (ligne).

       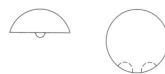

Drawing 7.2

Standard Button Sizes

Use this chart to determine the button size generally used in each garment type listed.

Garment	Button Size
Blouse/One-piece dress	$3/8$″ to $1/2$″
Jacket	$3/4$″ to $7/8$″
Coat	$3/4$″ to $1 1/4$″

Extension Overlap Allowances

Use this chart to determine the offset from the edge of the button to the extension edge in each garment type listed. The width of the extension is generally equal to the diameter of the button plus $1/8$″.

Garment	Button Offset
Shirt, blouse, one-piece dress	$3/8$″ to $1/2$″
Jacket, vest	$5/8$″
Coat	$3/4$″

Drawing 7.3. Extension allowance.

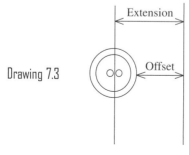

Drawing 7.3

Button Placements

On women's garments, buttons are placed on the left-hand side of the garment, and buttonholes are on the right-hand side. Generally, the first button is placed one half the button diameter plus $1/4''$ down from the neckline. However, on lapel collars the first button is placed either at the break point or $1/2''$ below it.

Drawing 7.4. Single.

- Measure in from the extension edge the diameter of the button plus $1/8''$.
- Draw a button placement line.
- Mark the first button at the desired location on the button placement line.
- Mark the next button at the waistline.
- Divide the space between the two buttons by the total number of buttons to be placed between them.
- Mark the buttons accordingly.
- * **Note:** Adjust the placement of the button nearest the bust line to prevent gaping.
- Mark the remaining buttons below the waistline.

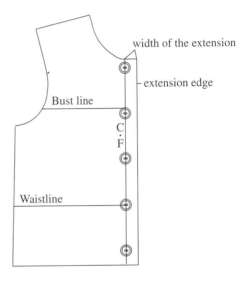

Drawing 7.4

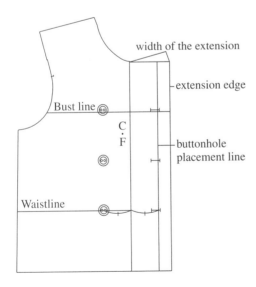

Drawing 7.5

Drawing 7.5. Double.

- Measure in from the extension edge the diameter of the button plus $1/8''$.
- Draw the buttonhole placement line.
- Measure in from the center front the distance between it and the buttonhole placement line.
- Mark the button placement.
- Follow the preceding instructions for single button placement to mark the remaining buttons.

Buttonhole

Buttonholes are the openings through which buttons are inserted. They must be positioned and made just wide enough to accommodate their corresponding buttons. Buttonholes can be applied vertically, horizontally, or at an angle, depending on the style.

There are three types of buttonholes: straight, keyhole, and bound. The straight buttonhole is the most common and is used on nearly all types of garments. It is made from a variety of fabrics, ranging from woven to knits and especially thin fabrics. The keyhole buttonhole is generally used on garments that require thicker fabrics, such as jackets and coats, or for garments with large buttons. The bound buttonhole is generally used on expensive garments and often functions as a decorative element, such as on the lapel of a jacket.

Drawing 7.6. Types of buttonholes.

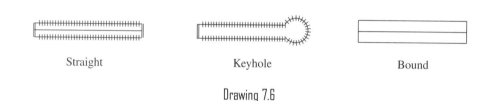

Straight   Keyhole   Bound

Drawing 7.6

Drawing 7.7. Buttonhole length.

• Proper buttonhole length is important to prevent pulling and puckering. It is generally equal to the width of the button plus $1/8''$. However, thicker customized buttons may require a larger allowance, which can be determined by slipping the button through a slit cut in a piece of test fabric.

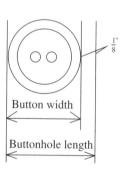

Drawing 7.7

Drawing 7.8. Horizontal buttonhole placements.

- Cross mark the buttonhole start $\frac{1}{8}$" out from the buttonhole placement line, toward the extension edge.
- Measure in the buttonhole length and cross mark the buttonhole end.

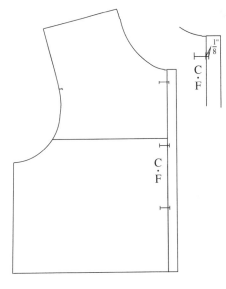

Drawing 7.8

Drawing 7.9. Vertical buttonhole placements.

- Cross mark the center of the button on the button placement line.
- Measure down the buttonhole length and cross mark the buttonhole end.

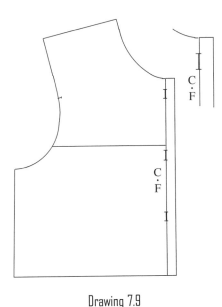

Drawing 7.9

Drawing 7.10. Waistband and cuff.

Button:
- Add an extension to one edge of the waistband or cuff.
- Measure in from the extension edge the width of the extension and draw a button placement line.
- Mark the button at the midpoint of the button placement line.

Buttonhole:
- At the opposite edge of the cuff, measure in the width of the extension and mark.
- Cross mark the buttonhole start $\frac{1}{8}$" out from the line.
- Measure in the buttonhole length and cross mark the buttonhole end.

Drawing 7.10

CUFFS

uffs are used to finish a hem, generally at the end of a sleeve. Although they are primarily used to enhance and support sleeve design, they can exert a design influence over the entire garment. Cuff width equals the circumference of the arm where the cuff will fall plus the desired ease. To accommodate the cuff height, the length of the sleeve pattern must generally be shortened by the cuff height minus $3/4$".

There are two basic types of cuffs: turned-back and sewn-on. Turned-back cuffs are an extension of the sleeve, and the sleeve length must thus be extended to accommodate their being rolled up. Sewn-on cuffs are integrated into the sleeve length, and their width must thus be subtracted from the total sleeve length desired. Examples of sew-on cuffs include band, barrel, French, and wing.

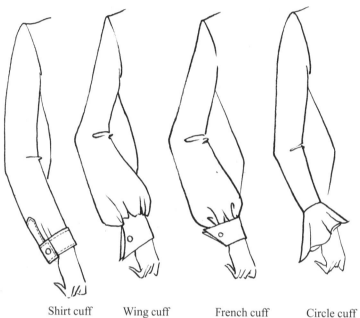

Illustration 7.1a

Shirt cuff   Wing cuff   French cuff   Circle cuff

Illustration 7.1b

Rolled-up cuff   Band cuff   Piping cuff

Sewn-on Cuffs.

The following dimensions will be used to develop
examples of barrel, French, and wing cuffs:

Cuff height = 2″.
Cuff width = 8″.
XX′ = 4″.
XX″ = 4″.

Drawing 7.11. Sleeve.

- Trace the straight sleeve pattern.
- Shorten the sleeve length by $1^1/_4″$ (cuff height minus $^3/_4″$).
- Measure out 4″ from both sides of the center line on the hem.
- **Note:** This sleeve pattern will be the foundation for all of the following sleeve examples.

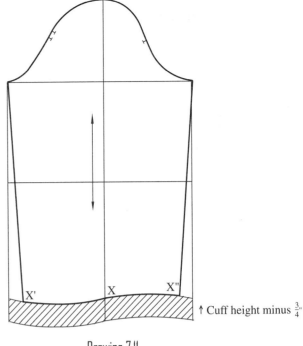

↑ Cuff height minus $\frac{3}{4}″$

Drawing 7.11

Drawing 7.12. Shirt Cuff.

- Draw the cuff 8″ wide and 2″ long.
- Add a $^3/_4″$ extension on one edge of the cuff.
- Mark the button placement(s).
- Measure in $^3/_4″$ on the opposite edge and mark.
- Measure out $^1/_8″$ from this mark and mark the buttonhole(s).
- Double the height of the cuff for the facing.

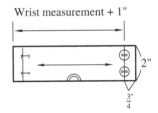

Drawing 7.12

Drawing 7.13. Wing Cuff.

- Draw a horizontal line 8″ long, labeling A and B.
- Square up 4″ from points A and B, labeling C and D.
- Connect point C to D.

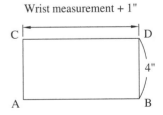

Drawing 7.13

Drawing 7.14.

- Measure out $^3/_4″$ from points A and B and label A′ and B′.
- Connect points C to A′ and D to B′.
- Mark in $^1/_4″$ from the midpoints of lines CA′, A′B′, and DB′ and reshape.

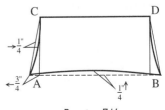

Drawing 7.14

Drawing 7.15. French Cuff.

- Draw a horizontal line 8″ long, labeling it A and B.
- Square up 2″ from points A and B, labeling it C and D.
- Connect point C to D.
- Add a 1″ extension to line DB for the button placement.

Drawing 7.15

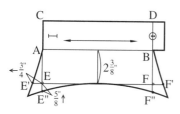

Drawing 7.16

Drawing 7.16.

- Square down $2^3/_8$″ from points A and B to label E and F, as shown.
- Connect point E to F.
- Extend out $3/_4$″ from points E and F, labeling E′ and F′.
- Measure down $5/_8$″ from points E and F and label E″ and F″.
- Draw the desired angle and height of the cuff, starting from point A and passing through point E′.
- Draw the same angle from point B passing through point F′.
- Connect the two angles with a curved line passing through points E″ and F″.

Drawing 7.17. Circle Cuff.

The cuff will be produced with a 3″ cuff height and a 8″ cuff width.
- Draw the cuff 8″ wide and 3″ long.
- Slash across, but not through, the cuff every 2″, as shown.

Drawing 7.18.

- Spread each slash line to form a circle, as shown.
- Retrace the cuff.

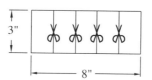

Drawing 7.17

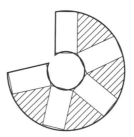

Drawing 7.18

Drawing 7.19. Piping Cuff.

- Draw the cuff the length of the arm circumference at the end of the sleeve and $1^1/_2$″ wide.
- **Note:** Ease may be added to the cuff width to accommodate arm movement.
- Double the height of the cuff for the facing.

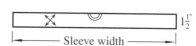

Drawing 7.19

Turned-back Cuff

Drawing 7.20. **Rolled turned-back cuffs.**

- Trace the sleeve pattern.
- Measure down 3″ from the biceps line and draw the hem.
- Measure down 3″ from the hem for the cuff.
- Mark the fold line at the center of the cuff.
- Add a $1^1/_4$″ hem.
- Fold along the fold line, then redraw the underarm seam.

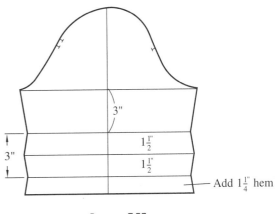

3″

3″

$1\frac{1}{2}$″

$1\frac{1}{2}$″

Add $1\frac{1}{4}$″ hem

Drawing 7.20

Faced turned-back Cuff

Drawing 7.21.

- Trace the straight sleeve pattern.
- Extend the sleeve length $2^1/_2$″ at the hem.
- Reshape the sleeve pattern, as desired.

Facing:
- Measure up $4^1/_2$″ from the new hemline and draw the facing line.
- Trace the facing separately.

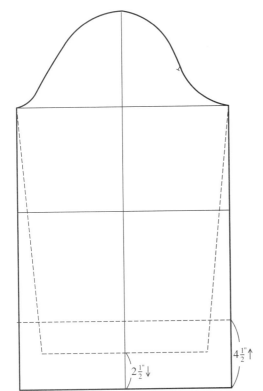

$4\frac{1}{2}$″ ↑

$2\frac{1}{2}$″ ↓

Drawing 7.21

FACINGS

*F*acings are used to give the raw edges of a garment a finished look. When made with special fabrics, they can also help to stabilize the shape of a garment. Facing widths generally range from 1″ to 3″, depending on location. There are two basic types of facings: stitched-on and fold-back.

Stitched-on facings are created by tracing the edge of a pattern piece so that a new piece of fabric can be cut out and then sewn over the raw edge. They offer the advantages of allowing a fabric different than the rest of the garment to be used, as well as the ability to be applied to edges of any shape, including waistlines, armholes, and necklines. Fold-back facings are created by extending the edge of the pattern piece and then folding that extension over on the finished garment. They offer the advantages of avoiding the seam line and extra fabric used when attaching a separate facing.

Drawing 7.22. Neckline and extension edge facing.

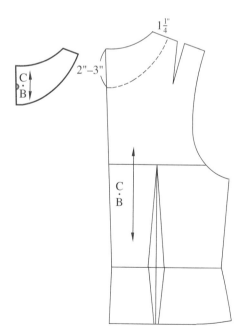

Drawing 7.23. Back.

- Measure in 1¼″ from the neck on the shoulder and mark.
- Measure down 2″ to 3″ from the neck at the center back and mark.
- Draw the facing line by connecting the marks.
- Trace the facing separately.

Drawing 7.24. Front.

- Measure in $1\frac{1}{4}''$ from the neck on the shoulder and mark.
- Measure in $1\frac{1}{2}''$ on the hem and mark.
- Draw the facing line by connecting the marks.
- Trace the facing separately.

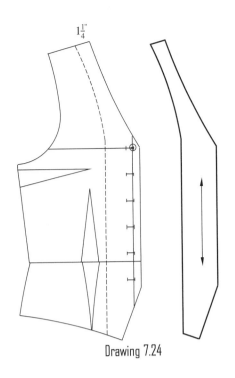

Drawing 7.24

Drawing 7.25

Drawing 7.25. All-in-one facing.

Drawing 7.26. Back.

- Measure down $2''$ from the underarm at the side seam and mark.
- Measure down $3''$ from the neck on the center back and mark.
- Draw the facing line by connecting the marks.
- Trace the facing separately.

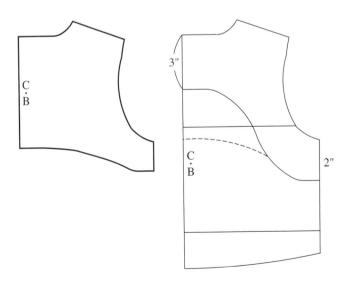

Drawing 7.26

Drawing 7.27. **Front.**

• Repeat the steps used for the back facing to complete the front facing.

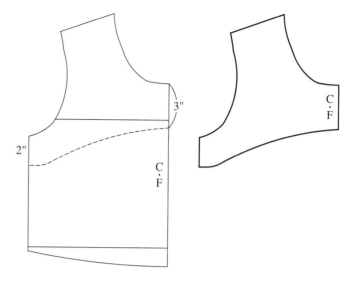

Drawing 7.27

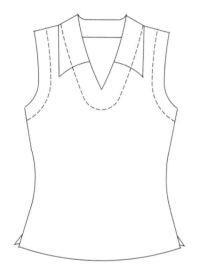

Drawing 7.28

Drawing 7.28. **Armhole and neckline facing.**

Drawing 7.29. **Back.**

• Measure down 2″ to 3″ from the neck at the center back and mark.
• Measure in 1¼″ at the neck on the shoulder and mark.
• Draw the facing line by connecting the marks.
• Measure in 1¼″ from the shoulder tip and mark.
• Measure down 1¼″ from the underarm at the side seam and mark.
• Draw the facing line by connecting the marks.
• Trace the facings separately.

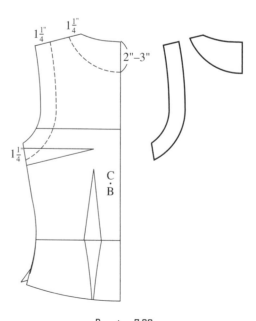

Drawing 7.29

Drawing 7.30. **Front.**

• Repeat the steps used for the back facing to complete the front facing.

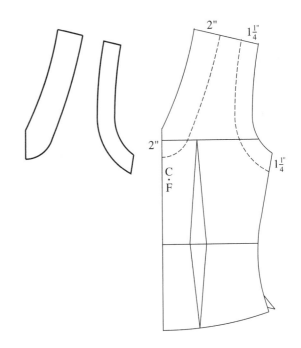

Drawing 7.30

Drawing 7.31. **Waistband facing.**

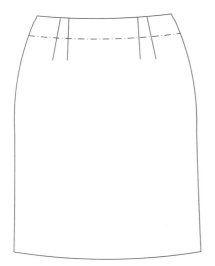

Drawing 7.31

Drawing 7.32. **Back.**

• Trace the back skirt pattern.
• Draw a line parallel to and 2″ down from the back waistline.
• Trace the facing separately.

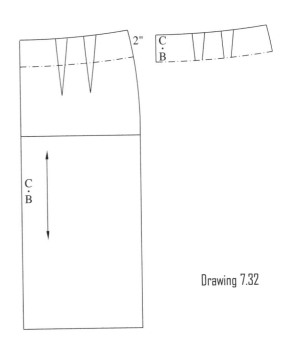

Drawing 7.32

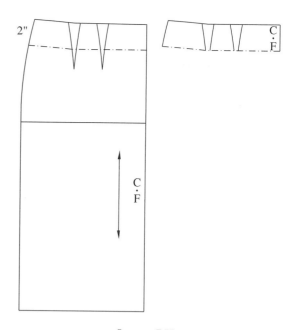

Drawing 7.33. Front.

- Repeat the steps used for the back facing to complete the front facing.

Drawing 7.33

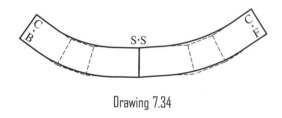

Drawing 7.34

Drawing 7.34.

- Close the darts, then reshape the facings.
- Flip the back piece over, then connect the front and back facings at the side seams.
- Trace the facing as one continuous piece.

NECKLINE

$\mathcal{T}$he neckline is the bodice opening through which the neck extends. There are three basic neckline types: round, square, and V-shaped. Numerous variations of the basic types can be created by altering neckline depth and width.

Necklines can fall high, low, wide, or at the natural position on the neck. The design of a given neckline will dictate various aspects of its construction, including its width, depth, squaring, and angle. Neckline styling is commonly manipulated to enhance the appearance of the upper garment, through modifications as subtle as varying shape, to more dramatic changes, such as adding a collar.

Neckline Variations

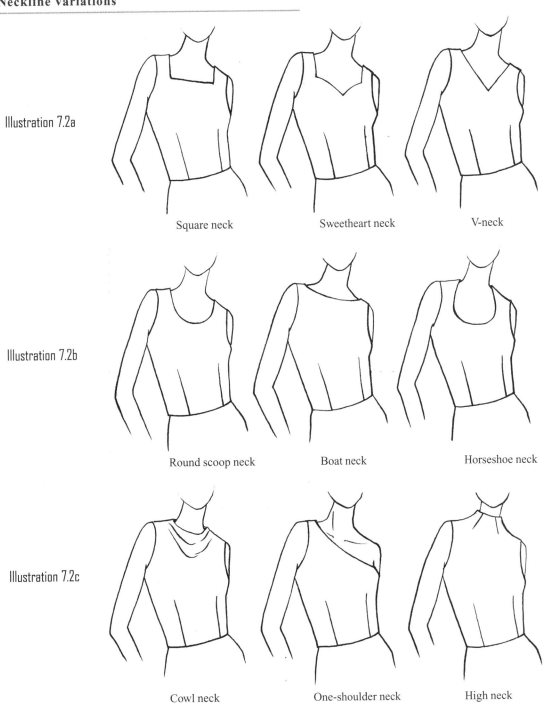

Illustration 7.2a

Square neck   Sweetheart neck   V-neck

Illustration 7.2b

Round scoop neck   Boat neck   Horseshoe neck

Illustration 7.2c

Cowl neck   One-shoulder neck   High neck

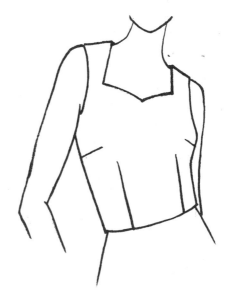

Illustration 7.3

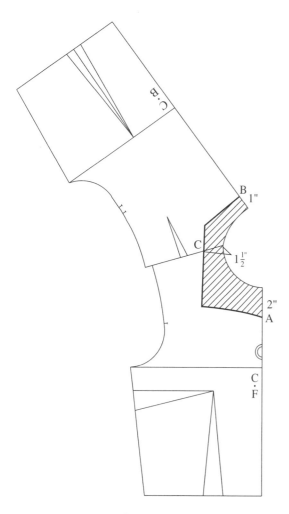

Drawing 7.35

Drawing 7.35.

- Trace the front bodice pattern.
- Match the neck points of the front and back bodices, aligning their shoulder lines.
- Trace the back bodice pattern.
- Measure down 2″ from the neck at the center front and label A.
- Measure down 1″ from the neck at the center back and label B.
- Measure in 1¹⁄₂″ from the neck on the shoulder line and label C.
- Connect point A to C and point B to C with slightly curved lines, as shown.
- Cut along the neckline.

V-Neckline

Illustration 7.4

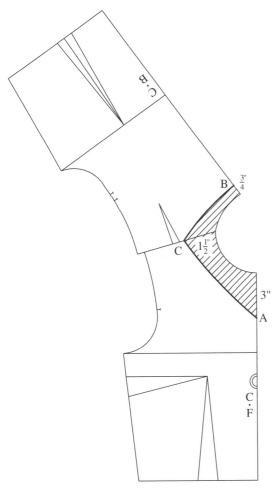

Drawing 7.36

Drawing 7.36.

- Trace the front bodice pattern.
- Match the neck points of the front and back bodices, aligning their shoulder lines.
- Trace the back bodice pattern.
- Measure down 3″ from the neck at the center front and label A.
- Measure down ³/₄″ from the neck at the center back and label B.
- Measure in 1¹/₂″ from the neck on the shoulder and label C.
- Connect point A to C and point B to C with slightly curved lines, as shown.
- Cut along the neckline.

Illustration 7.5

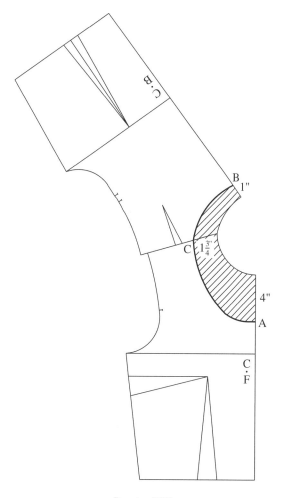

Drawing 7.37

Drawing 7.37.

- Trace the front bodice pattern.
- Match the neck points of the front and back bodices, aligning their shoulder lines.
- Trace the back bodice pattern.
- Measure down 4″ from the neck at the center front and label A.
- Measure down 1″ from the neck at the center back and label B.
- Measure in $1\frac{3}{4}$″ from the neck on the shoulder and label C.
- Connect point A to C and point B to C with curved lines, as shown.
- Cut along the neckline.

Low Cowl Neck

Illustration 7.6

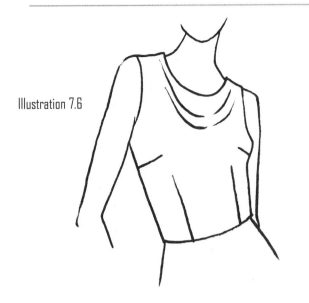

Drawing 7.38

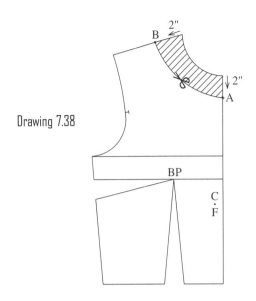

Drawing 7.38.

- Trace the front bodice sloper.
- Measure down 2″ from the neck at the center front and label A.
- Measure in 2″ from the neck on the shoulder line and label B.
- Connect point A to B.

Drawing 7.39.

- Cut along line AB.
- Measure down 4″ from A and label C.
- Connect point C to the shoulder tip with a curved line.
- Divide the shoulder line between B and the shoulder tip into two and mark, as shown.
- Divide line AC into two and mark, as shown.
- Connect the marks with curved lines, as shown.

Drawing 7.39

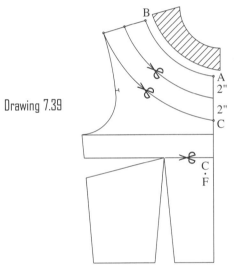

Drawing 7.40.

- Slash each line from the center front to, but not through, the shoulder line.
- Spread each slash line $1^1/_2$″.
- Square a line down from A to the hem.
- Square a line out from A to just over point B.
- Continue the shoulder line up from B to meet the line from A.
- Reshape the neckline and the center front.

Drawing 7.40

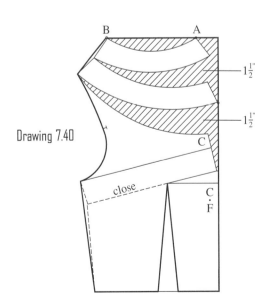

Illustration 7.7

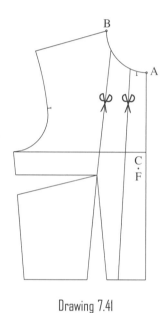

Drawing 7.41

Drawing 7.41.

- Trace the front bodice sloper.
- Label A at the neck on the center front.
- Label B at the neck on the shoulder.
- Divide the neckline (AB) into thirds and mark.

Drawing 7.42.

- Transfer the side dart to the neckline mark closest to B.
- Draw a slash line from the neckline mark closest to A to the waistline.
- Cut along the slash line to, but not through, the waistline.
- Spread the slash line 2″.
- Square a line out from B.
- Square a line up from A to meet the line from B.
- Reshape the neckline and side seam.

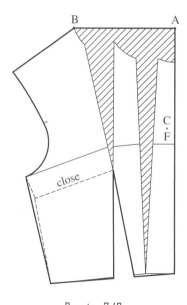

Drawing 7.42

High Neckline I

Illustration 7.8

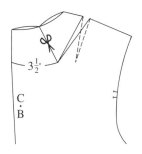

Drawing 7.43

Drawing 7.43. Back.

- Reposition the shoulder dart point to $3^1/_2''$ from the center back, as shown.
- Slash from the midpoint of the back neckline to the new dart point.
- Transfer the dart to the neck by closing the dart.

Drawing 7.44.

- Square up $1^1/_2''$ from the neck at the center back and label A.
- Square up $1^1/_2''$ from the neck at the shoulder.
- Square over $^1/_4''$ and label B.
- Connect B to the neck point.
- Shape the neckline from A to B, as shown.
- Measure in $2''$ from the neck on the shoulder and label C.
- Connect point B to C, blending into the shoulder line.

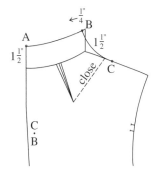

Drawing 7.44

Drawing 7.45

Drawing 7.45.

- Fold the paper at the original neckline, then trace the dart legs to the top of the collar through the paper.

Drawing 7.46.

• Unfold the pattern.

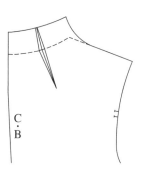

Drawing 7.46

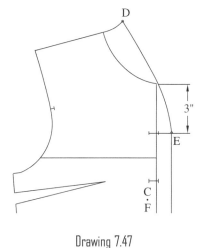

Drawing 7.47

Drawing 7.47. Front.

• Align the neck points of the front and back patterns, matching the shoulder line.
• Trace the back neckline onto the front, labeling D for B.
• Measure down 3″ from the neck at the center front and label E on the extension edge.
• Connect D to E with a slightly curved line, as shown.

Drawing 7.48.

• Transfer the side dart to the desired location on the neck, as shown.
• Redraw the dart legs to 4″ to 5″ length.
• Measure in $^1/_4$″ from each leg of the neck dart, then connect to the neckline, as shown.
• Close the side dart, then reshape the side seam.

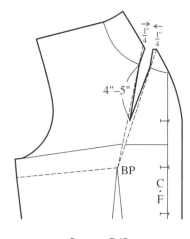

Drawing 7.48

Illustration 7.9

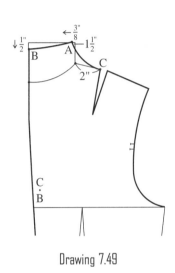

Drawing 7.49

Drawing 7.49. **Back.**

- Trace the back bodice pattern.
- Square up from the neck at the center back.
- Square $1\frac{1}{2}''$ up from the neck at the shoulder.
- Square over $\frac{3}{8}''$ and label A.
- Square over to intersect the first line, as shown.
- Square down $\frac{1}{2}''$ and label B.
- Shape the neckline from A to B, as shown.
- Measure $2''$ out from the neck at the shoulder and label C.
- Connect point A to C, blending into the shoulder line.

Drawing 7.50. **Front.**

- Trace the front bodice pattern.
- Square up $1\frac{1}{2}''$ from the neck at the center front.
- Square out $\frac{1}{2}''$ and label D.
- Draw a line from the bust line on the center front to D, as shown.
- Square up $1\frac{1}{2}''$ from the neck at the shoulder.
- Square over $\frac{3}{8}''$ and label E.
- Shape the neckline from E to D, as shown.
- Measure $2''$ out from the neck at the shoulder and label F.
- Connect point E to F, blending into the shoulder line.

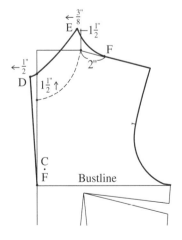

Drawing 7.50

PLACKETS

$\mathcal{P}$lackets are the finished openings of garments, used both to enhance the fit of and to aid getting in and out of an article of clothing. They generally include a closure device, such as buttons, hooks, ties, or Velcro. Plackets can be used on almost any type of garment and are usually found at the center front, center back, and sleeve. Placket width, length, and shape can vary with location and design but should be sufficient to allow easy opening.

Drawing 7.51. Placket variations.

Drawing 7.51

Bodice Placket

Drawing 7.52. Rugby Placket.

Drawing 7.52

Drawing 7.53. Bodice.

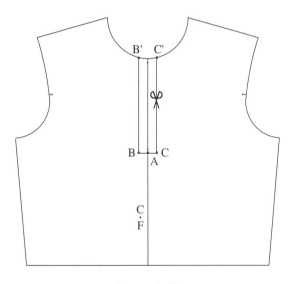

Drawing 7.53

- Trace the entire front bodice pattern.
- Mark the center front.
- Measure down 7″ (placket length) on the center front and label A.
- Square out $^3/_4$″ (half the placket width) on each side of A, labeling B and C.
- Square lines up from B and C to the neck, labeling B′ and C′ (placket lines).
- Mark the notches on the center line, at the neck and the bottom of the placket.
- Cut along line CC′.
- Mark the pattern "Right Side Up."

Drawing 7.54. Placket left side.

- Trace the placket separately (B′-C′-C-B-B′), including the notches.
- Extend the bottom of the placket 1″.

Drawing 7.54

Drawing 7.55. Placket right side.

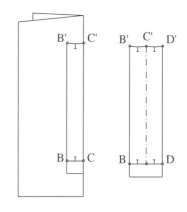

Drawing 7.55

- Trace the placket separately (B′-C′-C-B-B′), including the notches.
- Fold on line CC′, then trace the neck curve (B′C′) and notches onto the extension.
- Unfold the pattern and label DD′.
- Extend the line CC′ the width of the placket (BC).

Drawing 7.56. Shirt Placket.

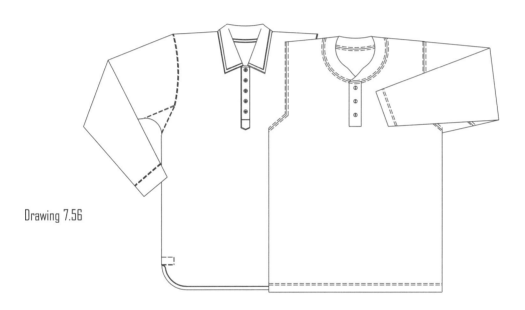

Drawing 7.56

Drawing 7.57.

- Trace the entire front bodice pattern.
- Mark the center front.
- Measure down 10″ (placket length) on the center front and label A.
- Square out $\frac{1}{2}$″ (half the placket width) on each side of A, labeling B and C.
- Square lines up from B and C to the neck, labeling B′ and C′ (placket lines).
- Measure in 2″ from the neck on the shoulder.
- Square out $1\frac{1}{2}$″ from B.
- Draw the facing line, as shown.
- Mark the notches at the neck and the bottom of the placket.

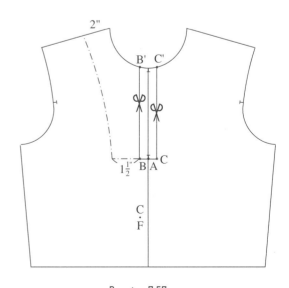

Drawing 7.57

Drawing 7.58. Bodice.

- Cut out section B'-B-C-C'-B'.
- Mark the pattern "Right Side Up."

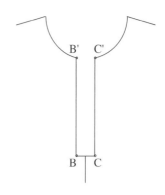

Drawing 7.58

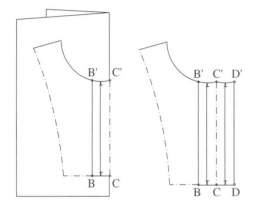

Drawing 7.59

Drawing 7.59. Placket left side.

- Trace the placket separately (B'-C'-C-B-B'), including the facing.
- Fold on line CC', then trace the neck curve (B'C'), including the notches.
- Unfold the pattern and label DD'.
- Extend line CC' the width of the placket (BC).

Drawing 7.60. Placket right side.

- Flip the left side placket over, then trace.
- Extend the bottom edge of the placket 1″ between points D and B.

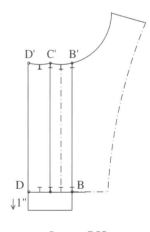

Drawing 7.60

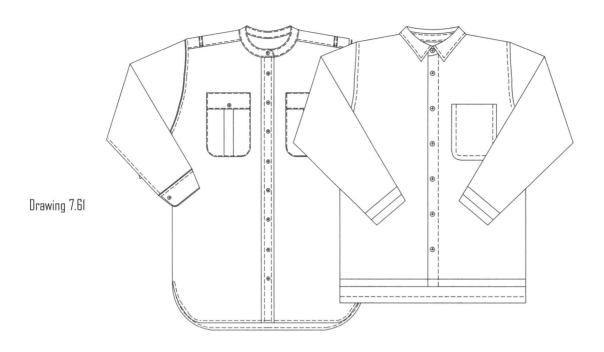

Drawing 7.61

Method A

Drawing 7.62. Left and right sides.

- Trace the front bodice pattern.
- Add a ⁵⁄₈″ extension to the center front, labeling A and A′ as shown.
- Measure in ⁵⁄₈″ from the center front and draw line BB′, as shown.

- Mark the notches at the neck and hem on the center front.
- Fold on line AA′, then trace the neck curve (BA) and notches.
- Unfold the pattern and label CC′.
- Extend the placket edge the width of the placket (BA).

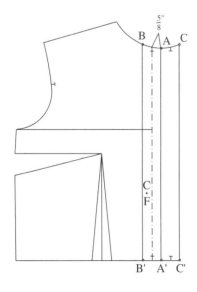

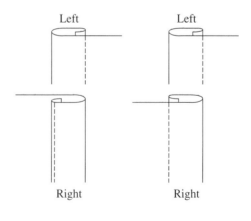

Drawing 7.62

Method B
Drawing 7.63. **Left side.**

• Develop the left side pattern, using the preceding procedure for Method A.

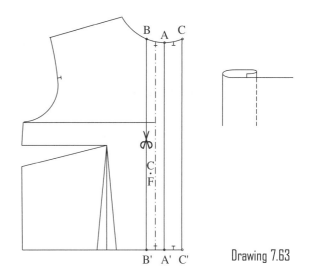

Drawing 7.63

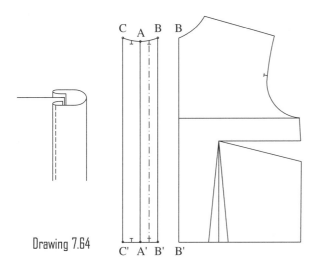

Drawing 7.64

Drawing 7.64. **Right side.**

• Trace the left side pattern.
• Cut along the placket line (BB′).

Method C
Drawing 7.65. **Left side.**

• Develop the left side pattern, using the previously described procedure for Method A.

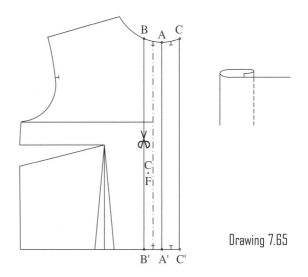

Drawing 7.65

Drawing 7.66. **Right side.**

• Trace the left side pattern.
• Cut along the placket line (BB′).
• Extend the bodice edge (BB′) 3/8″.
• Align the placket line to the bodice edge.
• Retrace the placket and bodice as a single, continuous piece, transferring all labels.
• Fold between the bodice and placket, matching BB′ on the bodice to BB′ on the placket.
• Fold on line AA′ then trace the neckline (BA).

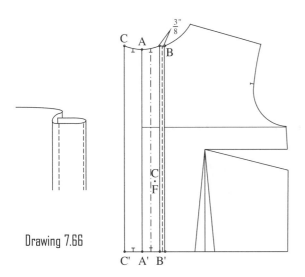

Drawing 7.66

Drawing 7.67. Slit Placket.

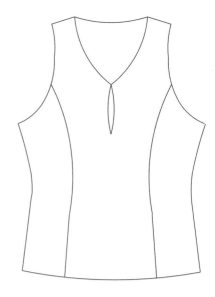

Drawing 7.67

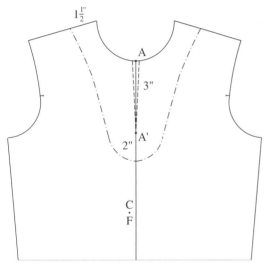

Drawing 7.68

Drawing 7.68.

- Trace the entire front bodice pattern.
- Measure down 3″ from the neck at the center front then label A and A′.
- Measure out ¼″ from both sides of A and mark.
- Connect A′ to the marks with dashed lines.

Facing:
- Measure in 1½″ from the neck on the shoulder.
- Measure down 2″ from A′ on the center front.
- Draw the facing line, as shown.

Drawing 7.69. Bodice.

- Slash line AA′.

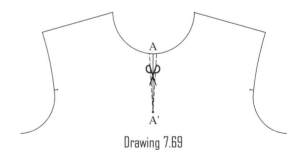

Drawing 7.69

Drawing 7.70

Drawing 7.70. Facing.

- Trace the facing separately.

Sleeve Plackets.

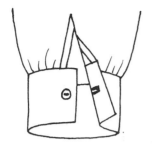

Petticoat

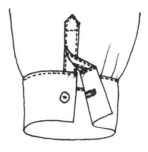
Shirt sleeve placket

Illustration 7.10

Petticoat Placket

Drawing 7.71. Sleeve.

- Trace the sleeve pattern.
- Measure in 2″ from the back underarm seam at the hem.
- Draw the placket slit line 2$\frac{1}{2}$″ long.

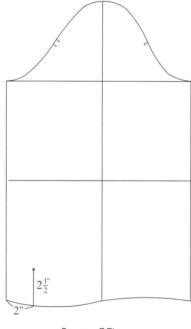

$2\frac{1}{2}$″

2″

Drawing 7.71

2″

Drawing 7.72

Drawing 7.72. Placket binding.

- Cut the placket binding 2″ wide and three times the length of the placket slit.

Drawing 7.73. **Sleeve.**

- Trace the sleeve pattern.
- Measure in 2″ from the back underarm seam at the hem and label Y.
- Square up $2^1/_2$″ from point Y and label Y′.
- Measure out $^1/_2$″ on both sides of Y, then square up 3″ from both points and mark.
- Connect the marks to Y′, as shown.
- Slash from Y to Y′, then slash to each mark.

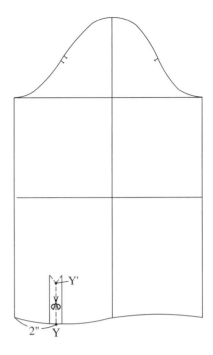

Drawing 7.73

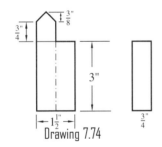

Drawing 7.74

Drawing 7.74. **Upper and under plackets.**

- Draw a rectangle 3″ long and $^3/_4$″ wide.
- Extend the top edge of the rectangle $^3/_4$″.
- Draw a $^3/_8$″ pointed extension to the top of the rectangle, as shown.
- Extend the right side of the rectangle $^3/_4$″.
- Draw a rectangle 3″ long and $^3/_4$″ wide.

POCKETS

Pockets are pouches created as a part of garments, which although historically conceived as functional elements now act as a significant design detail on nearly every kind of clothing. Traditionally, the only functional requirements of a pocket are that it be large enough for a hand to fit into it easily and deep enough to hold its contents securely. Pockets may be placed either straight or at an angle, and may be angular, rounded, or both, resembling virtually any geometric shape.

There are numerous styles of pockets. Those located on the outside of a garment are always "patch" pockets, whereas those located on the inside may be "front hip," "inseam," or "bound welt" pockets.

❖

Drawing 7.75. Pocket variations.

Drawing 7.75

Drawing 7.76. **Front hip pocket.**

Front hip pockets (continental pockets) are generally used on the fronts of pants and skirts. They consist of two separate inside pockets that have been sewn together to create a pouch, placed inside the garment. The garment is attached to the pockets to shape the entrance. Pocket size and placement may vary, depending on the desired style line.

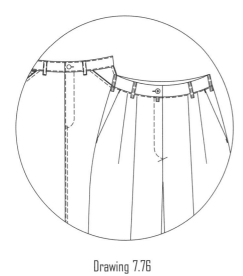

Drawing 7.76

Drawing 7.77. **Pocket placement.**

- Label A at the waistline on the side seam.
- Measure in 1″ from A and label B.
- Measure down 7″ from A, on the side seam, and label B′.
- Connect point B to B′.
- **Note:** this line may be either straight or curved, as desired.
- Measure out 2″ to 3″ (pocket width) from B at the waistline and label C.
- Measure down 2″ from B′, at the side seam, and label C′.
- Draw the inside pocket shape from point C to C′, as shown.
- **Note:** The resulting pocket should be at least 10″ deep and 7″ wide.

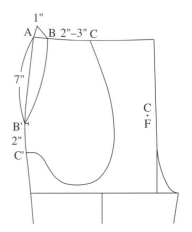

Drawing 7.77

Drawing 7.78. **Inside pockets.**

- Trace the inside pocket separately (A-C′-C-A).
- Trace the inside pocket facing separately (B-B′-C′-C-B).

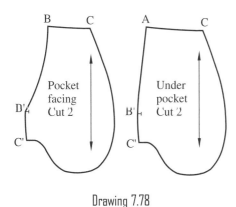

Drawing 7.78

Drawing 7.79. **Garment.**

- The garment includes the side seam up to and along the pocket style line (BB′).
- Separate section A-B-B′-A.

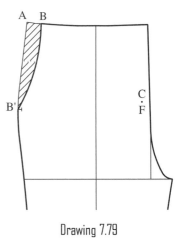

Drawing 7.79

Drawing 7.80. **Inseam pocket.**

Inseam pockets consist of two separate inside pockets that have been sewn together to create a pouch, placed inside the garment on an existing seam line. Because inseam pockets utilize an existing seam for their opening, they are virtually invisible compared with other kinds of pockets.

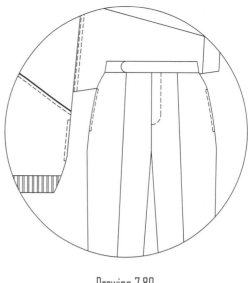

Drawing 7.80

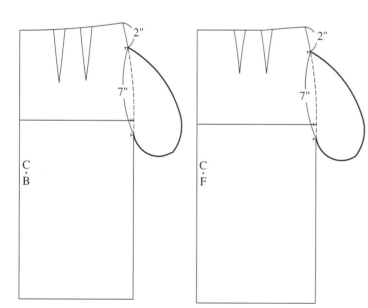

Drawing 7.81

Drawing 7.81. **Continuous inseam pocket.**

- Mark the pocket opening 5″ to 7″ long on the target seam.
- Draw the inside pocket shape at the entrance, as shown.
- Repeat for the back pattern piece.

Drawing 7.82. Separate inseam pocket.

- Mark the pocket opening 5″ to 7″ long on the target seam.
- Extend the pocket entrance edge 1″.
- Draw the inside pocket shape at the entrance, over the pattern, as shown.
- Trace the pocket shape separately.
- Repeat for the back pattern piece.

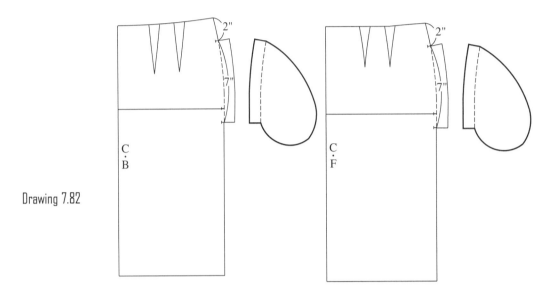

Drawing 7.82

Drawing 7.83. Bound pocket.

Bound pockets are inserted in a slash made in the garment. They can be either single or double welt and are generally found on jackets, coats, and the back of pants, but can be used on virtually any garment. Their openings can be straight, curved, or angled, as a design element, and their size will vary with garment type.

Drawing 7.83

Drawing 7.84.

- Draw the bound pocket, using the desired shape and dimensions.
- Mark the pocket placement on the pattern.

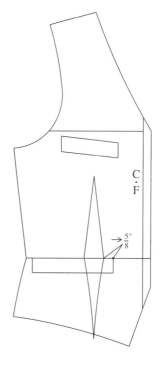

Drawing 7.84

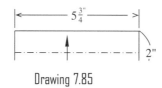

Drawing 7.85

Drawing 7.85. Welt.

- Flip the welt over, then trace as one piece, as shown.
- Mark the fold line with a dashed line.

Drawing 7.86. Inside pockets.

- Draw the first inside pocket piece as wide as the welt and as deep as desired.
- Draw the second inside pocket piece as wide as the welt and the same length as the first inside pocket piece minus the length of the welt.

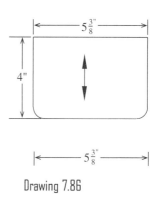

Drawing 7.86

Drawing 7.87. **Patch pocket.**

Patch pockets consist of a single piece, top-stitched directly onto the garment without separate facings. They are generally used in casual wear and can be of any size, shape, or location, depending on the intended use.

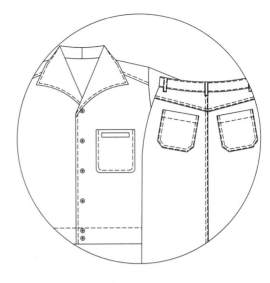

Drawing 7.87

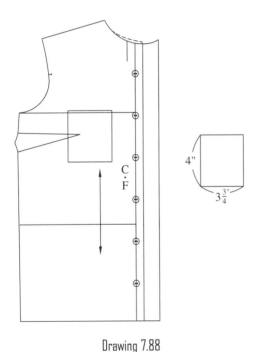

Drawing 7.88

Drawing 7.88. **Pocket.**

- Draw the patch pocket, using the desired shape and dimensions.
- Mark the pocket placement on the pattern.
- Trace the pockets separately.

Drawing 7.89 Pocket flap.

Pocket flaps can be used on any kind of pocket, almost always as a purely decorative element. However, some functional garments (e.g., uniforms, cargo pants) feature flaps with a functional component. They can be either angled or rounded and of virtually any shape.

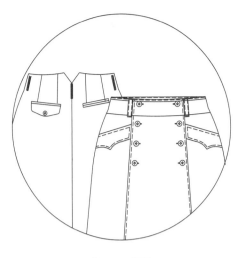

Drawing 7.89

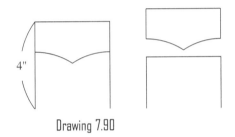

Drawing 7.90

Drawing 7.90. Separate flap.

- Once the pocket shape has been developed to the desired dimensions, its flap is then traced separately so that it can be developed to dimensions and shape appropriate for the pocket.
- Draw the flap on the pocket pattern, following the shape of the pocket.
- Trace the flap separately.

Drawing 7.91. Continuous flap (patch pocket).

- In this style, both the patch pocket and its flap are developed from a single piece.

Flap:
- Draw the pocket, using the desired shape and dimensions.
- Extend the top edge of the pocket, to create the flap.
- Mark the flap fold line along the center of the flap, as shown.

Facing:
- Trace the flap and pocket separately.

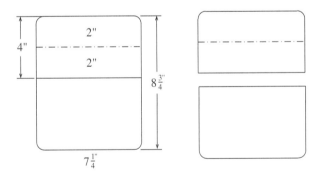

Drawing 7.91

WAISTBANDS

The waistband is a strip of fabric used to finish the waistline of a skirt or pants. Most waistbands feature a closure at the center back, center front or side seam. Those that do not generally use an elastic band. Waistband closures are fastened with a closure device, such as buttons, zippers, drawstrings or hooks, which act both to facilitate taking the garment on and off and to provide a secure fit. There are four types of waistbands: classic, pull-on, facing, and bias-binding.

Waistband variations

Draw-string   Classic waistband   Facing   Elastic   Bias binding

Illustration 7.11

Classic Waistband

The classic waistband is generally $1^1/_4''$ high and equal in length to the waist measurement plus $^1/_2''$ for ease. The ease allows for darts, tucks, and gathers, and helps to avoid a tight fit across the stomach or a rolled effect below the waistband on skirts. A $1''$ to $2''$ long extension is generally added to one side to accommodate button placement.

Illustration 7.12

Drawing 7.92.

- Draw the waistband, using the following dimensions:
    Length = Waist measurement plus $^1/_2''$ for ease.
    Height = $1^1/_4''$.
    Button extension = $1''$.
- Mark the button placement at the center of the center back.
- Mark the buttonhole $^3/_4''$ from the edge at center height.
- Mark the fold placement.

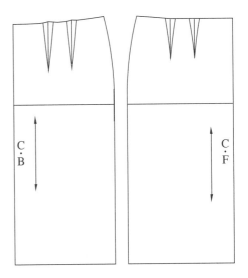

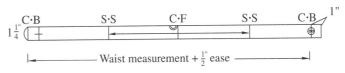

Drawing 7.92

Pull-on Waistband

The pull-on (elastic band) waistband is used in the absence of a closure. The band can be cut stretched, in which case it will be equal to the waist measurement plus a $1/2''$ seam allowance extension. It may also be cut unstretched, in which case it will be cut equal to the waist measurement, minus 2" to 5", plus a $1/2''$ seam allowance extension.

The elastic band should stretch enough to pull on easily over the hips, yet still fit snugly at the waistline. It is enclosed in a casing extended from the pattern by squaring a line up from the hip line a height that may vary with design.

Illustration 7.13

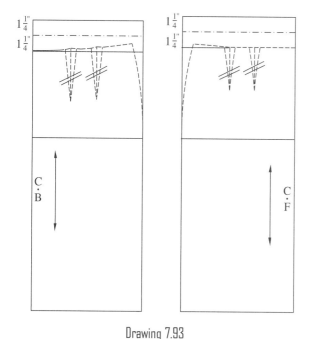

Drawing 7.93

Drawing 7.93.

- Trace the back and front patterns, but do not trace the darts.
- Square up $2^{1}/_{2}''$ from the center back at the waistline.
- Square out from this point, passing the side seam.
- Square up from the hip line at the side seam until the lines intersect.
- Reshape the waistline, as shown.
- Draw the casing fold line at the center of the casing, as shown.
- Repeat these steps from the center front on the front pattern.

Facing Waistband

Facing waistbands have no added waistband. Instead, the facing is attached to the waistline and then turned inside to make a finished waistline seam. The facing is generally 2″ and follows the curve of the waistline. It is created by measuring down 2″ from the waistline on the pattern, then tracing the waistline to a separate piece of paper, after which the darts are closed and the facing reshaped.

Illustration 7.14

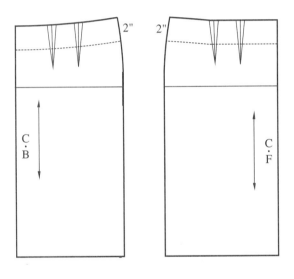

Drawing 7.94

Drawing 7.94.

- Draw a line parallel to and 2″ down from both the front and back waistlines.

Drawing 7.95.

- Trace the facings separately.
- Close the darts, then reshape the facings.

Drawing 7.95

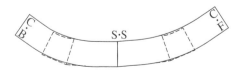

Drawing 7.96

Drawing 7.96.

- Flip the back piece over, then connect the front and back facings at the side seams.
- Trace the facing as one continuous piece.

Bias-Binding Waistband

The bias-binding waistband is cut 2″ wide and the length of the waist measurement plus 2″. It is attached at the waistline, then folded back inside for a $\frac{1}{2}$″ finished binding. Bias-binding waistbands usually feature hook-and-eye closures.

Illustration 7.15

Drawing 7.97.

• Draw the bias-binding, using the dimensions shown.

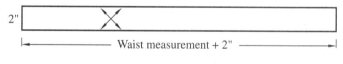

Drawing 7.97

Chapter Eight

THE COLLAR

INTRODUCTION TO THE COLLAR

_T_he collar is an element that is attached (permanently or removably) to the neckline of a garment and that can be functional, purely ornamental, or a combination of the two. A collar can enhance the appearance of a blouse, dress, or jacket by adding a point of focus or interest. Proximity to the face plays an important role in establishing the significance of a collar as a design detail.

It is the shape and attachment of the collar at the neckline that distinguishes the four basic collar categories: standing, rolled, flat, and lapel. Even though the shapes of collar edges and bodice necklines may change with fashion trends and styles, the fundamental structure of the collar neckline in these categories remains the same.

Collar Category Variations

| Standing | Rolled | Flat | Shawl | Notched |

Illustration 8.1

Drawing 8.1. Collar shapes by category.

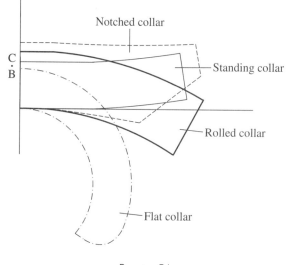

Drawing 8.1

Collar Components

Collar patterns are developed from the front and back neck measurements. The main components in the development of the collar pattern are the neckline edge, stand, roll line, collar height (fall), and collar edge. Any of these components can be stylized with different heights and shapes to create new collar designs.

Collar Neckline
The neckline edge is the point at which the collar is attached to the bodice. For proper fit, the neckline edge of the collar should be equal in length to the bodice neckline, although in industry it is usually increased $1/2''$ for ease.

Collar Stand
The stand is attached to the neckline and is hidden by the collar fall. The collar stand can be of any prac- tical height and can begin at the center back and fade to the center front, or begin at the center front and fade to the back.

Collar Fall
The fall is the visual part of the collar and can vary greatly in size and shape. Its height at the center front or back must be at least $1/8''$ longer than the col- lar stand to hide the neckline seam.

Roll Line
The roll line is the line along which the collar stand and the collar height meet.

Collar Edge
The collar edge (collar outline) is the outermost edge of the collar and can vary greatly in length and shape.

Drawing 8.2. Collar component placement in various collar styles

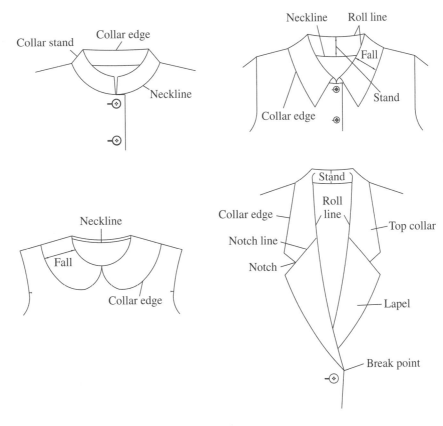

Drawing 8.2

STANDING COLLAR

erived from Chinese costume garments, the standing collar is the oldest known collar design. It is essentially a bare collar stand with no added fall—the collar stand is also the collar fall. The basic pattern is a rectangle, extending up from the neckline either as a single-width band or as a double-width band that is folded in half. By adjusting the fullness, shirring, length, and width of the rectangle, various styles can be created.

Standing Collar Groups

Illustration 8.2

Standing   Mandarin   Ruffle   Ribbon

The pattern is initially developed in a rectangular shape from the front and back neck measurements. Changing the length of BB′ will determine how the collar fits around the neck. If BB′ is shorter, the collar edge will fit loosely around the neck. If BB′ is longer, the collar edge will fit tightly around the neck.

Drawing 8.3. Standing collar.

- Reshape the front and back necklines to the width and depth of the desired design.
- Develop the pattern from the front and back neck measurements.

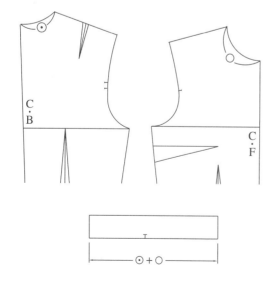

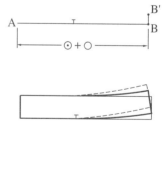

Drawing 8.3

Standing Collar Foundation

The following steps are used to create a generic standing collar, which can then be modified to create any of various types of standing collars. Descriptions and patterns for several specific types of standing collars follow.

Drawing 8.4.

- Measure and record the front and back necklines.

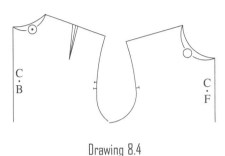

Drawing 8.4

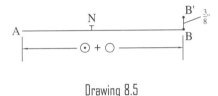

Drawing 8.5

Drawing 8.5.

- Draw a line the combined length of the front and back necklines.
- Label A and B, as shown.
- Measure in the length of the back neckline from A, then label N and mark a notch.
- Square up $^3/_8''$ from B and label B′.

Drawing 8.6.

- Divide line AB into thirds, then label X at two thirds of AB.
- Connect point X to B′, then reshape line AB′.
- Square up 1″ from A and label C.
- Square up 1″ from B′, perpendicular to line B′X, and label C′.
- Connect point C to C′ with a line parallel to AB′.
- **Note:** The collar edge may take on any shape, and the collar point can be finished at any angle desired.

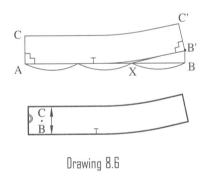

Drawing 8.6

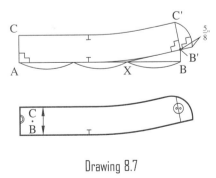

Drawing 8.7

Drawing 8.7. Standing collar with extension.

- Extend a line $^5/_8''$ from B′ then connect to C′ with a curved line, as shown.
- **Note:** The collar extension should be equal to the garment extension.
- Mark the grain line as shown.

Mandarin Collar

This collar is an example of the standing collar. The actual name for this collar is the stand-up collar. This collar may be cut on the bias or straight grain, and its shape can vary.

Illustration 8.3

Drawing 8.8.

- Refer to the standing collar foundation instructions from Drawing 8.4 to develop the mandarin collar, using a 1″ collar height.

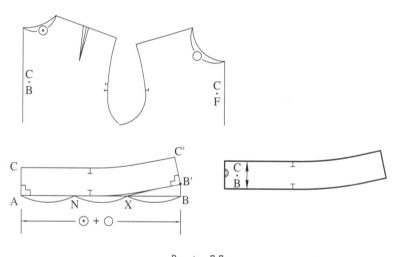

Drawing 8.8

Ribbon Collar

Also called a tie collar, this collar is similar to the mandarin collar, but it is tied in a knot or bow at the center front or shoulder of the neckline. Depending on the width of the tie, the effect will be different. The bias cut of this collar creates a very soft effect.

Illustration 8.4

Drawing 8.9.

- Reshape the front and back necklines as desired.
- Refer to the standing collar foundation instructions from Drawing 8.4 to develop the ribbon collar, using a $2^3/_4''$ collar height.
- Extend the collar length as necessary to accommodate the tie.

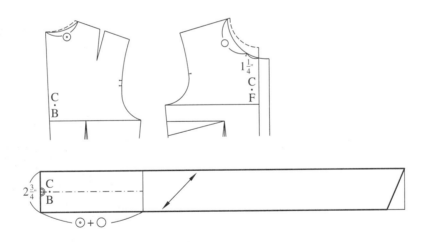

Drawing 8.9

Ruffle Collar

This is a rectangular collar that flares out as it rises from the neckline. This flaring is accomplished by use of two to three times the necessary collar length, which is then shirred at the neckline.

Illustration 8.5

Drawing 8.10.

- Reshape the front and back necklines as desired.
- Refer to the standing collar foundation instructions from Drawing 8.4 to develop the ruffle collar, using a $2^3/4''$ collar height.
- Extend the collar length two to three times the length of the front and back neck measurements to create the ruffling.

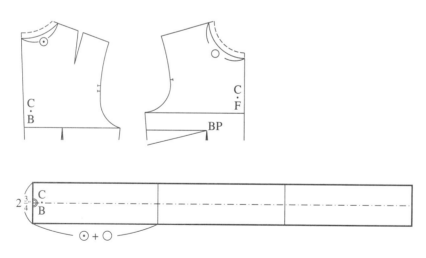

Drawing 8.10

ROLLED COLLAR

The rolled collar starts at the neckline, stands up, then falls back onto the shoulder line. The fold line and roll line are the same, so the roll line will determine the height of both collar and stand. The collar stand begins at center front or center back, curves around the neckline, then fades as the collar ends, following the shape of the roll line. The shape of the collar neckline and the length of its outer edge together determine how the collar will fall onto the shoulders. The collar height should be at least $3/16''$ larger than the stand so that when the collar is down, the seam line between the bodice and stand will be hidden. The collar point may be rounded, pointed, or angled.

* * *

Rolled Collar Groups

Illustration 8.6

Italian   Convertible   Shirt

Patterns are initially developed in a rectangular shape, from the front and back neck measurements. Changing the length of the collar edge results in different collar neckline shapes. As AA′ is decreased, the neckline becomes less curved, resulting in a shorter collar edge, which causes the collar to stand up more. As AA′ is increased, the neckline becomes more curved, resulting in a longer collar edge, which causes the collar to lie flatter.

Drawing 8.11. Rolled collar.

- Reshape the front and back necklines to the width and depth of the desired design.
- Develop the pattern from the front and back neck measurements.

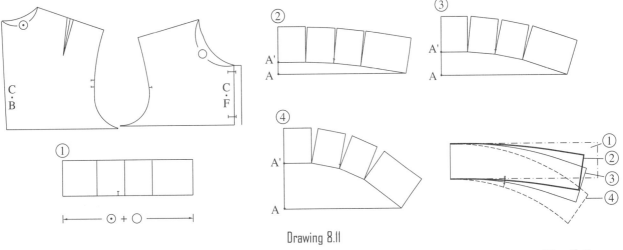

Drawing 8.11

Shirt Collar

The shirt collar is a combination of the rolled and stand collars. It features a stand that rolls naturally away from the neck to a rounded or angled edge.

Illustration 8.7

Drawing 8.12.

- Reshape the front and back necklines.
- Measure and record the front and back necklines.

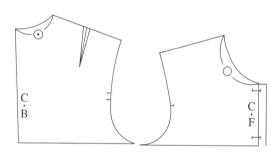

Drawing 8.12

Drawing 8.13.

- Draw a guideline and label A at the beginning point.
- Square up $^3/_4''$ to 3″ from point A and label A′.
- Square in the length of the back neckline from A′, then label N and mark a notch.
- Draw a line the length of the front neckline from N to the guideline, and label B.

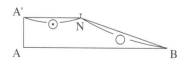

Drawing 8.13

Drawing 8.14.

- Square up 1″ from A′ and label C (A′C = collar stand).
- Square up $^3/_8''$ from B and label B′.
- Square in from C to just above N and label N′.
- Connect point N′ to B′.
- Square up $1^3/_4''$ from point C (the desired collar height) and label D.
- **Note:** CD should be at least $^1/_8''$ longer than A′C.
- Draw the collar edge extending 3″ from B′, then label E at the end point.
- **Note:** The collar edge may be shaped and the collar point at any angle, as desired.
- Square in from D to just above N′, then curve down slightly to connect to E, as shown.

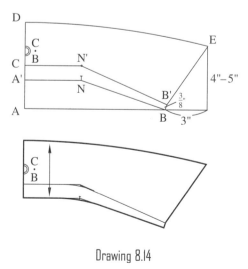

Drawing 8.14

Convertible Collar

This style of collar is found on many sportswear garments. It is a rolled collar that, when worn open, shows facings, but when worn closed, has the appearance of a regular shirt collar.

Illustration 8.8

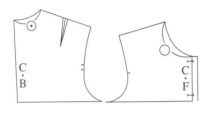

Drawing 8.15

Drawing 8.15.

- Reshape the front and back necklines as desired.
- Measure and record the front and back necklines.

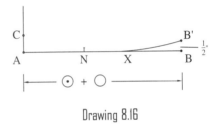

Drawing 8.16

Drawing 8.16.

- Draw a line the combined length of the front and back necklines, then label A and B, as shown.
- Measure in the length of the back neckline from A then label N and mark a notch.
- Square up 1″ from A and label C (AC = collar stand).
- Square up ¹/₂″ from B and label B′.

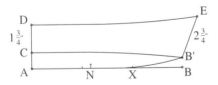

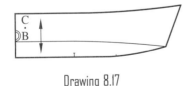

Drawing 8.17

Drawing 8.17.

- Divide line AB into thirds, then label X at two thirds of line AB.
- Connect point X to B′, then reshape line AB′.
- Square in from C to over N, then curve down slightly to connect to B′, as shown.
- Square up 1³/₄″ from C and label D (CD = collar height).
- * **Note:** Line CD should be at least ¹/₈″ longer than line AC.
- Draw the collar edge extending 2³/₄″ from B′ then label E at the end point.
- * **Note:** The collar edge may be shaped and the collar point at any angle, as desired.
- Square in from D to just above N, then curve up slightly to connect to E, as shown.

Shirt Collar with Separate Stand

This collar features collar height and stand that are developed separately.

Illustration 8.9

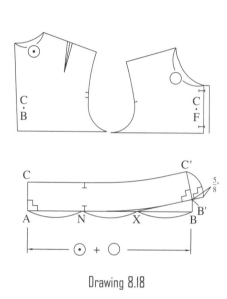

Drawing 8.18

Drawing 8.18.

- Measure and record the front and back necklines.
- Refer to the standing collar with extension instructions from Drawing 8.7 to develop the collar stand, as shown.

Drawing 8.19.

- Measure in $^1/_8''$ from point C' and mark.
- Square up $1^3/_8''$ from C and label D.
- Square in from D the length of line AN and mark a notch, then curve down to connect to the mark, as shown.
- Draw the collar edge extending 3'' from the mark, then label E at the end point.
- **Note:** The collar edge may be shaped and the collar point at any angle, as desired.
- Square up $1^3/_4''$ from D and label F.
- Square in from F to just above the notch, then curve up to connect to E, as shown.
- Trace the collar and stand separately.

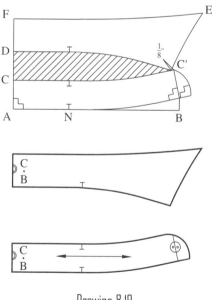

Drawing 8.19

Italian Collar

This is a shirt collar that is attached near or below the midpoint of a V-shaped neckline.

Illustration 8.10

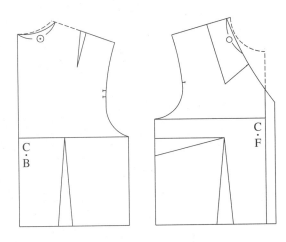

Drawing 8.20

Drawing 8.20. Italian collar.

- Reshape the front and back necklines as desired.
- Draw the Italian collar shape on the front bodice.
- Mark notches on the neckline where the collar will start.
- Measure and record the front neckline from notch to shoulder, and the full length of the back neckline.

Drawing 8.21.

- Refer to the shirt collar instructions from Drawing 8.13 to develop the Italian collar, using the following dimensions:

  AA′ = 1″.
  A′C = 1″.
  CD = 1⅝″.
  BB′ = ³⁄₈″.
  B′E = 4″.

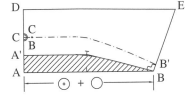

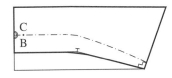

Drawing 8.21

FLAT COLLAR

$\mathcal{T}$he flat collar lies flat along the shoulder, generally with $1/8''$ to $1/2''$ of collar stand. Flat collars are developed by joining the front and back bodices at the neck point and then overlapping their shoulder tips $1/2''$ to create a flat collar with minimal stand and natural roll.

Flat Collar Groups

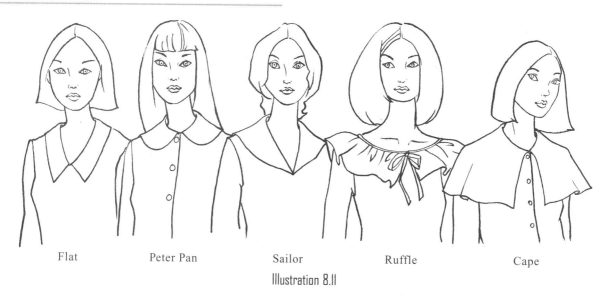

| Flat | Peter Pan | Sailor | Ruffle | Cape |

Illustration 8.11

The amount of overlap determines both the neckline shape and the length of the collar edge. If there is less overlap, the collar edge is longer, resulting in a smaller collar stand. If there is more overlap, the collar edge is shorter, resulting in a higher collar stand. As the maximum overlap is exceeded, the neckline will begin to take on a pointed shape. If the shoulder tips are not overlapped at all, the collar will lie flat and will ruffle.

Drawing 8.22. Flat collar.

- A = 0″ overlap.
- B = $3/4''$ overlap.
- C = 2″ overlap.

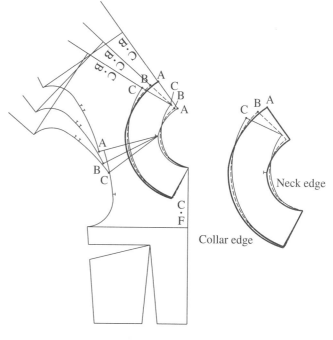

Drawing 8.22

Flat Collar Foundation

The following steps are used to create a generic flat collar, which can then be modified to create any of various types of flat collars. Descriptions and patterns for several specific types of flat collars follow.

Drawing 8.23.

- Trace front bodice from the bust line to the neckline.
- Match the neck points of the front and back bodices, aligning their shoulder lines.
- Secure the back bodice at its neck point with a pushpin.
- Rotate the back bodice to overlap the shoulder tips $1/2''$.
- *** Note:** Do not overlap the neck points.
- Trace the back bodice.
- Mark a notch where the front and back neck points meet on the shoulder.

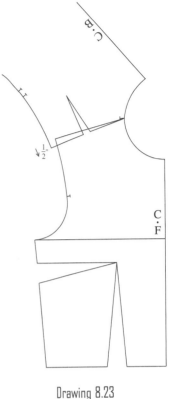

Drawing 8.23

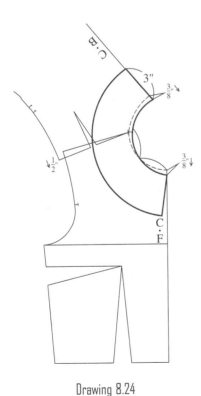

Drawing 8.24

Drawing 8.24.

- Raise the neck $3/8''$ at the center back and lower the neck $3/8''$ at the center front.
- Reshape the neckline, passing through the midpoint of the front neckline.
- Measure down $3''$ (collar height) from the neck at the center back and mark.
- Draw the collar edge as desired.
- Trace the collar separately.

Drawing 8.25. Under collar.

- Mark the grain line, as shown.

Drawing 8.25

Drawing 8.26

Drawing 8.26. Upper collar.

- Trace the under collar.
- Add $^1/_8''$ to the collar edge, starting at the center back and fading to the center front.
- Mark the grain line, as shown.

Peter Pan Collar

The shape and design of this collar is a reference to the English children's book character, Peter Pan. This collar has a gradually rounded point at the center front neckline. If the collar point is angled, it is referred to as a Soutien collar, otherwise it is called a Puritan or Pilgrim collar.

Illustration 8.12

Drawing 8.27.

- Refer to the flat collar foundation instructions from Drawing 8.23 to develop the Peter Pan collar, using a 2″ collar width and ½″ overlap.

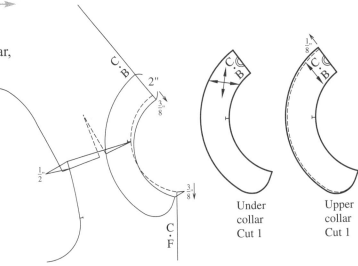

Drawing 8.27

Illustration 8.13

Drawing 8.28.

- Refer to the flat collar foundation instructions from Drawing 8.23 to develop the ruffle collar, using a 4″ collar width and no overlap.

Ruffle Collar

This collar has a softly and wavy curved shape. The slash and spread method can be used to add fullness. Either gathers or tucks can be used to construct the ruffle. The number of slashes put into the collar determines the degree of waviness.

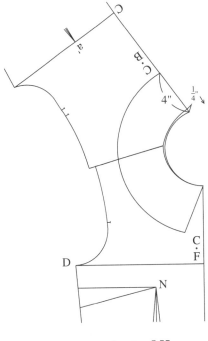

Drawing 8.28

Drawing 8.29. Finished pattern.

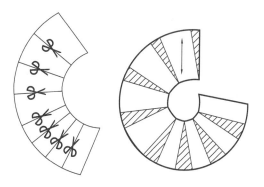

Drawing 8.29

- Trace the collar separately.
- Draw slash lines from the collar edge to the neck-line, as shown.
- Cut along the slash lines from the collar edge to, but not through, the neckline.
- Spread the slash lines to form a circular shape, making certain to leave a seam allowance at each edge.
- Retrace the collar, rounding the edges.
- Mark the grain line, as shown.

Illustration 8.14

Sailor Collar

Derived from navy uniforms, the shape of the sailor collar goes from front to back in a square panel that falls flat down the back.

Drawing 8.30.

- Refer to the flat collar foundation instructions from Drawing 8.23 to develop the sailor collar, using a 4″ collar width, 1″ overlap, and shaping as shown.

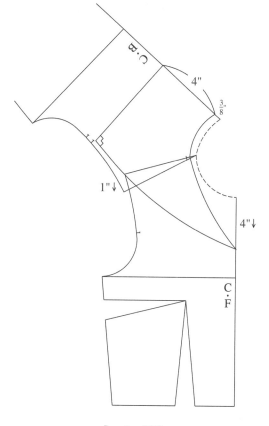

Drawing 8.30

Drawing 8.31. Finished pattern.

- Trace the over and under collar patterns.
- Mark the grain lines, as shown.

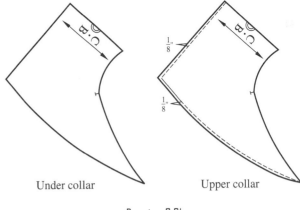

Under collar   Upper collar

Drawing 8.31

Illustration 8.15

Drawing 8.32. Cascading collar.

- Lower the neck $1/2''$ on the back bodice.
- Measure out 4″ from the neck on the shoulder and down 4″ from the neck at the center back.
- Draw the collar edge with a slightly curved line.
- Lower the neck 5″ at the center front and measure in $1/2''$ at the neck on the shoulder.
- Reshape the neckline.
- Measure in 4″ from the neck on the shoulder.
- Draw the collar edge with a slightly curved line.
- * **Note:** The front and back collar widths at the shoulder seam should be equal.

Cascade Collar

The appearance of the cascade collar is reminiscent of a waterfall. It is created using the slash and spread method along the length of the front of the outer edge. The more curved the collar pattern is, the more the fabric will "fall." The shape of the finished collar is determined largely by the location of the collar placement slashes on the bodice pattern.

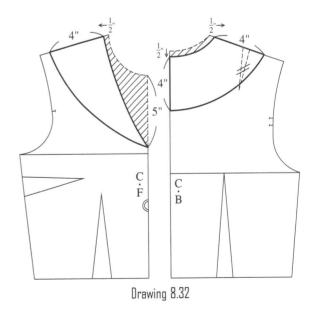

Drawing 8.32

Drawing 8.33. Cascading collar.

- Trace the collar separately.
- Connect the front and back collars at the shoulder seam.
- Draw the slash lines on the collar, as desired.
- *** Note:** More of the slash lines should be placed toward the front, so that the collar falls there.

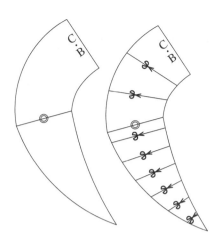

Drawing 8.33

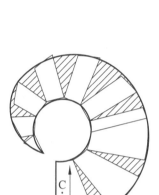

Drawing 8.34

Drawing 8.34.

- Cut along the slash lines to, but not through, the neckline.
- Spread the slash lines open until the collar creates a 360-degree circle.
- *** Note:** Center front and center back should be 1″ apart to allow for seam allowances.
- Reshape the neckline and collar edge.

Cape Collar

This collar falls over the shoulders. It is a large collar and has the shape of the garment for which it is named.

Illustration 8.16

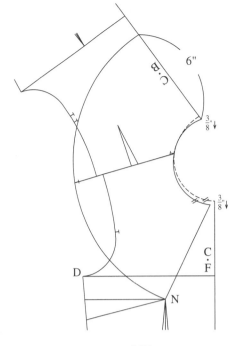

Drawing 8.35.

- Refer to the flat collar foundation instructions, earlier, to develop the cape collar, using a 6″ collar width, no overlap, and shaping as shown.

Drawing 8.35

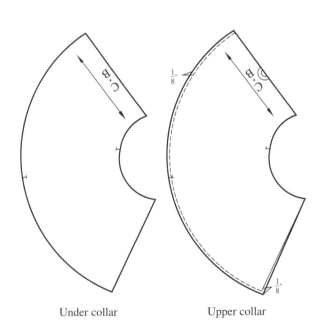

Under collar   Upper collar

Drawing 8.36

Drawing 8.36. Finished pattern.

- Trace the over and under collars separately.
- Mark the grain lines, as shown.

LAPEL COLLAR

*L*apel collars are open collars. Their necklines are generally V-shaped to accommodate the lapel, as they extend from the front bodice and fold back to reveal the facing. The top collar can be part of the lapel, such as in the shawl and wing collars, or it can be separate from the lapel, such as in the notched, Napoleon, and oblong collars.

Lapel Collar Groups

Wing   Oblong   Shawl   Open   Napoleon

Illustration 8.17

Drawing 8.37. **Lapel collar.**

- The back collar is shaped by extending the neckline at the shoulder and then swinging that line to define the collar stand, generally $^3/_4''$.

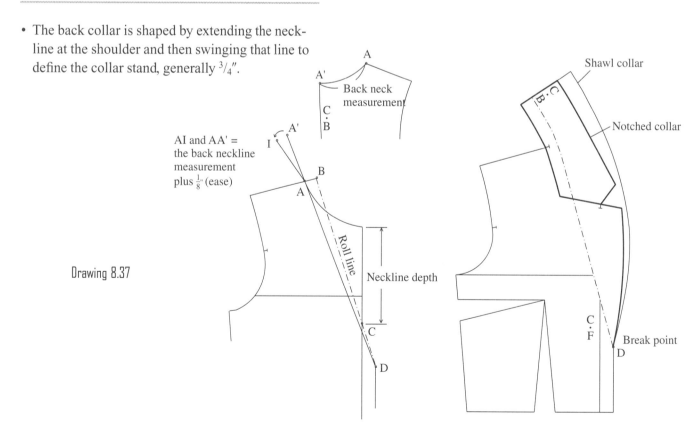

Drawing 8.37

- Swinging the back neckline more results in a longer collar edge, and a shorter, flatter stand. Likewise, swinging it less results in a shorter collar edge, and a longer, higher collar stand.

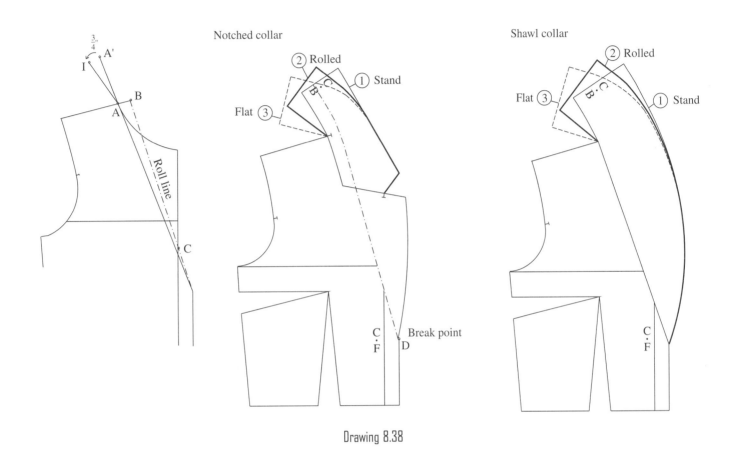

Drawing 8.38

Lapel Collar Neckline Variations

The width and depth of the neckline determine the shape of a lapel collar. Narrowing the neckline width and increasing its depth results in a narrower collar, whereas widening the neckline and decreasing its depth makes it wider.

Illustration 8.18

Drawing 8.39.

- Neckline depth = $7^1/_4''$.
- Neckline width = Unchanged.

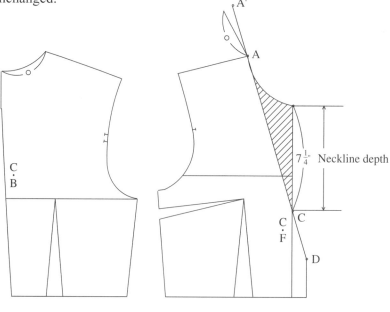

Drawing 8.39

Drawing 8.40.

- Neckline depth = $4^3/_4''$.
- Neckline width = $1^1/_2''$.

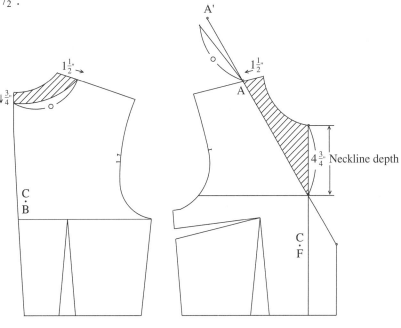

Drawing 8.40

Drawing 8.41.

- Neckline depth = $3^1/_2''$.
- Neckline width = $3^1/_2''$.

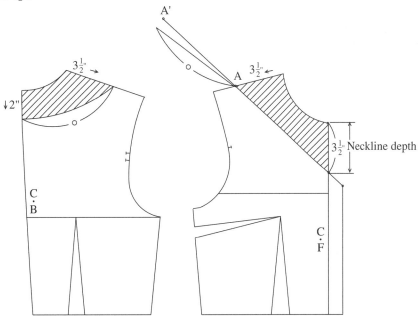

Drawing 8.41

Shawl Collar

The shawl collar is structurally similar to the notched
collar described in the next section. It differs in that
it does not contain a top collar, its lapel is derived
from a single piece, and it has a center back seam.

Shawl collar variations

Illustration 8.19

Drawing 8.42. Lapel variations.

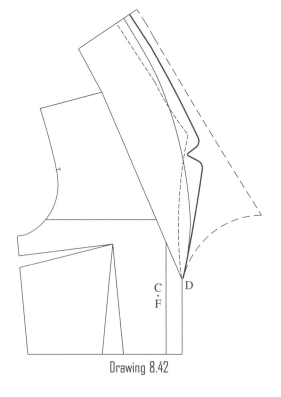

C
•
F

D

Drawing 8.42

Drawing 8.43. Back.

- Trace the back bodice sloper.
- Lower the neckline 1″.
- * **Note:** The shoulder dart on the back will be eased in as it is sewn.

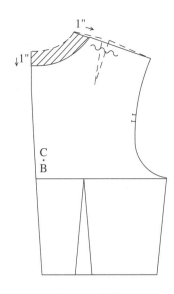

Drawing 8.43

Drawing 8.44. Front.

- Trace the front bodice sloper.
- Measure in 1″ from the neck on the shoulder and label A.
- Reshape the neckline.

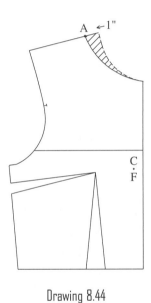

Drawing 8.44

Drawing 8.45.

- Extend the shoulder line 1″ from A and label B (AB = collar stand).
- Add a 1″ extension to the center front.
- Measure down 4″ (neckline depth) from the neck at the center front and label C.
- * **Note:** The placement of point C (neckline depth) may vary.
- Draw a line from B to the extension edge, passing through C, and label D (BD = roll line).
- Create the lapel shape as desired.

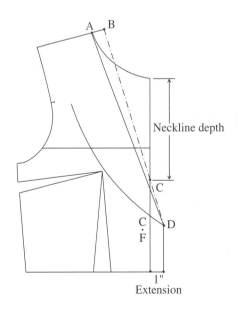

Drawing 8.45

Drawing 8.46.

- Fold under the pattern along the line BD.
- Trace the lapel.

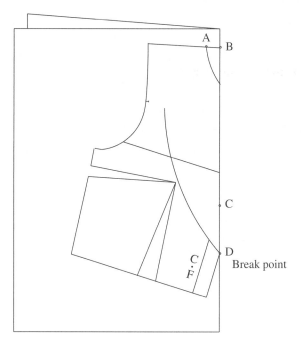

Drawing 8.46

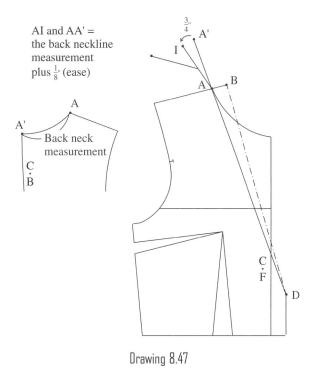

AI and AA' =
the back neckline
measurement
plus $\frac{1}{8}''$ (ease)

Back neck
measurement

Drawing 8.47

Drawing 8.47.

- Unfold the paper and mark the lapel.
- Connect point A to D.
- Extend line AD up from A, the length of the back neck measurement, and label A'.
- Swing line AA' over $^3/_4''$ and label I (AI = AA').
- **Note:** As AA' is swung more, the collar edge is increased, resulting in a flatter stand.
- Connect point A to I.

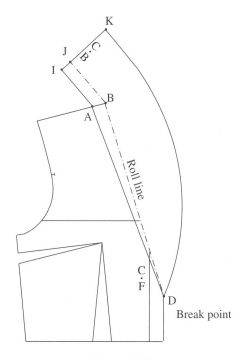

Drawing 8.48

Drawing 8.48.

- Square out $3^1/_2''$ from I and label K (IK = collar height).
- **Note:** Collar height can vary as long as it is square on the corners at I and K.
- Shape the lapel as desired.
- Measure in 1" from I and label J (IJ = stand).
- Connect point J to B (JBD = roll line).

Drawing 8.49. Back facing.

- Measure down 2″ to 3″ from the neck on the center back.
- Measure in 1³/₄″ from the neck on the shoulder.
- Draw the facing from the shoulder to the center back, as shown.
- Trace the facing separately.

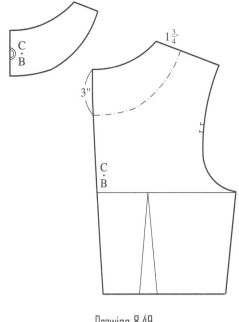

Drawing 8.49

Drawing 8.50. Front facing.

- Measure in 2¹/₂″ from the center front on the hem.
- Measure in 1³/₄″ from the neck on the shoulder.
- Draw the facing from the shoulder to the hem.
- Trace the facing separately.

- Cut along the roll line and shift outward ¹/₈″ to add ease.
- Measure out ¹/₈″ at the lapel edge, blending to nothing at the break point.
- Add ¹/₈″ to the hem.

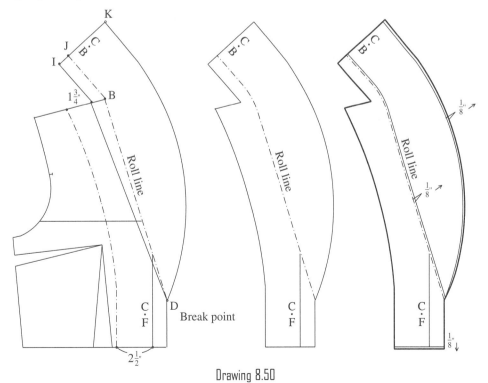

Drawing 8.50

- Mark the notches and grain lines, as shown.

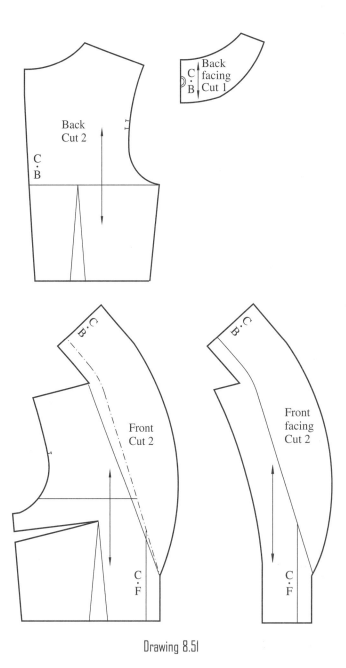

Drawing 8.51

Notched Collar

Named for the "notch" formed at the intersection of its collar and lapel, the notched collar is the standard collar used in most tailored jackets. The upper collar is attached to the bodice facing and the under collar to the bodice. Style variations are achieved by manipulating the placement of the collar break, width or shape of the lapel, and placement of the notch, and by using a double- or single-breasted closure.

Lapel and Notch Placement Variations

Illustration 8.20

Drawing 8.52. Lapel and notch placement variations.

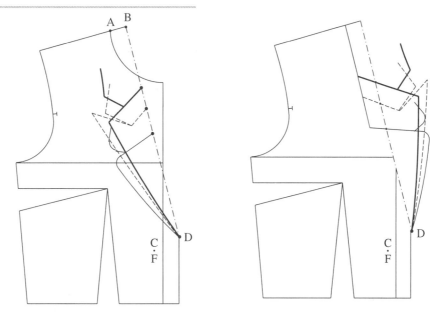

Drawing 8.52

Drawing 8.53. Back and Front.

• Trace the back and front bodice slopers.
• Lower the neckline ¹/₂″.

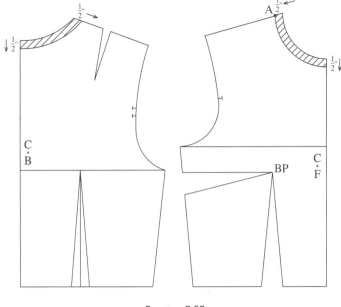

Drawing 8.53

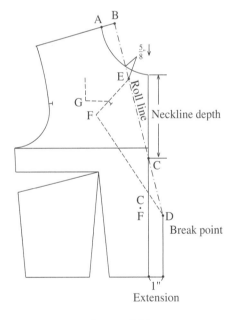

Drawing 8.54

Drawing 8.54.

• Label A at the neck on the shoulder.
• Extend the shoulder line 1″ from A and label B
  (AB = collar stand).
• Add a 1″ extension to the center front.
• Measure down 5¹/₂″ (neckline depth) from the
  neck at the center front and label C.
• **Note:** The placement of point C (neckline depth)
  may vary.
• Draw a line from B to the extension edge, passing
  through point C and label D (BD = roll line).
• Measure down ⁵/₈″ at the intersection of the neck-
  line and roll line and label E.
• Create the lapel as desired by forming a triangle
  from points E, F, and D.
• Design the top collar as desired, and label G at the
  collar point.

Drawing 8.55. Lapel and shape variations.

- Point E can be placed anywhere on the roll line (BD).

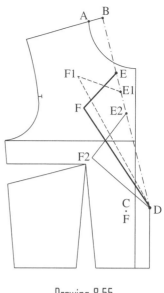

Drawing 8.55

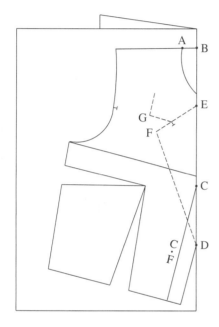

Drawing 8.56

Drawing 8.56.

- Fold the pattern under on line BD.
- Trace the lapel (EFD) and top collar, including the notch.

Drawing 8.57.

- Unfold the paper.
- Draw a guideline down from A, perpendicular to the shoulder seam.
- Extend line FE to intersect that line, labeling H where the two intersect.
- Extend HA up from A the length of the back neck measurement and label A′.
- Swing line AA′ over $^3/_4''$ and label I (AI = AA′).
- Connect point A to I.

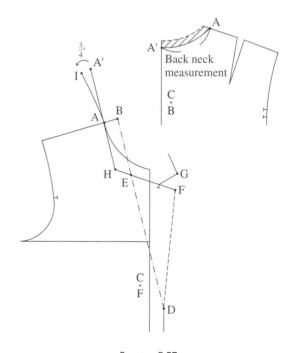

Drawing 8.57

Drawing 8.58.

- Square out $3^{1}/_{2}''$ from I and label K.
- Connect K to G and shape with a slightly inward curved line.
- Draw a slightly outward curved line from F to D.
- Blend IAH with a slightly inward curved line.
- Measure in 1″ from I on IK and label J (IJ = collar stand).
- Connect J to B (JBD = roll line).
- Mark the notch at point A on the shoulder.
- Mark the notch where the top collar and lapel meet.
- Separate the top collar, including the notch.

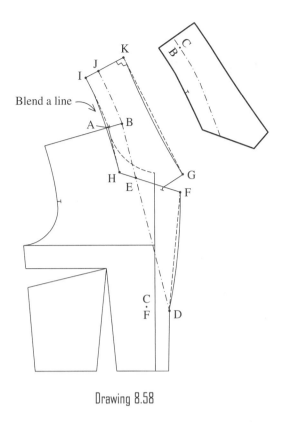

Drawing 8.58

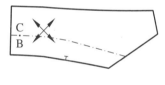

Drawing 8.59

Drawing 8.59. Under collar.

- Mark the grain line and notch, as shown.

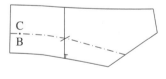

Drawing 8.60

Drawing 8.60. Upper collar.

- Trace the under collar.
- Draw a line parallel to the center back through the notch.

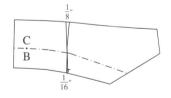

Drawing 8.61

Drawing 8.61.

- Slash from the top edge of the collar to, but not through, the roll line.
- Slash from the bottom neckline of the collar to, but not through, the roll line.
- Spread $^{1}/_{8}''$ at the collar edge, letting the bottom neckline overlap $^{1}/_{16}''$.

Drawing 8.62.

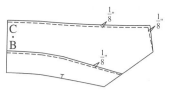

Drawing 8.62

- Cut along the roll line.
- Shift the top part up $^1/_8''$.
- Add $^1/_8''$ to the top edge of the collar.
- Add $^1/_8''$ to the collar tip and blend to nothing, as shown.

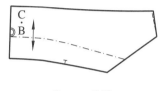

Drawing 8.63

Drawing 8.63.

- Mark the grain line and notch, as shown.

Drawing 8.64. Back facing.

- Measure down 3″ from the neck at the center back.
- Measure in $1^3/_4''$ from the neck on the shoulder.
- Draw the facing from the shoulder to the center back.
- Trace the facing separately.

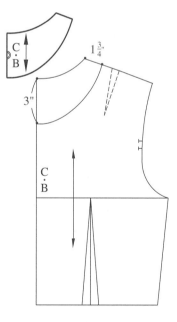

Drawing 8.64

Drawing 8.65. Front facing.

- Measure in $2\frac{1}{2}''$ from the center front on the hem.
- Measure in $1\frac{3}{4}''$ from the neck point on the shoulder.
- Draw the facing from the shoulder to the hem.
- Trace the facing separately.

- Cut along the roll line and shift the lapel outward $\frac{1}{8}''$ for the ease.
- Measure out $\frac{1}{8}''$ at the lapel tip, then blend to nothing at the break point and the neck point, as shown.
- Add $\frac{1}{8}''$ to the hem.

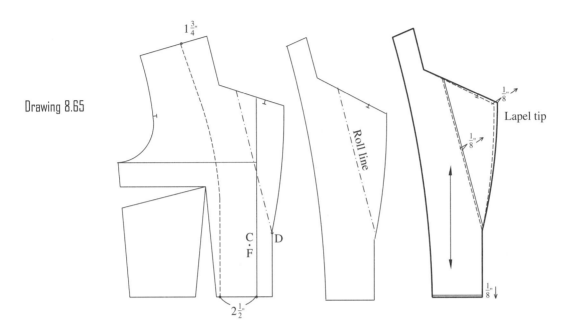

Drawing 8.65

Drawing 8.66. Finished patterns.

- Mark the notches and grain lines, as shown.

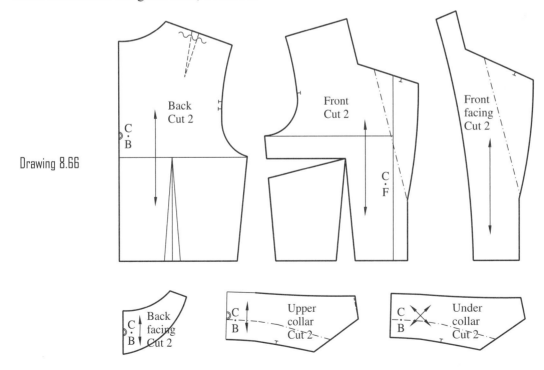

Drawing 8.66

Open Collar

The open collar is similar to the convertible collar, except that the roll line for the open collar extends into the bodice. When it is open, its appearance is similar to that of the notched collar. This collar is generally used on sportswear shirts or blouses.

Drawing 8.67.

- Add an extension to the center front.
- Extend the shoulder line 1″ from A and label B.
- Measure up $1^3/_4$″ from the bust line on the extension edge and label D.
- Connect point B to D.
- Refer to the notched collar instructions from Drawing 8.57 to develop the open collar as shown, using the following dimensions:

    AB = 1″ (collar stand).

    IJ = 1″ (collar stand).

    IK = $2^3/_4$″ (collar height).

Illustration 8.21

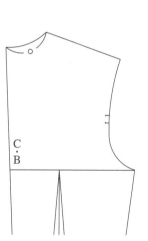

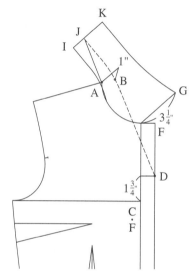

Drawing 8.67

Drawing 8.68. Finished patterns.

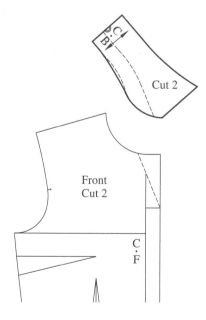

Drawing 8.68

Oblong Collar

This collar is similar to the shawl collar, only with a seam line going through it. It is connected to the edge of the bodice extension with its roll line extending into the bodice. When the collar is open, the lapel spreads open into a V-neck.

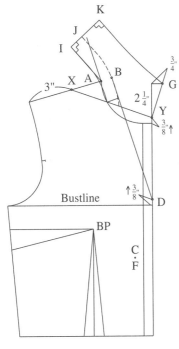

Drawing 8.69

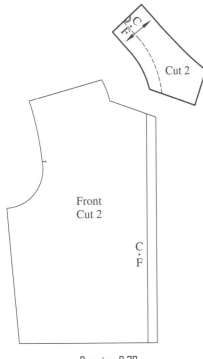

Drawing 8.70

Illustration 8.22

Drawing 8.69.

- Add an extension to the center front.
- Extend the shoulder line $3/4''$ from A and label B.
- Measure up $3/8''$ from the bust line on the extension edge and label D.
- Connect point B to D.
- Measure 3″ in from the shoulder tip and label X.
- Measure $3/8''$ up from the neck at the extension edge and label Y.
- Connect X and Y.
- Refer to the notched collar instructions from Drawing 8.57 and 8.58 to develop the oblong collar as shown, using the following dimensions:
    AB = $3/4''$.
    IJ = $3/4''$.
    IK = $2^1/2''$.

Drawing 8.70. Finished patterns.

Wing Collar

This collar is reminiscent of the open wings of a bird. It is similar to the shawl collar, except that its fall has a higher lift. It can be created as part of the bodice or as a separate collar connected to the bodice.

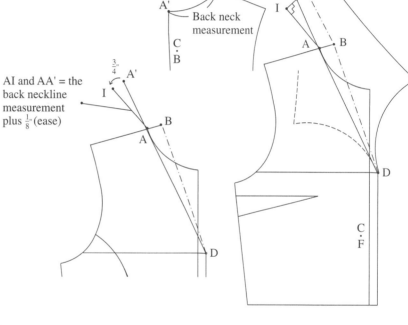

Illustration 8.23

Drawing 8.71.

- Add a $5/8''$ extension to the center front.
- Extend the shoulder line $1''$ from A and label B.
- Label D on the extension edge at the bust line.
- Refer to the shawl collar instructions from Drawing 8.45 to develop the wing collar as shown, using the following dimensions:

    AB = $1''$.
    IJ = $1''$.
    IK = $3''$.

AI and AA' = the back neckline measurement plus $\frac{1}{8}''$ (ease)

Drawing 8.71

Drawing 8.72. Finished patterns.

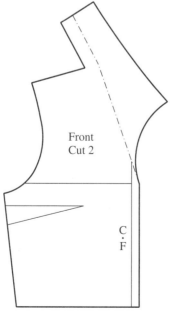

Front
Cut 2

C·F

Drawing 8.72

Napoleon Collar

The Napoleon collar is generally used on double-breasted coats. The stand for this collar can be extremely high with very large lapels. The stand and shirt collar are completely separate, and the top collar has its own separate stand as well.

Illustration 8.24

Drawing 8.73. **Lapel.**

- Measure in $3/8''$ from the neck on the shoulder and label M.
- Measure up $2^3/8''$ from the waistline on the extension and label N.
- Connect point M to N.
- Measure down $3/8''$ from the neck at the center front and label G.
- Square out from G to the extension line and label H.
- Square in from G to line MN, labeling I at the intersection.
- Square in $3/4''$ from I and label J.
- Connect points M, J, and N (JN = roll line).
- Reshape HN with slight outward curve, as shown.

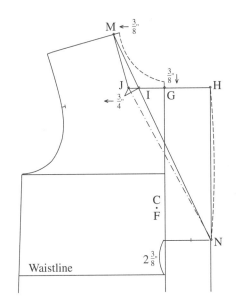

Drawing 8.73

Drawing 8.74. **Collar.**

- Measure and record the front and back necklines.
- Refer to the standing collar foundation instructions from Drawing 8.4 to develop the collar stand, using the following dimensions:

    AC = $1^5/8''$.
    BB′ = $1^1/4''$.
    B′C′ = $1^3/8''$.

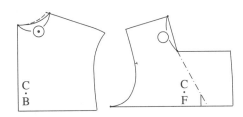

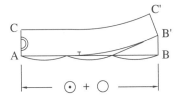

Drawing 8.74

Drawing 8.75.

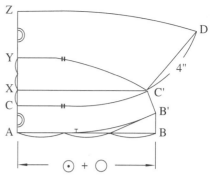

- Draw a line from C′, perpendicular to center back, and label X.
- Square up two times the length of CX and label Y.
- Connect Y to C′, mirroring the curve of line CC′.
- Square up 3″ from Y and label Z (collar height).
- Draw the collar point from C′, at any angle and length, and label D.
- Connect point D to Z, ending square to YZ as shown.

Drawing 8.75

Drawing 8.76. Finished pattern.

- Separate the collar stand and collar, as shown.

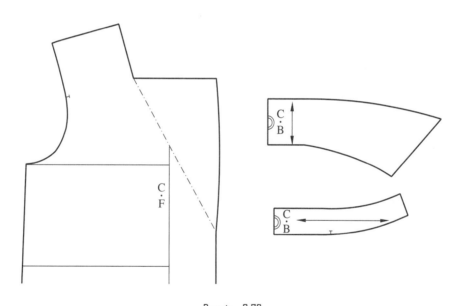

Drawing 8.76

Head Measurements for Hood

A = Head circumference. Measure around the head at its widest point.

B = Back hood length. Measure from the neck at the center front to the center top of the head.

C = Back hood length. With head tilted, measure from the shoulder at the neck to the center top of the head.

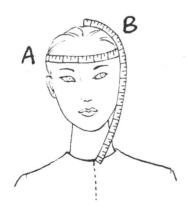

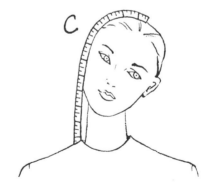

Drawing 8.77.

- Trace the portion of the front pattern that lies above the bust line.
- Label A at the neck on the center front.
- Label B at the neck on the shoulder.
- Square a line up from the extension edge.
- Draw a line from B, perpendicular to the extension edge, labeling C where the two lines intersect.
- Square a line up from A, labeling D where it intersects CB.
- Measure in the front neck measurement from D and label E.
- Measure out the back neck measurement from E and label F.

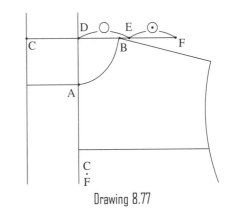

Drawing 8.77

Drawing 8.78.

- Square up 14″ (hood measurement) from C and label G.
- Square in 4″ (extension) from G and label H.
- Square out 1″ from G then square down $1/2$″ and label J.
- Connect point J to H.
- Connect point J to C, square at first, then bending inward as shown.
- Square out 11″ (hood width) from H and label I.
- Connect point I to F.
- Draw the neckline from A to F, as shown, making certain that it is equal in length to the combined front and back neck measurements.
- Measure in the front neck measurement from A on AF and mark a notch.
- Shape the back of the hood as shown.

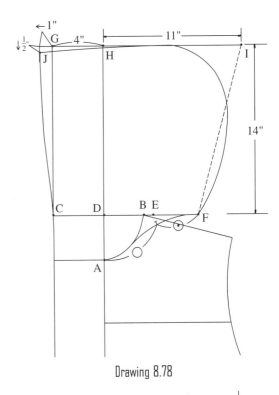

Drawing 8.78

Drawing 8.79. Finished pattern.

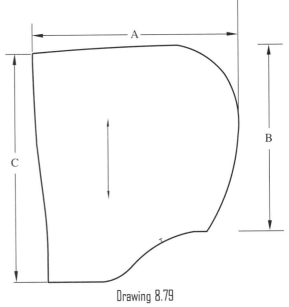

Drawing 8.79

Drawing 8.80. Hood with dart.

- Extend line DF $1\frac{1}{2}''$ for the dart intake.
- Measure out $1\frac{1}{2}''$ from the notch and mark.
- Draw the dart legs 4″ long, using the notch and mark, as shown.

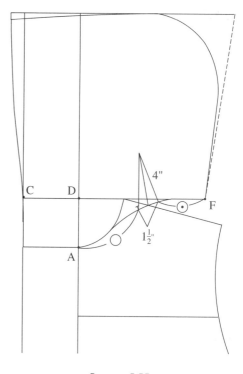

Drawing 8.80

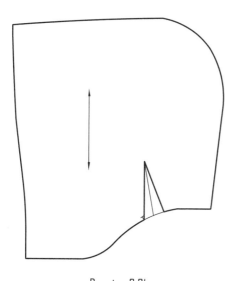

Drawing 8.81

Drawing 8.81. Finished pattern.

Chapter Nine

THE SLEEVE

INTRODUCTION TO THE SLEEVE

 *S*leeves wrap around the arms and hang from the outer edge of the shoulders. Most garments feature them as decorative or functional elements. As a decorative element, a sleeve should compliment the bodice. As a functional element, a sleeve should allow for ease of movement and comfort.

All sleeves fall into one of three categories, based on how they are cut and constructed: set-in, kimono, and raglan styles. Set-in sleeves are separate from the bodice and connected to it with a seam at the armhole. Kimono sleeves are literally a continuation of the bodice, and thus are not sewn at all. Raglan sleeves are set into the bodice, and extend into part of the neckline and armhole.

Sleeves can be finished with cuffs, lace, or ruffles to enhance the overall design. The silhouette of a sleeve can vary with its length, width, and design details such as flares, gathers, and pleats. The shape of a sleeve can be altered using the slash and spread method to add fullness. Instructions for drafting various sleeve patterns can also be found in Chapters 10, and 11, covering blouses and one-piece dresses.

Sleeve Variations

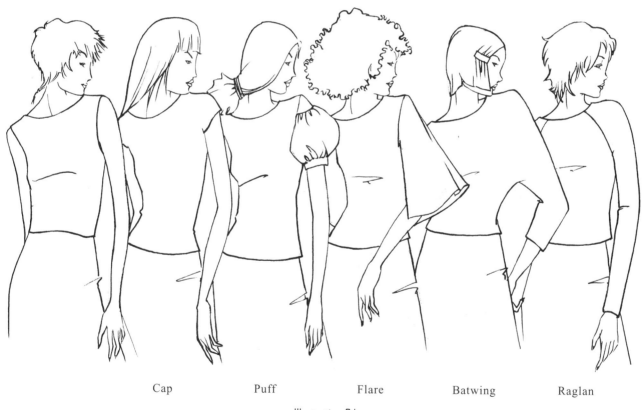

Cap   Puff   Flare   Batwing   Raglan

Illustration 9.1

Sleeve Cap Height

The arm angle upon which a particular sleeve sloper is based is dictated largely by the sleeve cap height. Changes made to the cap height directly affect the comfort and mobility of the garment. Decreasing the cap height widens the biceps line and increases the under sleeve length, thus opening the armhole for an increase in overall comfort and mobility. Likewise, increasing the cap height narrows the biceps line and decreases the under sleeve length, thus closing the armhole for a tighter fit and a more structured armhole.

The following illustrations demonstrate the results of varying cap height on the final sleeve pattern and range of arm motion in the finished garment.

Illustration 9.2

Drawing 9.1. Cap height.

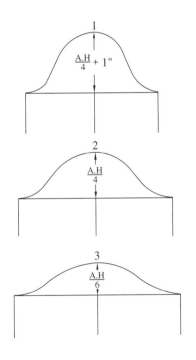

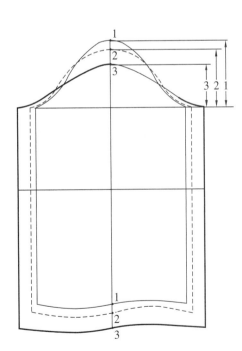

Drawing 9.1

Sleeve Cap and Armhole Position

As the armhole is lowered, the biceps line of the sleeve must be raised and widened correspondingly. This will shorten the cap height, thus allowing for a larger, more open armhole. For example, if the armhole is lowered 2″, the biceps line must be raised 2″ and extended beyond the underarm seam lines, after which the sleeve cap is reshaped to equal the armhole measurement on the bodice.

The following illustrations depict the results of varying armhole positions on the sleeve cap in the finished garment and final sleeve pattern.

Illustration 9.3

Drawing 9.2. Armhole variations.

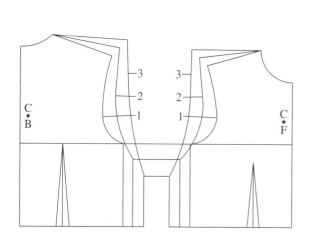
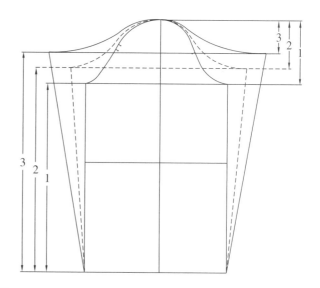

Drawing 9.2

SET-IN SLEEVE

One-Piece Sleeve Styles

The set-in sleeve is sewn into the bodice and may be of any length, depending on garment design and function. Set in sleeves can fit smoothly in the armhole or with gathers or tucks for more fullness at the sleeve cap. There are many design variations for set-in sleeves, ranging from fitted to full.

Set-in sleeve patterns are developed from sleeve slopers. By slashing and spreading for fullness at various locations, such as the sleeve cap and hem, numerous styles can be created, including cap, tulip, and flared sleeves. When constructed, set-in sleeves can be cut in one, one-and-a-half or two pieces.

Illustration 9.4

Drawing 9.3. Basic set-in sleeve patterns.

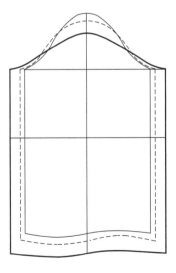

Drawing 9.3

Puff Sleeves

Puff sleeves feature gathers or tucks at the armhole, hem, or both, to create a "puffed" shape and a very soft appearance overall. They are generally short; longer variations are referred to as bishop or melon sleeves.

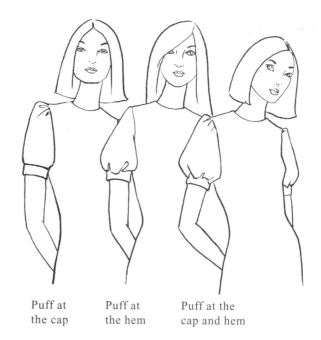

Puff at   Puff at   Puff at the
the cap   the hem   cap and hem

Illustration 9.5

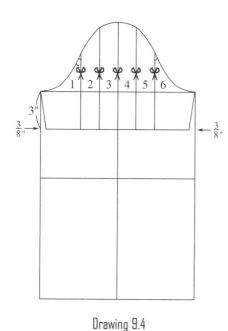

Drawing 9.4

Drawing 9.4. Puff sleeve at the cap.

- Trace the straight sleeve sloper.
- Measure down 3″ from the biceps line for the sleeve length.
- Taper in $^3/_8$″ at each side.
- Draw the slash lines, between the notches, spaced 2″ apart.
- * **Note:** Generally, the slash lines are evenly spaced.
- Number each section, as shown.

Drawing 9.5. Finished pattern.

- Cut along the slash lines, from the cap to, but not through, the hem.
- Draw a horizontal guideline
- Spread the slash lines at the hem, as desired.
- Spread each piece $^3/_4$″ apart.
- Measure up 1″ from the center line and reshape the cap to this measurement for a smooth, contoured shape.
- * **Note:** Do not change the sleeve cap below the notches.

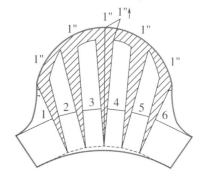

Drawing 9.5

Drawing 9.6. Puff sleeve at the hem.

- Follow the preceding instructions for the puff sleeve at the cap (Drawing 9.5) to develop the puff sleeve at the hem pattern.

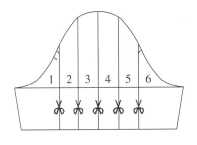

Drawing 9.6

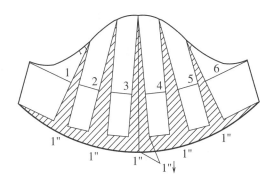

Drawing 9.7

Drawing 9.7. Finished pattern.

- Cut along the slash lines, from the hem to, but not through, the cap.
- Draw a horizontal guideline
- Spread the slash lines at the hem, as desired.
- Spread each piece 1″ apart.
- Measure down 1″ from the center line and reshape the hem with a curved line.

Drawing 9.8. Puff at the cap and hem.

- Follow the earlier instructions for the puff sleeve at the cap (Drawing 9.5) to develop the puff sleeve at the cap and hem pattern.

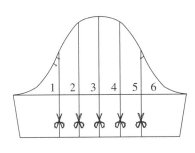

Drawing 9.8

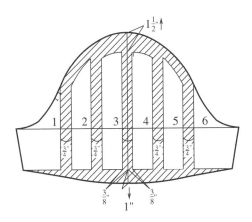

Drawing 9.9

Drawing 9.9. Finished pattern.

- Cut along the slash lines.
- Draw a horizontal guideline with a vertical guideline intersecting at its center.
- Match the biceps line to the horizontal guideline, as shown.
- Place sections 3 and 4, $^3/_8$″ from the vertical guideline.
- Spread the remaining pieces $^3/_4$″ apart.
- Measure up $1^1/_2$″ from the center line and reshape the cap to this measurement for a smooth, contoured shape.
- * **Note:** Do not change the sleeve cap below the notches.
- Measure down 1″ from the center line and reshape the hem with a curved line.

Petal Sleeve

This sleeve features a rounded shape and the overlapping style, generally at the front, reminiscent of overlapping flower petals.

Illustration 9.6

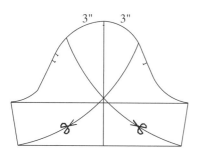

Drawing 9.10

Drawing 9.10. **Plain petal sleeve.**

- Trace the sleeve sloper.
- Shorten the sleeve length as desired.
- Measure out 3″ on both sides of the sleeve center line and mark.
- Connect the marks to the hem at the side seams, as shown.

Drawing 9.11. **Finished pattern.**

- Trace the back and front sleeve patterns separately, including the notches.

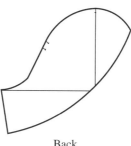 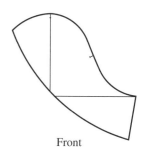

Back   Front

Drawing 9.11

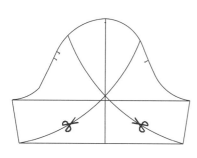

Drawing 9.12

Drawing 9.12. **Petal sleeve with shirring at the cap.**

- Follow the earlier instructions for the plain petal sleeve (Drawing 9.10), then proceed to complete the front and back sleeve patterns.

Drawing 9.13.

- Draw the slash lines between the notches.

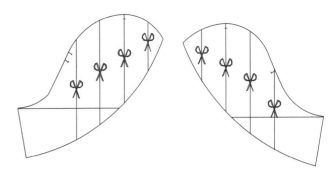

Drawing 9.13

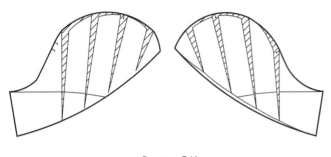

Drawing 9.14

Drawing 9.14. Finished pattern.

- Cut along the slash lines, from the cap to, but not through, the hem.
- Spread the slash lines at the cap, as desired.
- Reshape the cap.

Drawing 9.15. Petal sleeve with flare at the hem.

- Follow the earlier plain petal sleeve instructions (Drawing 9.10), then proceed to complete the front and back sleeve patterns.

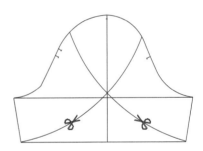

Drawing 9.15

Drawing 9.16.

- Draw the slash lines between the notches.

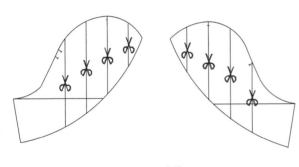

Drawing 9.16

Drawing 9.17. Finished pattern.

- Cut along the slash lines, from the hem to, but not through, the cap.
- Spread the slash lines at the hem, as desired.
- Reshape the hem.

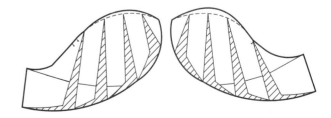

Drawing 9.17

Bishop Sleeve

This subcategory of puff sleeves extends all the way to the wrist and is shirred into the cuff.

Illustration 9.7

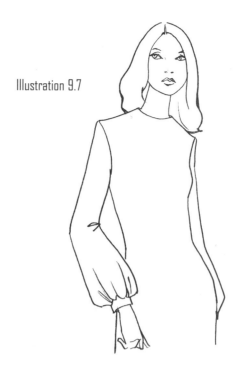

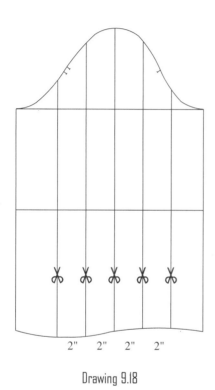

2" 2" 2" 2"

Drawing 9.18

Drawing 9.18.

- Trace the straight sleeve sloper.
- Draw the slash lines on each side of the center line, spaced 2″ apart, as shown.
- Cut along the slash lines, including the center line to, but not through, the sleeve cap.

Drawing 9.19. **Finished pattern.**

- Spread each slash line $1^1/_2$″ at the hem.
- Reshape the hem.

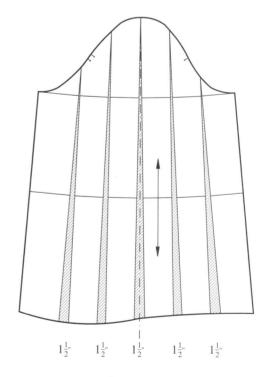

$1\frac{1}{2}$″ $1\frac{1}{2}$″ $1\frac{1}{2}$″ $1\frac{1}{2}$″ $1\frac{1}{2}$″

Drawing 9.19

Leg-of-Mutton Sleeve

This sleeve, named for the shape of a roast leg of lamb, features a full cap that tapers to a tight fit near the wrist.

Illustration 9.8

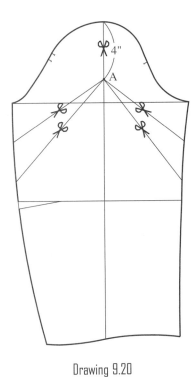

Drawing 9.20

Drawing 9.20.

- Trace the tight sleeve sloper.
- Measure down 4″ from the cap on the center line and label A.
- Mark both side seams between the biceps and elbow lines into thirds.
- Connect A to each mark, as shown.

Drawing 9.21 Finished pattern.

- Slash on the center line, from the cap to A.
- Slash from A to each mark, as shown.
- Spread the slash line at the cap 2¹/₂″ on each side of the center line.
- Reshape the cap.

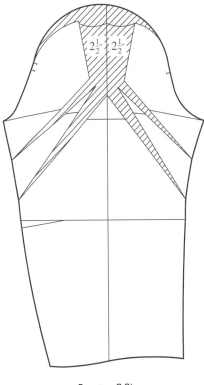

Drawing 9.21

Cowl Sleeve

This sleeve is very soft in appearance, with draped pleats falling around the upper arm. It is generally cut on the bias to create the fullness necessary for the pleats to drape properly.

Illustration 9.9

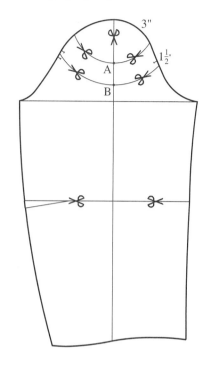

Drawing 9.22

Drawing 9.22.

- Trace the tight sleeve sloper.
- Measure down 3″ from the cap on the center line and label A.
- Measure out 3″ on both sides of the sleeve center line and mark.
- Connect the marks to A with curved lines.
- Measure down $1\frac{1}{2}$″ from A and label B.
- Measure out $4\frac{1}{2}$″ on both sides of the sleeve center line and mark.
- Connect the marks to B with curved lines.

Drawing 9.23. Finished pattern.

- Slash on the center line, from the cap to the elbow line.
- Slash from the elbow line to, but not through, the underarm seams, as shown.
- Slash the curved lines through A and B to, but not through, the cap, as shown.
- Spread the slashed lines as desired.
- Reshape the cap.

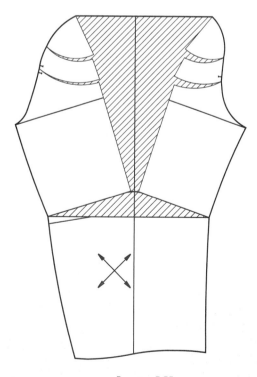

Drawing 9.23

Lantern Sleeve

This sleeve is relatively plain, with fullness added between the upper and under pieces, creating a lantern shape. The finished sleeve can be of almost any length from short to long.

Illustration 9.10

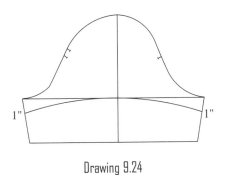

Drawing 9.24

Drawing 9.24.

- Trace the sleeve sloper.
- Shorten the sleeve length, as desired.
- Measure down 1″ from the biceps line on both ends of the underarm seam and mark.
- Connect the marks with a curved line, passing through the biceps line at the sleeve center line, as shown.

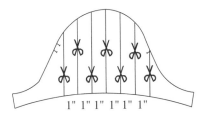

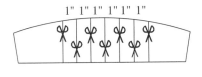

Drawing 9.25

Drawing 9.25.

- Separate the sleeve.
- Draw three slash lines, 1″ apart, on each side of the center line of both sleeve pieces.

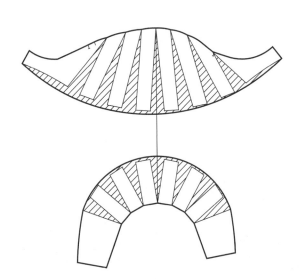

Drawing 9.26

Drawing 9.26. Finished pattern.

- On the sleeve cap, cut along the slash lines from the biceps line to, but not through, the cap.
- On the lower sleeve piece, cut along the slash lines from the biceps line to, but not through, the hem.
- Spread the slash lines open 1″ then reshape the cap and hem.

Cap Sleeve

This sleeve extends from the shoulder line, with a silhouette reminiscent of the bill of a cap. The bulk of the sleeve is at the shoulder, often not requiring that the sleeve extend around the entire armhole. Cap sleeves can be constructed in either a set-in or a kimono style. They can feature a seam line at the armhole or be extended from the bodice shoulder to a point a few inches down the arm.

With armhole   Without armhole

Illustration 9.11

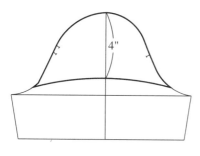

Drawing 9.27

Drawing 9.27. With armhole seam.

- Trace the sleeve sloper.
- Measure down 4″ from the top of the cap on the center line.
- Draw a curved hemline, as shown.

Drawing 9.28. Without armhole seam I.

- Measure up $3/8''$ from the shoulder tip and out $2^1/_2''$ and mark.
- Draw a new shoulder line from the neck point to the mark, as shown.
- Draw a line from the underarm point, ending square at the mark.
- Reshape the armhole.

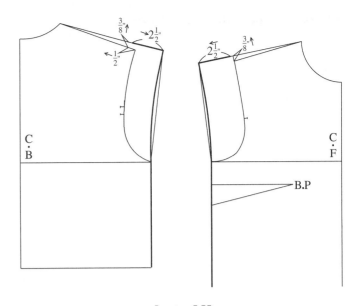

Drawing 9.28

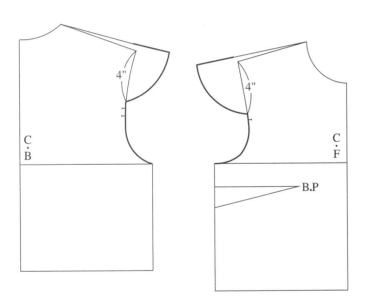

Drawing 9.29

Drawing 9.29. Without armhole seam II

- Measure up $3/8''$ from the shoulder tip and out $2^1/_2''$ and mark.
- Draw a new shoulder line from the neck point to the mark, as shown.
- Measure down $4''$ from the shoulder tip on the armhole, then draw the sleeve hem, as shown.

One-and-One-half-Piece Sleeve

This sleeve is fitted at the elbow. Its elbow dart can be either transferred to the sleeve hem and stitched as a dart or used as an opening slit.

Illustration 9.12

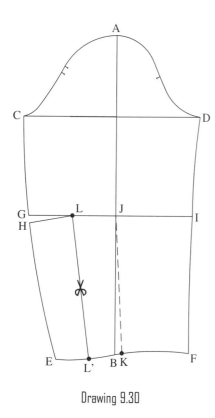

Drawing 9.30

Drawing 9.30.

- Trace the tight sleeve sloper.
- Label all points on the sloper, as shown.
- Find the midpoint of line EF (wrist) and label K.
- Connect points J and K with a dashed line.
- Find the midpoint of EK and label L′, then connect to point L.

Drawing 9.31

- Slash the line LL′ from point L′ to, but not through, point L.
- Close the elbow dart and the slash line LL′ will be open.
- Reshape the line CE with a slightly curved line.

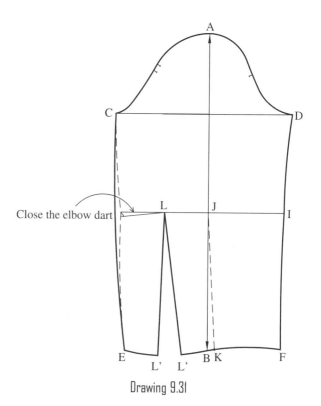

Close the elbow dart

Drawing 9.31

Two-Piece Sleeve

This sleeve is cut in two pieces: one for the underarm and one for the over arm. It is shaped with a bend at the elbow, which allows the sleeve to follow the natural curve of the arm. It is generally used in men's and women's tailored suit jackets.

Illustration 9.13

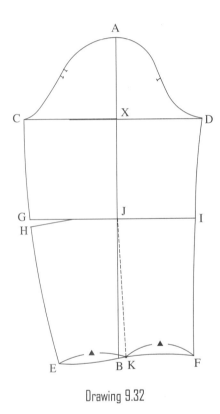

Drawing 9.32

Drawing 9.32. Two-piece sleeve I.

- Trace the tight sleeve sloper.
- Label all points on the sloper as shown.
- Label K at the midpoint of line EF.
- Connect point J to K with a dashed line.

Drawing 9.33.

- Fold the upper back underarm seam of the sleeve, matching line CG to XJ.
- Fold the lower back underarm seam of the sleeve, matching line HE to JK.
- Fold the excess paper at point J in the form of an elbow dart.
- Mark points L, M, and N.
- Slash from point I to the midpoint of IJ.

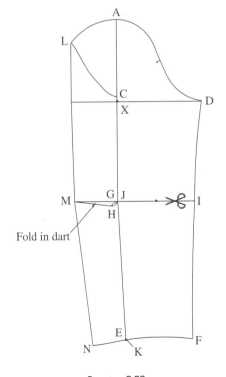

Fold in dart

Drawing 9.33

- Fold the upper front underarm seam of the sleeve, matching line DI to XJ.
- Fold the lower back underarm seam of the sleeve, matching line IF to JK.
- Mark points O, P, and Q, as shown.
- * **Note:** The wrist measurement of the sleeve may be increased by extending the wrist measurement from point N as much as desired, as per points N and N′.

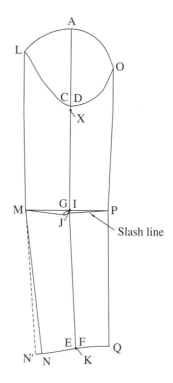

Drawing 9.34

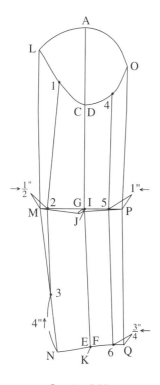

Drawing 9.35

Drawing 9.35.

Back underarm seam:
- Mark the center point of line LC and label 1.
- Measure in $1/2''$ from point M and label 2.
- Connect point 1 and 2.
- Measure up 4″ from point N and label 3. Connect point 2 to 3.

Front underarm seam:
- Mark the center point of line OD and label 4.
- Measure in 1″ from point P and label 5.
- Connect point 4 to 5.
- Measure in $3/4''$ from point Q and label 6.
- Connect point 5 to 6.

Drawing 9.36. **Marking notches.**

- Measure up 3″ from point 5 and mark notch 7.
- Measure down 2″ from point 5 and mark notch 8.
- Measure the distance from point 4 to 7, then measure that distance down from 1 and mark notch 9.
- Measure the distance from point 6 to 8, then measure that distance up from N and mark notch 10.

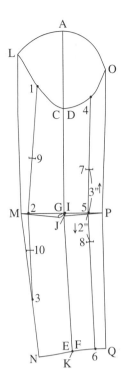

Drawing 9.36

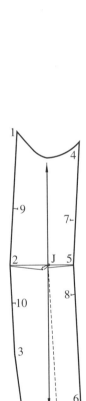

Drawing 9.37

Drawing 9.37. **Undersleeve section.**

- Cut out and remove the section on line (1-2-3-N-K-6-5-4-C-1).
- Trace this piece on another piece of paper.
- Trace notches 7, 8, 9, and 10.
- Reshape the lines, blending at each point.
- Mark the grain line from point C to B with a straight line.

Drawing 9.38. Over arm section.

- Open the folded side sections (1-2-3) and (4-5-6) remaining on each side of where the underarm was removed.

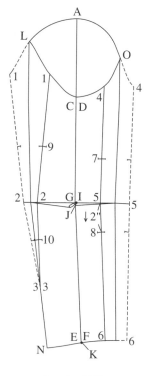

Drawing 9.38

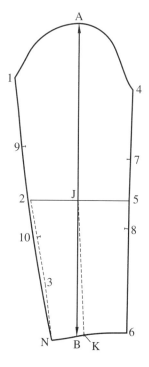

Drawing 9.39

Drawing 9.39.

- Relabel 1, 2, and 3 on the side that is now facing up.
- Relabel 4, 5, and 6 on the side now facing up.
- Re-mark notches 7, 8, 9, and 10 on the side now facing up.
- Mark the grain line from point A to B with a straight line.
- Reshape the lines, blending at each point.

Drawing 9.40. Finished patterns.

• Mark the notches and grain lines, as shown.

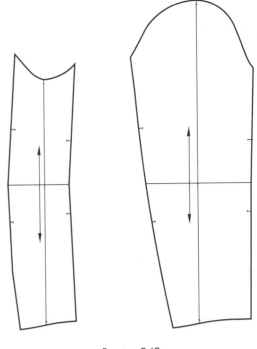

Drawing 9.40

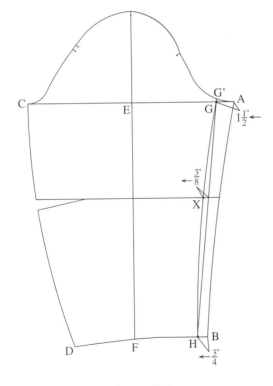

Drawing 9.41

Drawing 9.41. Two-piece sleeve II.

• Trace the tight sleeve sloper and label, as shown.
• Measure in $1^1/_2$" from point A and label G.
• Measure in $^3/_4$" from point B and label H.
• Connect G to H with a straight line.
• Extend HG to the sleeve cap, labeling G′ where it intersects the sleeve cap.
• Measure in $^3/_8$" from GH on the elbow line and label X, then draw a curved line from G to H, passing through X.

Drawing 9.42.

- Measure $1\frac{1}{2}''$ to the right from point E on the biceps line and label I.
- Measure $\frac{3}{4}''$ to the right from point F on the hemline and label J.
- Connect I to J with a straight line.
- Measure in $\frac{3}{8}''$ from IJ on the elbow line and label Y, then draw a curved line from I to J, passing through Y.

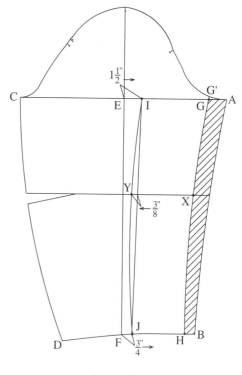

Drawing 9.42

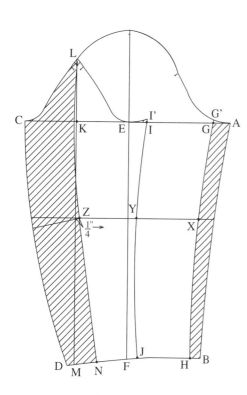

Drawing 9.43

Drawing 9.43.

- Label K at the midpoint of line CE.
- Draw a guideline running parallel to EF, passing through K.
- Extend this line to the sleeve cap, labeling L where it intersects the sleeve cap.
- Measure in $\frac{1}{4}''$ from LM on the elbow line and label Z.
- Label N at the midpoint of line DF.
- Connect L to N with a slightly curved line, passing through Z.

Drawing 9.44.

- Fold at line LK, matching point C to E.
- Trace line LC to create line LE, as shown.
- Fold over, matching point A to E.
- Trace line AG′ to create line EI′, as shown.

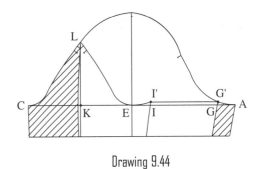

Drawing 9.44

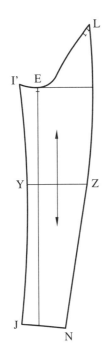

Drawing 9.45

Drawing 9.45. Under sleeve.

- Trace the over and under sleeves separately.
- Under sleeve: Trace L-Z-N-J-Y-I′-E-L, as shown.
- Flip the under sleeve over, as shown.

Drawing 9.46. Over sleeve.

- Over sleeve: Trace L-Z-N-H-X-G′-L, as shown.

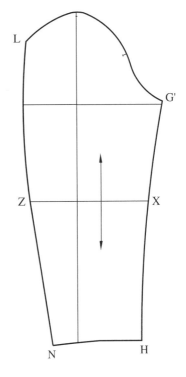

Drawing 9.46

KIMONO SLEEVE

*K*imono sleeves are connected to the bodice to form a distinctive square-shaped silhouette, with variations ranging from loose to tight in fit. Derived from the Japanese kimono, this sleeve style is also commonly referred to as the Kabuki or mandarin sleeve.

Kimono Sleeve Styles

Illustration 9.14

Batwing   Dolman   French

Batwing Sleeve
This style is a variation of the dolman sleeve and is very full. The armhole extends to the waist, and it has a very tight wrist. With arms extended away from the body, it has the appearance of a bat's wing.

Dolman Sleeve
This style is the largest variation of the kimono sleeve. The armhole is extremely deep and the wrist very fitted. Viewed from the back, it has the appearance of a cape.

French Sleeve
This style is a short variation of the kimono sleeve. It may be made like the traditional kimono sleeve or have an armhole seam line.

Drawing 9.47. Kimono sleeve pattern variations.

Kimono sleeve patterns can be developed from a sleeve sloper or by extending the sleeve from the bodice. The greater the angle from the bodice at which the sleeve is developed, the more excess fabric and greater the range of arm motion in the resulting sleeve.

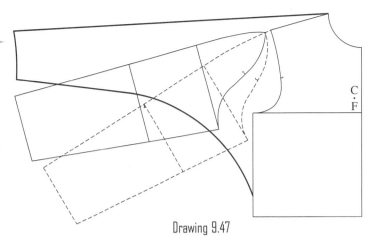

Drawing 9.47

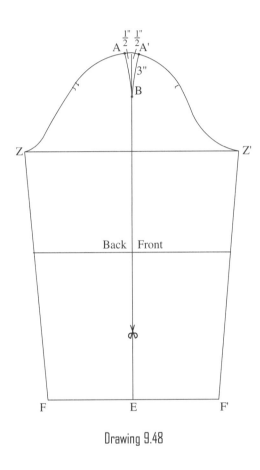

Drawing 9.48

Drawing 9.48. Kimono sleeve foundation.

- Trace the straight sleeve sloper.
- Measure out $1/2''$ on each side of the center line and label A and A′.
- Measure down 3″ from the sleeve cap on the center line and label B.
- Draw the dart legs by connecting points A and A′ to B.
- Label points Z and Z′ at the biceps line.
- Label points E, F, and F′ at the wrist line.

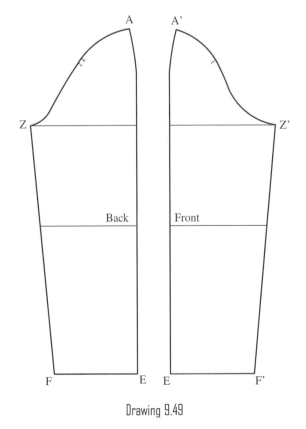

Drawing 9.49

Drawing 9.49.

- Cut along the center line, eliminating the dart intake.
- Label the sleeve pieces back and front.

Drawing 9.50. **Back.**

- Trace the back bodice sloper.
- Extend the shoulder line $\frac{3}{4}''$ to $1\frac{1}{4}''$ from the shoulder tip and mark.
- Place the back kimono sleeve foundation on the back bodice, matching A to the mark.

- Leave a $1\frac{1}{4}''$ space between the underarm point and Z, as shown.
- * **Note:** Increasing the distance between the underarm point and B results in both a greater range of motion for the arm as well as increased excess fabric in the underarm.
- Reshape the shoulder line and underarm side seam.

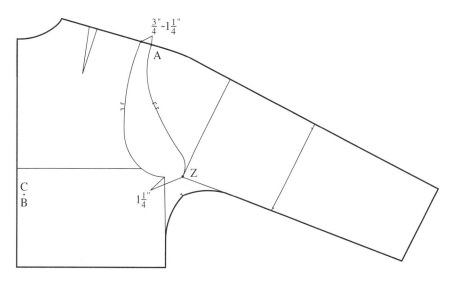

Drawing 9.50

Drawing 9.51. **Front.**

- Develop the front sleeve the same as the back.

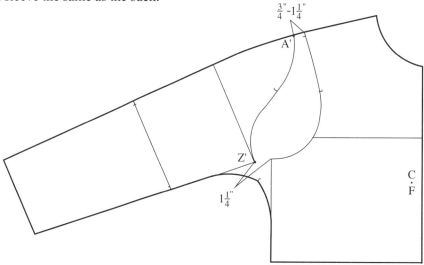

Drawing 9.51

Drawing 9.52. Batwing sleeve.

Back and front:
- Trace the bodice sloper.
- Place the back kimono sleeve foundation on the back bodice, matching A to the shoulder tip.

- Leave a 4″ space between the underarm point and Z, as shown.
- Reshape the over arm seam from the neck point to the hem in a straight line.
- Reshape the underarm seam from the waistline to the elbow line in a curved line.

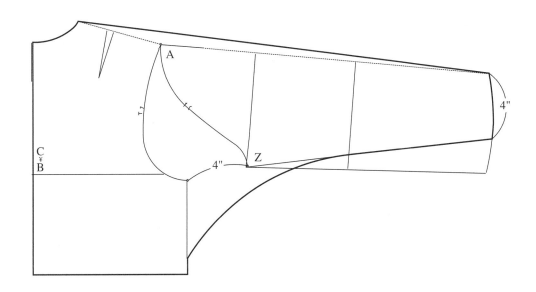

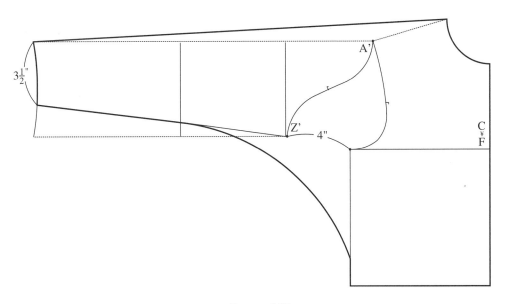

Drawing 9.52

Drawing 9.53. Dolman sleeve.

Back and front:

- Trace the bodice sloper.
- Measure in ³/₄″ from the shoulder tip and mark.

- Place the back kimono sleeve foundation on the back bodice, matching A to the mark.
- Leave a 2″ space between the underarm point and Z, as shown.
- Reshape the shoulder line and underarm side seam.

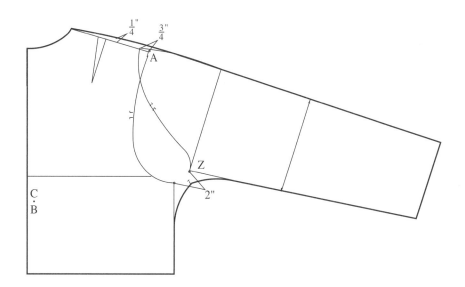

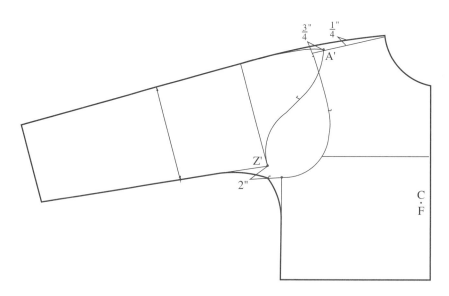

Drawing 9.53

Drawing 9.54. French sleeve.

Back and front:

- Trace the bodice sloper.
- Extend the shoulder line 5″, then square down $^3/_4″$ and label A.
- Measure down 2″ at the underarm point on the side seam, then square out $1^1/_2″$ and label B.
- Connect point A to B, ending square at each point.
- Reshape the shoulder line and underarm side seam.

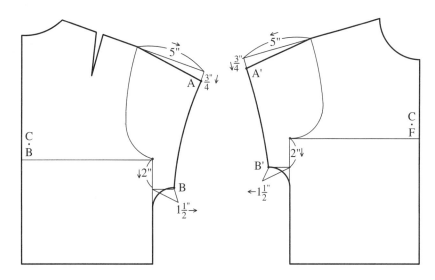

Drawing 9.54

RAGLAN SLEEVE

Ragan sleeves fall somewhere between the set-in and kimono styles. They extend past the armhole to the neckline, similar to a kimono sleeve, and are connected to the bodice with a seam, similar to a set-in sleeve. The raglan seam begins at the neckline and extends diagonally to the underarm, resulting in enhanced range of motion and comfort. Raglan sleeves may be constructed from one or two pieces, and can be varied by changing the shape of the armhole line, or by adding shirring or pleats at the armhole.

Raglan Sleeve Variations

Illustration 9.15

Drawing 9.55. Raglan style lines.

• The raglan style line may be straight, curved, or a squared curve, depending on the design. It can start from any point along the neckline, but generally begins within the first third of the neckline. The curve of the front bodice style line is deeper than that of the back.

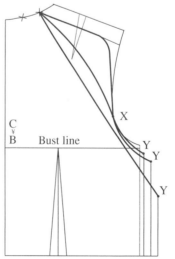
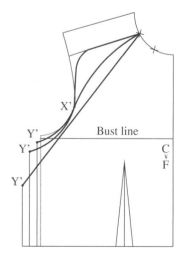

Drawing 9.55

Raglan sleeve pattern Variations.

Raglan sleeve patterns can be developed using a
sleeve sloper or by extending the sleeve from the
bodice.

1. Raglan Sleeve without Sleeve Sloper

Drawing 9.56. Raglan sleeve with dart.

Back:
*   Trace the back bodice sloper.
*   Lower the armhole and extend the bodice at the
    side seam, as desired.
*   Label Y at the underarm point on the side seam of
    the bodice.
*   Square up no more than $2^3/_4''$ from the bust line to
    the armhole and label X.
*   Divide the neckline into thirds.
*   Label 1 at the first one-third of the neckline.
*   Draw the raglan style line from point 1 to point X.
*   The style line extends from point X to point Y,
    blending with the underarm curve of the bodice.
*   Label 2 at the neck on the shoulder line.

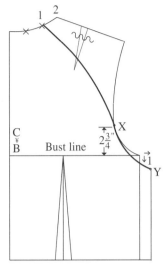

Drawing 9.56

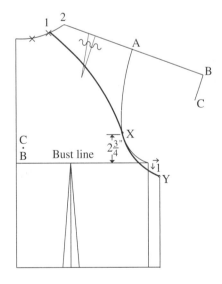

Drawing 9.57

Drawing 9.57.

*   Extend the shoulder line $5^3/_8''$ from point A and
    label B.
*   Square down 2″ from point B and label C.
*   **Note:** Generally, for these styles, the length of line
    BC is as follows:
    Blouse/Dress: $1^5/_8''$.
    Jacket = 2″.
    Coat = $2^1/_2''$.

Drawing 9.58. Raglan sleeve angle variations.

- When the measurement of line BC is shorter, the sleeve will fit more comfortably and allow for more mobility of the arm. This is because the bodice and sleeve are overlapped less at the side seam.
- When the measurement of line BC is longer, the sleeve will fit more tightly and allow for less mobility of the arm. This is because the bodice and sleeve are overlapped more at the side seam.

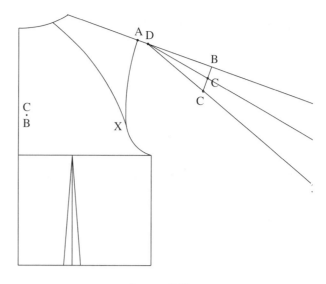

Drawing 9.58

Drawing 9.59.

- Measure out $^3/_8$″ to 2″ from point A, to allow for ease, and label D.
- * **Note:** Ease is added to the sleeve cap to allow for a smoother fit around the shoulder. Generally, the amount of ease added is as follows for these styles:
    Blouse/Dress = $^3/_8$″.
    Jacket = $^3/_4$″ to 1″.
    Coat = $1^3/_8$″ to 2″.
- Draw a line from point D, equal to the sleeve length measurement, passing through point C.
- Label E at the end of the sleeve.
- Square down $5^3/_4$″ from point E and label F.
- Line EF = Width of the sleeve.
- The width of the sleeve may be adjusted according to the design desired.
- Measure down the cap height, $5^3/_8$″ from point A, and mark.
- * **Note:** Generally, the cap height is as follows for these styles:
    Blouse/Dress = 5″ to $5^1/_2$″.
    Jacket = $5^1/_2$″ to 6″.
    Coat = 6″ to $6^3/_8$″.
- Square down from this mark, half of the biceps measurement plus 1″ or more for ease.
- Label Z at the end point of the biceps line.

- Draw the new underarm curve of the raglan sleeve, blending down from point X to point Z at the biceps line of the sleeve.
- * **Note:** Line XZ should be equal in length to line XY.
- If line XZ is too long or short, adjust the biceps line by extending or shortening it to match the length of line XY.
- Draw the underarm seam from point Z to F.

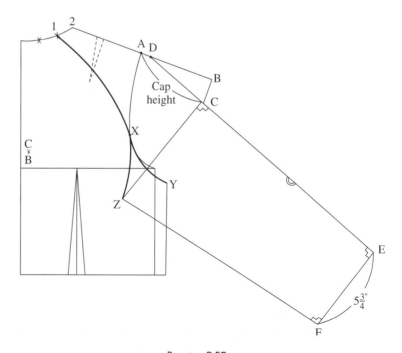

Drawing 9.59

Drawing 9.60.

Front

- The development of the front sleeve is the same as the back, except that the following measurements are changed:
- A'B' = 5³/₈"

- A'D' = ³/₈" to 2" (same as AD from Drawing 9.59)
- B'C = ³/₈" longer than BC on the back:
    Ex: Blouse/Dress = 2".
        Jacket = 2³/₈".
        Coat = 2¹/₂" to 3".
- E'F' = 5³/₈" (front sleeve is ³/₈" smaller than the back).

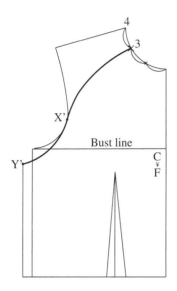

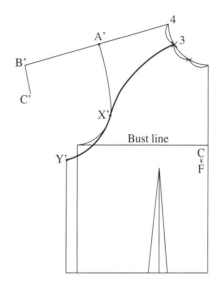

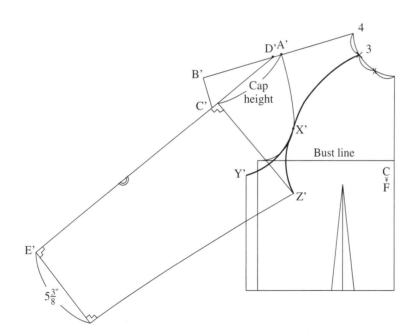

Drawing 9.60

Drawing 9.61. Back.

- Trace the back bodice and the sleeve separately.
- Bodice: 1-X-Y- side seam.
- Sleeve: 1-X-Z-F-E-D-2-1.
- Blend the shoulder line with a slightly curved line.

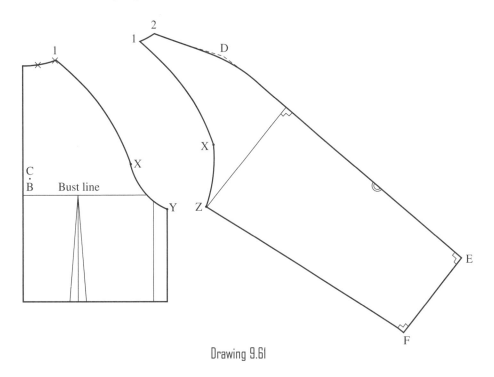

Drawing 9.61

Drawing 9.62. Front.

- Trace the front bodice and the sleeve separately.
- Bodice: 3-X′-Y′-side seam.
- Sleeve: 3-X′-Z′-F′-E′-D′-4
- Blend the shoulder line with a slightly curved line.

Drawing 9.62

Drawing 9.63. **One-piece sleeve.**

- Attach the front and back sleeve patterns, matching points E and E′.

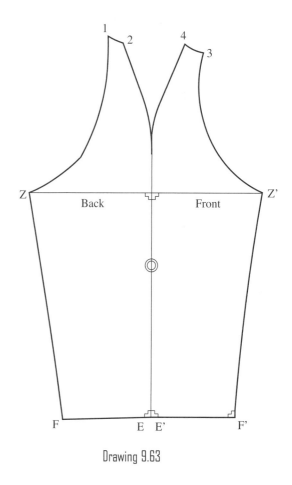

Drawing 9.63

Raglan Sleeve without Dart.

Raglan sleeves constructed without a shoulder dart have a less rounded shoulder line. Such sleeves are developed without a sleeve sloper and extend from the shoulder line of the bodice sloper. To develop a raglan sleeve without a dart, use the previous instructions for constructing this sleeve with a dart with the following adjustments.

Drawing 9.64. **Back.**

- Draw a line from point A, equal to the sleeve length measurement.
- Label E at the end of the sleeve.
- Square down $5^3/_4''$ from point E and label F.
- EF = $5^3/_4''$, Sleeve width.
- AB = $3^1/_2''$, Cap height.

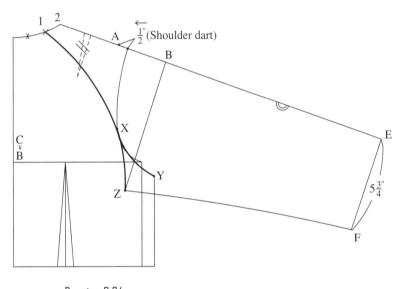

Drawing 9.64

Drawing 9.65. **Front**

- E'F' = $5^3/_8''$, Sleeve width.
- AB = $3^1/_2''$, Cap height.

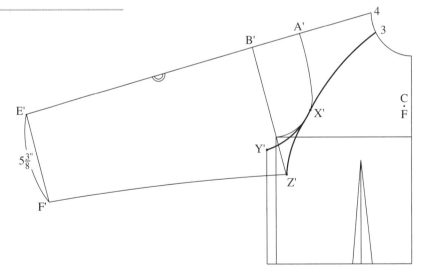

Drawing 9.65

Drawing 9.66. **Front and back.**

- Trace the bodice and sleeve separately.
- Blend the shoulder line with a slightly curved line.

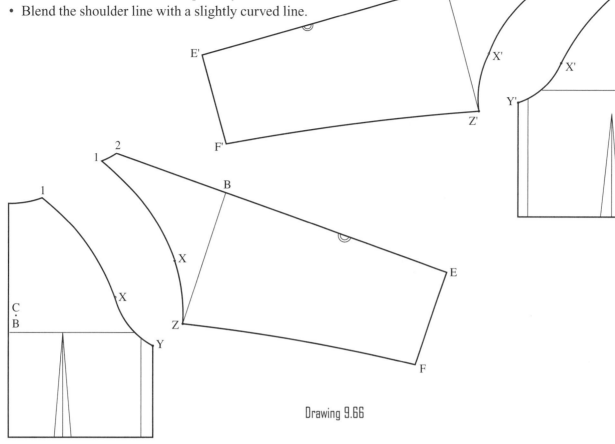

Drawing 9.66

Drawing 9.67. **One-piece sleeve.**

- Attach the front and back sleeve patterns, matching points 2 to 4, and E to E′.

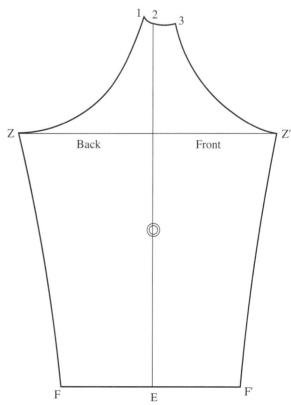

Drawing 9.67

2. Raglan Sleeve with Sleeve Sloper

Drawing 9.68. Back.

- Trace the back bodice sloper.
- Square up $2^3/_4''$ from the bust line, then square over to intersect the armhole and label X.
- Label Y at the underarm point of the bodice at the side seam.
- Divide the neckline into thirds and label 1 at the first one third.
- Draw the desired style line from point 1 to point X.
- * **Note:** The style line generally starts from the mid-point of the neckline; however, it can start from any point on the neckline.
- The style line extends to point Y, blending with the under armhole curve of the bodice.
- Label 2 at the intersection of the shoulder and neck.

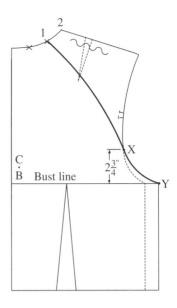

Drawing 9.68

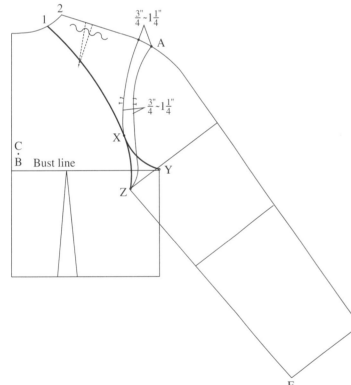

Drawing 9.69

Drawing 9.69.

- Extend the shoulder $^3/_4''$ to $1^1/_4''$ and mark.
- Place the back kimono sleeve foundation (Drawing 9.48) on the back bodice, matching point A to the mark.
- * **Note:** The distance from sleeve cap to mid-armhole ranges from $^3/_4''$ to $1^1/_4''$. The longer this distance, the more comfortable and functional the sleeve.
- Label Z at the underarm point of the sleeve.
- Draw the underarm curve, blending down from X to Z at the biceps line of the sleeve.
- XZ = XY.
- * **Note:** If line XZ is too long or short, adjust the biceps line by extending or shortening it to match with line XY.
- Reshape the underarm seam from Z to F.

Drawing 9.70. **Front.**

- Trace the front bodice sloper.
- Square up no more than $2^3/_4''$ from the bust line to intersect with the armhole and label X′.
- Label Y′ at the underarm point of the bodice at the side seam.
- Divide the neckline into thirds and label 3 at the first one third.
- Draw the desired style line from point 3 to point X′.
- *** Note:** The style line generally starts from the first one third of the neckline; however, it can start from any point on the neckline.
- The style line extends to point Y′, blending with the under armhole curve of the bodice.

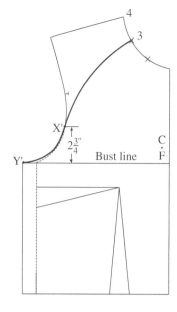

Drawing 9.70

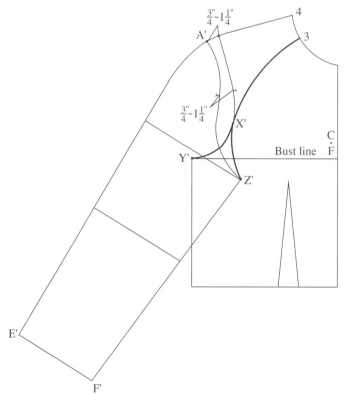

Drawing 9.71

Drawing 9.71.

- Extend the shoulder line $^3/_4''$ to $1^1/_4''$ and mark.
- Place the front kimono sleeve foundation (Drawing 9.48) on the front bodice, matching point A′ to the mark.
- *** Note:** The distance from sleeve cap to mid-armhole ranges from $^3/_4''$ to $1^1/_4''$. The longer this distance, the more comfortable and functional the sleeve.
- Label Z′ at the underarm point of the sleeve.
- Draw the underarm curve, blending down from point X′ to point Z′ at the biceps line of the sleeve.
- X′Z′ = X′Y′.
- *** Note:** If line X′Z′ is too long or short, adjust the biceps line by extending or shortening it to match with line X′Y′.
- Reshape the underarm seam from point Z′ to F′.

Drawing 9.72. **Back.**

- Trace the back bodice and sleeve separately.
- Bodice: 1-X-Y-side seam.
- Sleeve: 1-X-Z-F-E-2.
- Blend the shoulder line with a slightly curved line.

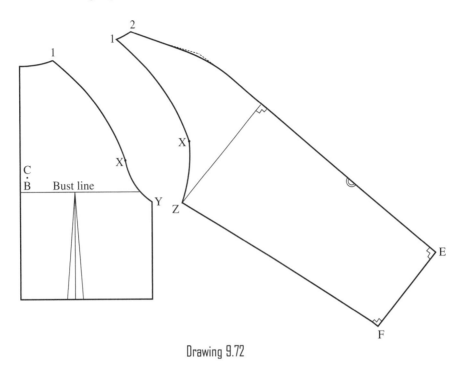

Drawing 9.72

Drawing 9.73. **Front.**

- Trace the front bodice and sleeve separately.
- Bodice: 3-X'-Y' side seam.
- Sleeve: 3-X'-Z'-F'-E'-4.
- Blend the shoulder line with a slightly curved line.

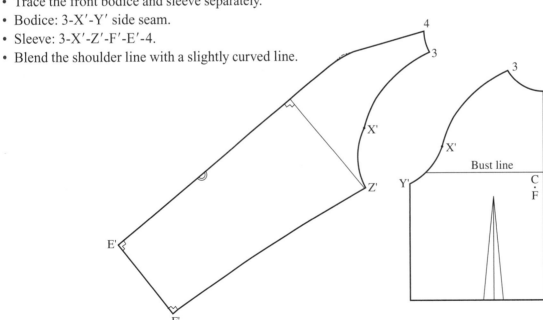

Drawing 9.73

Drawing 9.74. One-piece sleeve.

- Attach the front and back sleeve patterns, matching E on each pattern.

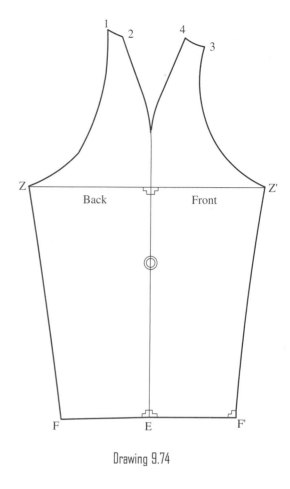

Drawing 9.74

Illustration 9.16

Raglan Sleeve Examples

This style has the top of the shirt yoke attached to the sleeve to create a one-piece sleeve.

Drawing 9.75.

- Begin development of the raglan sleeve foundation using the instructions from Drawings 9.64 and 9.65.
- Draw the raglan style line, as shown.

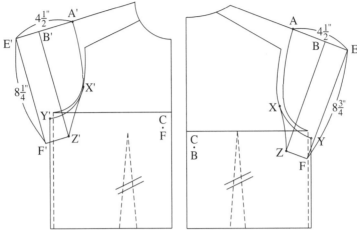

Drawing 9.75

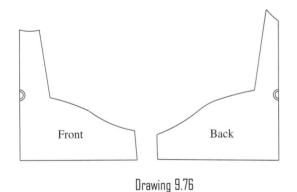

Drawing 9.76

Drawing 9.76.

- Separate the sleeve from the bodice.

Drawing 9.77.

- Align the back and front sleeves at the center line.
- Draw the slash lines, as shown.

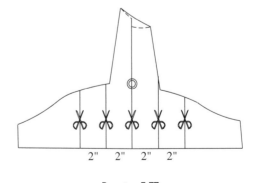

Drawing 9.77

Drawing 9.78. **Finished pattern.**

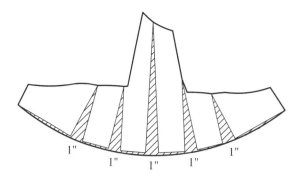

Drawing 9.78

- Spread the slash lines 1″ apart.
- Measure down 1″ from the hem at the center line.
- Reshape the hem.

2. Folklore Sleeve

These loose-fitting sleeves are historically associated with ethnic costumes, such as Gypsy attire. They are essentially raglan sleeves with shirring added at the neckline and hem for generous fullness.

Illustration 9.17

Drawing 9.79.

- Begin development of the raglan sleeve foundation using the instructions from Drawing 9.56.
- Draw the raglan style line, as shown.

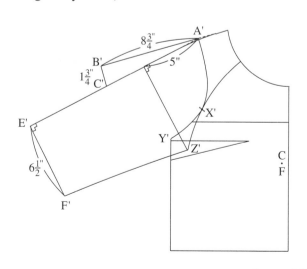

Drawing 9.79

Drawing 9.80.

• Separate the sleeve from the bodice.

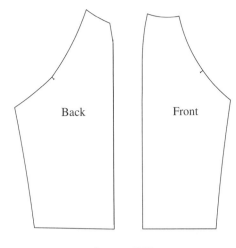

Drawing 9.80

Drawing 9.81

Drawing 9.81. Finished pattern.

• Align the back and front sleeves, separated 2″ at the center line, as shown.
• Retrace, reshaping the top and bottom as shown.

Chapter Ten

THE BLOUSE

INTRODUCTION TO THE BLOUSE

*B*louses (shirts) cover the upper torso. They feature an infinite variety of style lines, depending on their design details and the occasions for which they are designed. Depending on their fabric and decoration, blouses can be worn casually, for work, or for formal occasions. Design features, such as sleeves, collars, cuffs, and plackets, can be used to alter or enhance the overall appearance of a blouse.

Drawing 10.1. Blouse components.

A. Collar.
B. Front bodice.
C. Sleeve.
D. Armhole seam.
E. Buttonhole.
F. Button.
G. Facing.
H. Dart.
I. Shoulder seam.
J. Side seam.
K. Hem.
L. Cuffs.
M. Placket.
N. Pleat.
O. Back bodice.

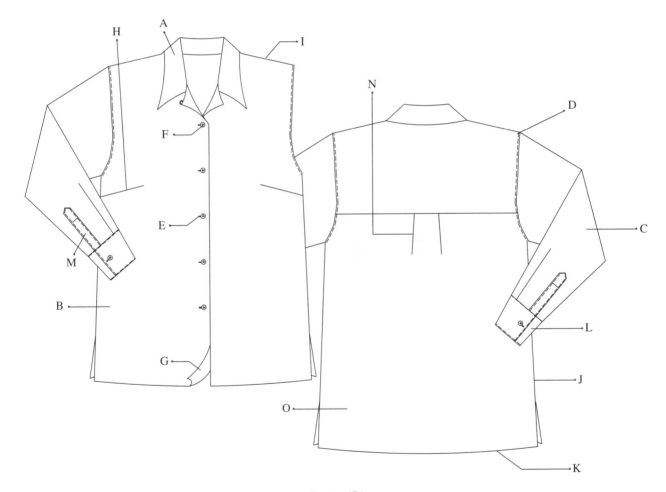

Drawing 10.1

Blouse Style Variations

Blouses may be worn either outside of or tucked into a skirt or pants. Because the length of a tucked-in blouse should be sufficient that arm movement will not pull it from the waistband, the length should extend to between the waistline and the hip line on the bodice sloper.

1. Over Blouse

Shell   Middy   Peplum   Tunic

Illustration 10.1

Shell
This is a pull-on, sleeveless style of blouse that can be made of a knit or woven fabric for different effect and designs.

Middy Blouse
This is a pull-on style of blouse, fashioned after the tops traditionally worn by naval midshipmen. It has been adopted as a women's fashion article, influencing school uniforms, tennis wear, and sports clothing.

Peplum Blouse
This blouse has a skirtlike panel extension (peplum) at the waistline, which can be straight or flared.

Tunic Blouse
Thigh length and slightly fitted or boxy, this blouse may be worn over a skirt or pants, with or without a belt.

Gypsy   Tuxedo   Stock-tie

Illustration 10.2

Gypsy Blouse
This blouse features a drawstring neckline and often
includes puffed style sleeves.

Tuxedo Blouse
Similar to the man's evening shirt, this style has
design variations created by tucks, ruffles, or
shirring.

Stock-Tie Blouse
This is a plain blouse, featuring an ascot-style tie
connected at the neckline.

Blouse Silhouette Variations

Blouse silhouettes can be categorized into three basic groups: straight, A-line, and fitted.

Straight

The waist dart is not sewn and the side dart can be either sewn or eliminated. The side dart can also be repositioned to the shoulder, neck, or various other locations, resulting in a straight side seam.

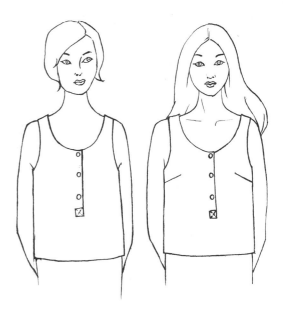

Illustration 10.3

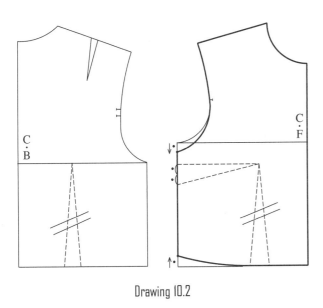

Drawing 10.2

Drawing 10.2. **Without the side dart**

- Eliminate the side dart by deepening the armhole half of the dart width.
- Eliminate the remaining half of the dart by shortening the hem at the side seam.

Drawing 10.3. **With the side dart**

- Sew the side dart but not the waist dart.

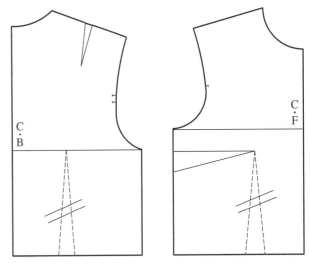

Drawing 10.3

A-Line

The waist darts are not sewn. The side dart may be
either sewn or transferred to the hem. The slash and
spread method can be used for additional fullness at
the hem.

Illustration 10.4

Drawing 10.4. With the side dart

- Sew the side dart but not the waist dart.
- Add fullness at the side seam on the hem.

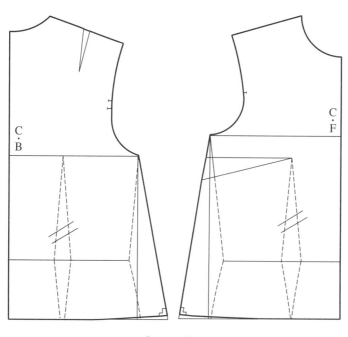

Drawing 10.4

Drawing 10.5. Without the side dart

- Do not sew the waist darts.
- Redraw the side seams to be perpendicular to the hipline.
- Close the front side dart and back shoulder dart, then transfer both to the hem.

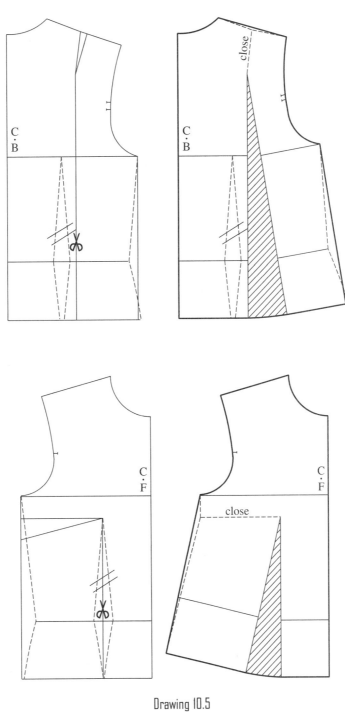

Drawing 10.5

Fitted

The side and waist darts are both sewn and manipulated to achieve varying degrees and types of fit.

Illustration 10.5

Drawing 10.6. Side and waist darts

• Sew the side and waist darts.

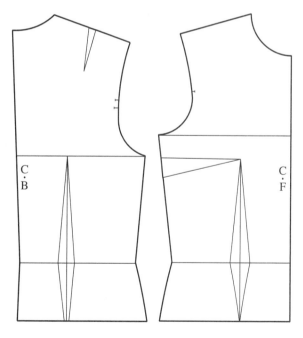

Drawing 10.6

Drawing 10.7. Princess line

- Reposition the waist dart to create a princess line.
- Close the front side dart and remove the back shoulder dart from the shoulder tip.

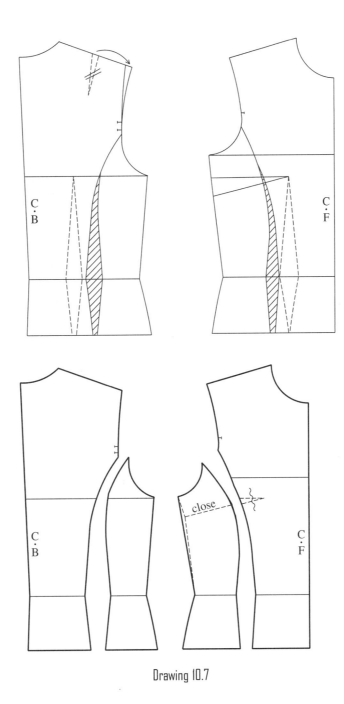

Drawing 10.7

Drawing 10.8. Multiple waist darts

- Split the back and front waist darts into two darts apiece.
- Transfer the side dart to the waist dart.

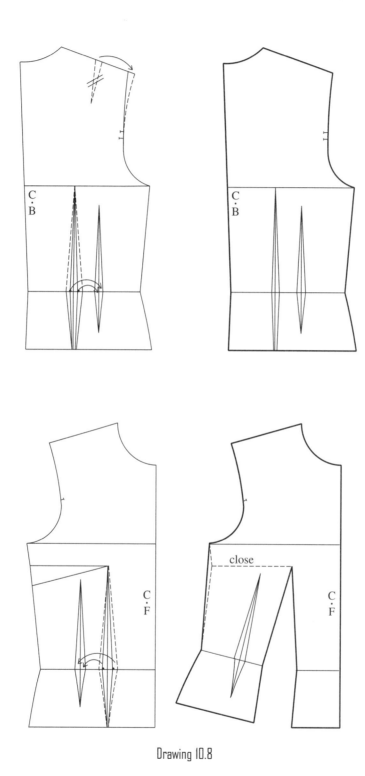

Drawing 10.8

BLOUSE FOUNDATION

The blouse foundation is initially developed from a tight bodice sloper, after which it can be manipulated to create a variety of designs, enhanced by the addition of details (e.g., collars, sleeves), and given color and texture through the use of different fabrics.

Drawing 10.9. Back and front.

- Trace the back fitted bodice sloper.
- Extend the bodice length 8″ down from the waistline at center back.
- Square out the measurement of ($H/4 + 3/8″$) one fourth of the hip measurement plus $3/8″$.
- Draw the curve of the hip from the waistline to the hip line.

Back:
- Reshape the center back with a straight line.
- Measure in $5/8″$ from the center back at the waistline.
- Measure in $3/8″$ from the center back at the hip line.
- Reshape the center back line.
- Extend the back dart length $5^1/2″$ to 6″.
- Draw the dart legs to meet at the waistline.

Front:
- Extend the front dart length $4^1/4″$ to $4^3/4″$.
- Draw the dart legs to meet at the waistline.

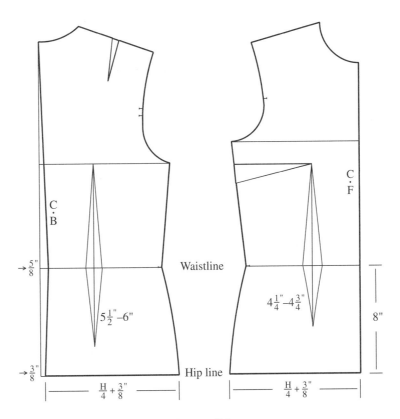

Drawing 10.9

Drawing 10.9a. Straight Sleeve.

- Trace the straight sleeve sloper.

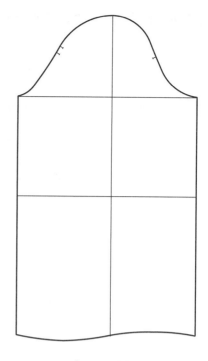

Drawing 10.9a

Drawing 10.9b. Tight sleeve.

- Trace the tight sleeve sloper.

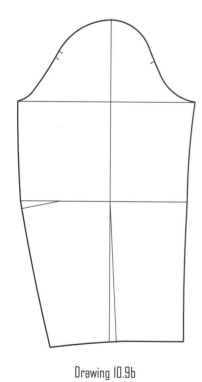

Drawing 10.9b

SHIRT COLLAR BLOUSE

Pattern Analysis

- Waist darts are not sewn and side seams are straight, creating a box silhouette.
- There is a yoke covering the front and back of the shoulders.
- Two knife pleats are added at the back, below the yoke, for comfort.
- Detail patterns developed for the shirt collar blouse are:

    Shirt collar with stand.
    Patch pocket.
    Shirt sleeve with cuffs and classic sleeve placket.
    Classic tailored shirt placket.

Illustration 10.6

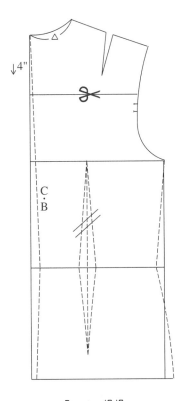

Drawing 10.10

Drawing 10.10.

- Trace the back blouse foundation, but do not trace the waist dart.
- Redraw the center back line to be perpendicular to the hip line.
- Redraw the side seam to be perpendicular to the hip line.
- Measure and record the back neckline.
- Measure down 4″ from the neck at the center back and draw the yoke style line.

Drawing 10.11.

- Cut along the yoke style line.
- Transfer the shoulder dart to the yoke line and reshape the yoke.
- Measure in 3″ from the armhole and draw a slash line perpendicular to the hem.

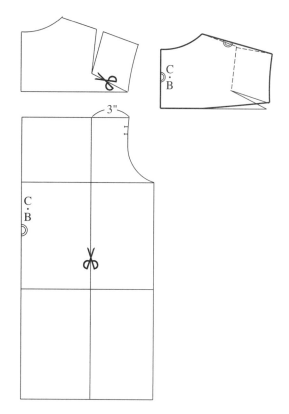

Illustration 10.11

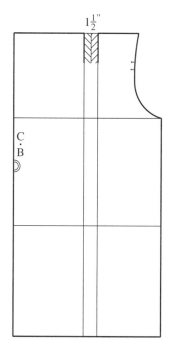

Drawing 10.12

Drawing 10.12.

- Cut along the slash line.
- Space the two piece 1¹/₂″ apart for the pleat.
- Mark the center of the pleat and draw the pleat lines 2″ long.

Drawing 10.13.

- Trace the front blouse sloper, but do not trace the waist dart.
- * **Note:** Leave 3″ of paper at the center front for the facing.
- Redraw the side seam, perpendicular to the hip line.
- Reposition the side dart point 1¼″ from the bust point.
- Lower the neck ³/₁₆″ at the center front then reshape the neckline.
- Measure and record the front neckline.
- Measure down 1¼″ from the shoulder line and draw the yoke line.

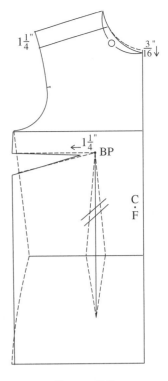

Drawing 10.13

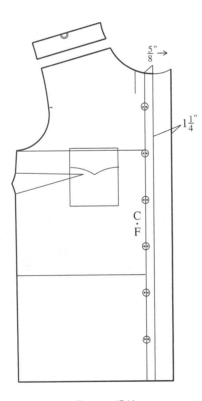

Drawing 10.14

Drawing 10.14.

- Add a ⁵/₈″ extension to the center front.
- Cut along the yoke style line.

Placket:
- Refer to the instructions given in the Bodice Placket section of Chapter 7 to complete the shirt placket as shown, using the following dimensions: Placket width: ³/₄″.

Button placement:
- Mark the first button 3″ down from the neck on the center front.
- Refer to the instructions given in the Button Placement section of Chapter 7 to mark the remaining button and buttonhole placements, as shown.

Drawing 10.15. Pocket.

- Draw the pocket $3^3/_4''$ wide and $4''$ long.
- Draw the pocket flap $3^3/_4''$ wide and $2''$ long, with the stylized line, as shown.
- Mark the pocket placement $2^1/_2''$ in from the center front on the bust line.

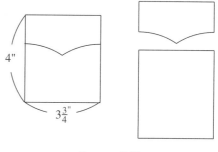

Drawing 10.15

Drawing 10.16. Yoke.

- Attach the back and front yoke along the shoulder line.

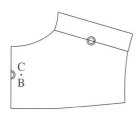

Drawing 10.16

Drawing 10.17. Sleeve.

- Trace the straight sleeve foundation.
- Shorten the sleeve length $2^1/_4''$ to allow for $3''$ cuff height.
- Label X at the midpoint of the hem.
- Measure out $5^1/_2''$ on each side of point X and label these points X' and X''.
- Draw the new underarm seam from the biceps line to points X' and X''.

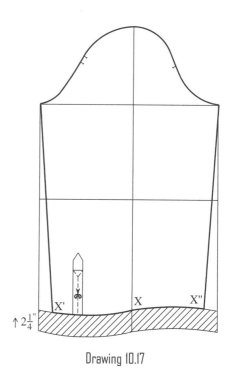

Drawing 10.17

Drawing 10.18. Placket placement.

- Measure in $1^1/_2''$ from point X' and label Y.
- Square up $2^1/_2''$ from point Y and label Y'.
- Measure $1/_2''$ on both sides of Y and square up $3''$ from these points.
- Connect these points to Y', as shown.

Pleats placement:
- Measure in $1^1/_2''$ from point Y and mark the first pleat, making it $1^1/_2''$ wide.
- Measure $1/_2''$ from the first pleat and mark the second pleat, which is also $1^1/_2''$ wide.

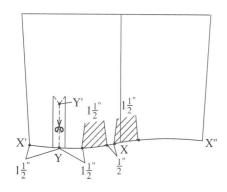

Drawing 10.18

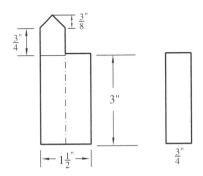

Drawing 10.19

Drawing 10.19. **Upper and under plackets.**

- Draw the upper and under plackets, using the dimensions shown.

Drawing 10.20. **Shirt cuffs.**

- Refer to the shirt cuff instructions at Drawing 7.12 in Chapter 7 (Details), using the following dimensions:

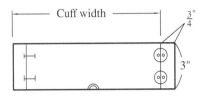

Drawing 10.20

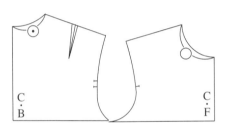

Drawing 10.21

Drawing 10.21. **Shirt collar with separate stand.**

- Measure and record the front and back necklines.
- Refer to the shirt collar with separate stand instructions from Drawing 8.18 in Chapter 8 (Collar), using the following dimensions:
AC = 1″.
BB′ = $^3/_8$″.
DF = 1$^3/_4$″.

Drawing 10.22.

- Trace the collar and stand separately.
- Mark the grain lines as shown.

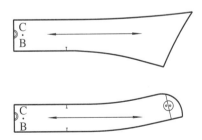

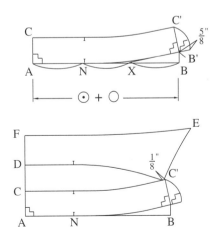

Drawing 10.22

Drawing 10.23. Finished patterns.

• Label the pattern pieces and mark the notches and grain lines, as shown.

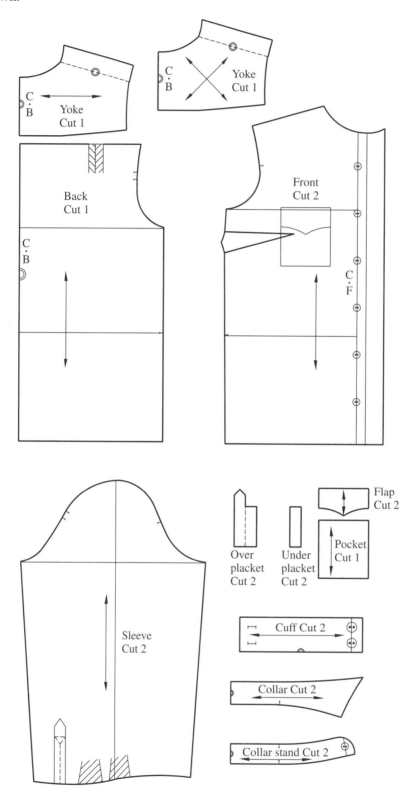

Drawing 10.23

Drawing 10.24. Seam allowances.

Center back, side, and shoulder seams = $^5/_8''$.
Hems = $1^1/_4''$.

- Add seam allowances:
  Pocket, collar, sleeve cap, vent, armholes, necklines, front extension, and facing = $^3/_8''$.

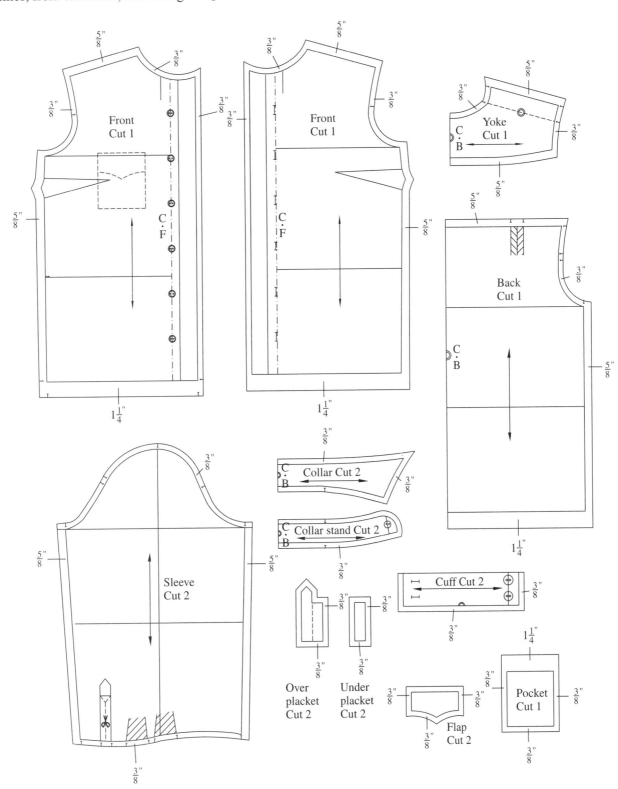

Drawing 10.24

Drawing 10.25. Garment Marker.

- The garment marker is produced by laying all of the pattern pieces out on the fabric. The pattern pieces should be placed so that their grain lines match the straight grain of the fabric. The width of the fabric and sizes of the pattern pieces will dictate how the pieces are laid. Much of this process is handled by computers in industry, but it is still important to be familiar with the relationship between fabric and pattern.

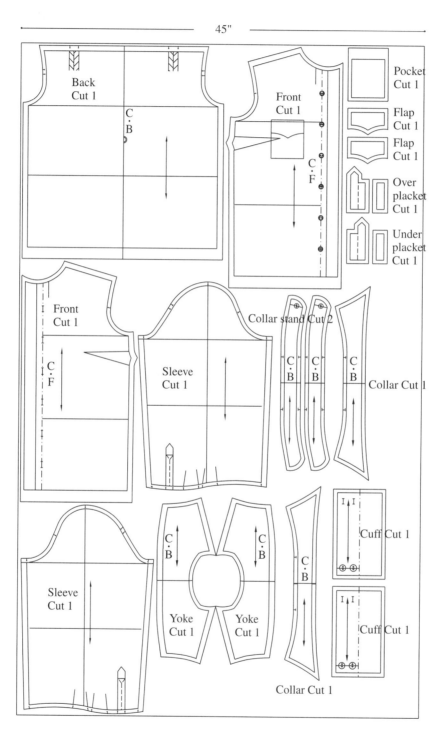

Drawing 10.25

BLOUSE CONSTRUCTION

Drawing 10.26. Preparation.

- Attach the interfacing to the facing and placket of the shirt front, over collar, outer stand, cuffs, pocket flap, and the top of the pocket.

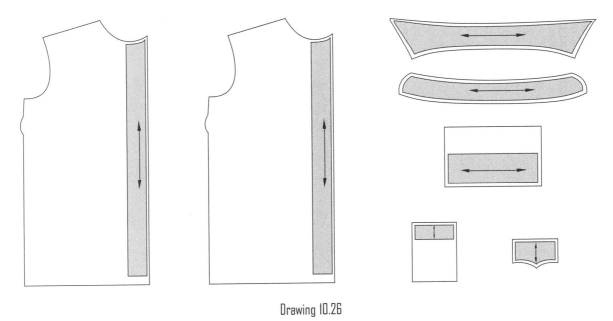

Drawing 10.26

Drawing 10.27. Construction.

- Sew the front darts, then press them up toward the shoulder.
- Fold the facing over as marked, then fold over again and stitch.
- Construct the pocket, then attach it to the left front bodice.

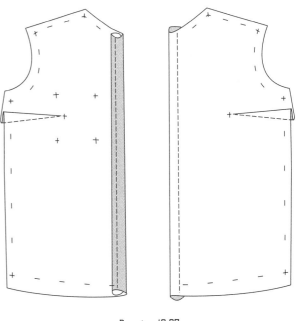

Drawing 10.27

Drawing 10.28. Pocket construction.

- Place the right sides of the pocket flaps together and stitch.
- Trim and clip the seam allowances.

- Turn the right side out and press.
- Topstitch around the edge of the pocket flap.
- Fold the top of the pocket down on the pocket line.
- Fold the hem up $1/2''$ then stitch.
- Fold in the pocket sides and bottom, then press.

Drawing 10.28

Drawing 10.29.

- Pin the pocket in place on the left side of the bodice, following the markings.
- Stitch around the pocket, making certain to tack down the corners at the pocket opening.

- Place the flap $5/8''$ above the pocket, then stitch into place.
- Trim the seam allowances to $1/4''$.
- Fold the flaps down, then topstitch across their upper edge.

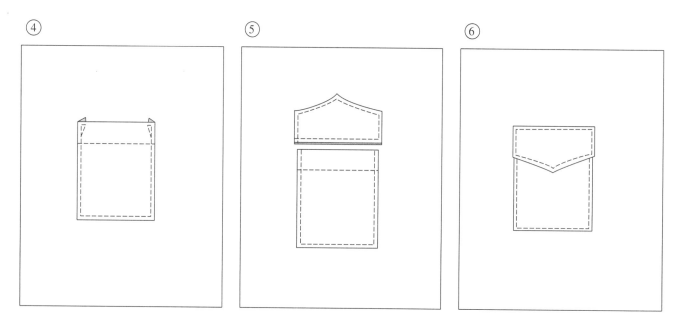

Drawing 10.29

Drawing 10.30. Back bodice.

- Sew the pleats on the back panel, then baste.
- Place the yoke pieces with right sides together.
- Place the back panel between the yoke panels, then stitch.
- Press the yoke upward, then topstitch.

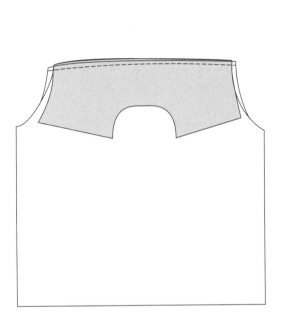

Drawing 10.30

Drawing 10.31. Front and back bodice attachment.

- Place the right sides of the front and back bodices together.
- Stitch the yoke and the front bodice together at the shoulders.
- Press the seam allowances toward the yoke.

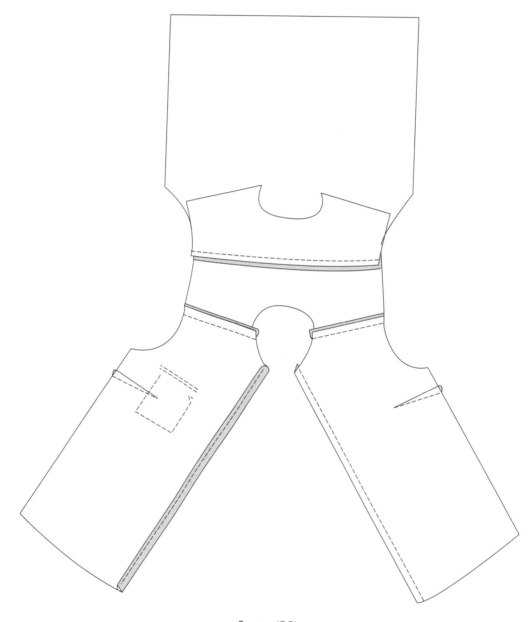

Drawing 10.31

- Fold the inner yoke over the front bodice.
- Topstitch the edges of the yoke, making certain that the seam allowances are pressed toward the inside.

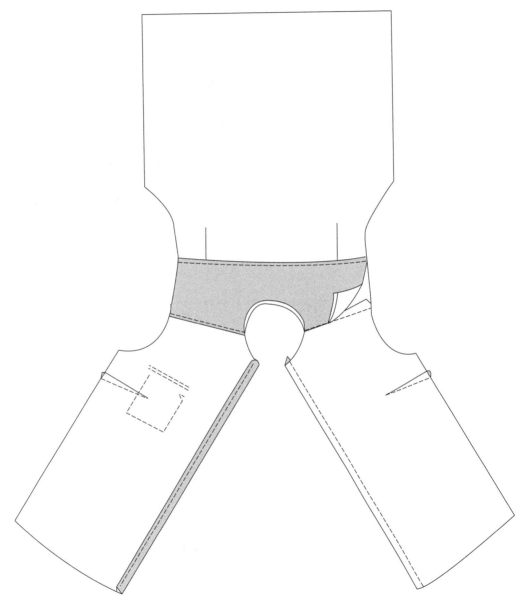

Drawing 10.32

Drawing 10.33. Placket.

- Fold the under placket in half, and the under placket seam allowances inward, then press.
- Clip the shirt sleeve slit opening in a Y-shape.
- Place the under placket around the slit edge closest to the underarm seam, then stitch into place from the right side of the sleeve.

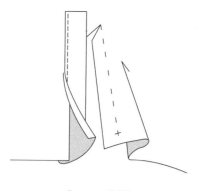

Drawing 10.33

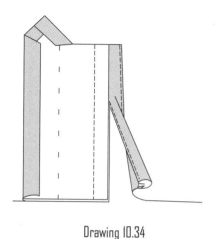

Drawing 10.34

Drawing 10.34.

- Prepare the over placket, folding all of the seam allowances inward.
- Clip the seam allowance at the base of the triangle.
- Place the right side of the over placket against the wrong side of the shirt fabric on the other slit, then stitch.

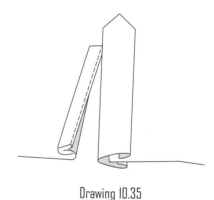

Drawing 10.35

Drawing 10.35.

- Fold the over placket toward the right side of the sleeve.

Drawing 10.36.

- Topstitch the outer edge and over triangle of the placket, using a tack stitch at the bottom edge of the triangle for reinforcement.

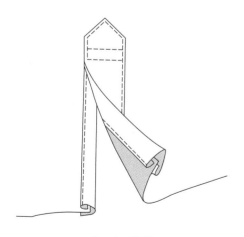

Drawing 10.36

Drawing 10.37. Sleeves to bodice attachment.

- Pin the sleeve cap to the bodice armhole with the right sides together.
- Stitch the armhole.
- Serge or zigzag the seam allowances.
- Press the seam allowances toward the sleeve.

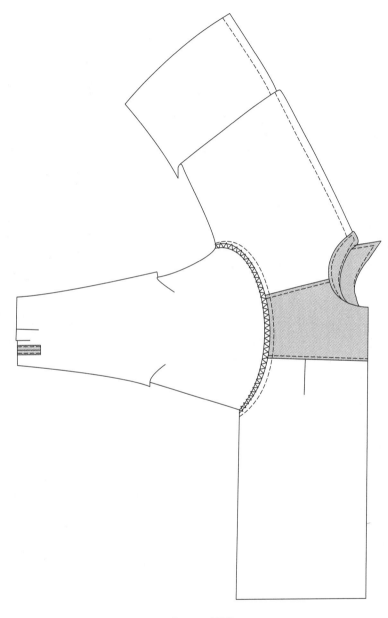

Drawing 10.37

- With the front and back bodices pinned right sides together, stitch the side seams and underarm seams along the bodice and sleeve.
- Serge or zigzag the seam allowances, then press toward the back bodice.

Rolled hem application:
- Fold the hem up $1/4''$ twice.
- Press and stitch.

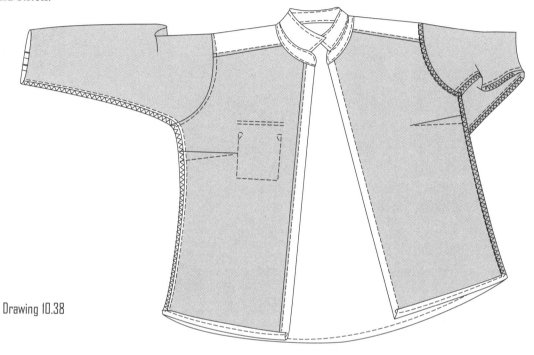

Drawing 10.38

Drawing 10.39

Drawing 10.39. Cuffs.

- Fold in the cuff edge seam allowances, then press.
- Fold the cuffs in half, right sides together, then stitch the outer edges.
- Trim the seam allowances.

Drawing 10.40.

- Turn the cuff right side out and press.

Drawing 10.40

Drawing 10.41.

- Place the cuff on the sleeve, right sides together, then stitch.
- Turn the cuffs and press the seam allowances inward.
- Topstitch the cuffs closed.

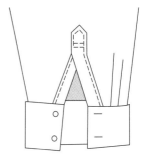

Drawing 10.41

①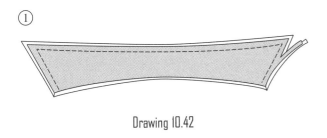

Drawing 10.42

Drawing 10.42. Shirt collar construction.

- Place the right sides of the shirt collar together, then stitch.
- Trim and clip the seam allowances.

Drawing 10.43.

- Turn the right side out, then press and topstitch.

②

Drawing 10.43

③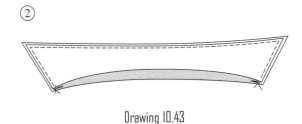

Drawing 10.44

Drawing 10.44.

- Fold up the outer stand seam allowance, then press.
- Place the inner and outer stand pieces together, then place the collar between the stand pieces.
- Stitch around the outer edge of the stand.
- Trim and clip the seam allowances.

• Turn the right side out and press.

④

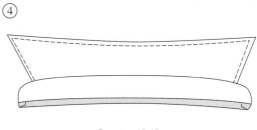

Drawing 10.45

Drawing 10.46. **Shirt collar construction.**

• Place the collar on the shirt neckline with the right
  sides together and stitch.
• Fold the collar up, then press.
• Push the seam allowances in toward the collar
  stand.
• Stitch the neckline closed from the inside of the
  garment.
• Stitch around the collar stand on the neckline
  edge, from the center back to the center front.
• Repeat on the other side of the collar stand, from
  the center back to the center front.

⑤

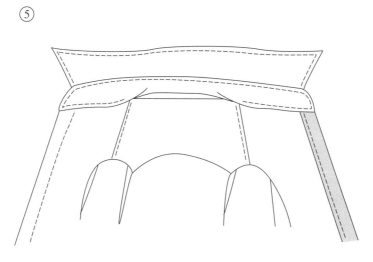

Drawing 10.46

PRINCESS LINE BLOUSE

Illustration 10.7

Pattern Analysis
- Waist darts are converted to a princess line.
- The front neckline is lowered for a more comfortable fit.
- There is a front facing.
- Detail patterns developed for the princess line blouse are:
  Convertible collar.
  Tight sleeve.

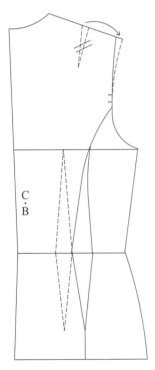

Drawing 10.47

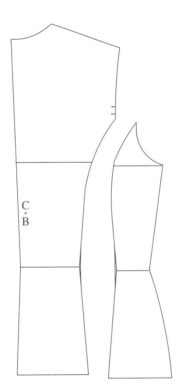

Drawing 10.48

Drawing 10.47. **Back.**

- Trace the back blouse foundation.
- Remove the shoulder dart at the shoulder tip.
- Reposition the waist dart one times its width toward the side seam.
- Draw the princess style line from the armhole to the hem, blending into the waist dart.

Drawing 10.48.

- Cut along the princess line, eliminating the waist dart.
- Smooth the princess line.

Drawing 10.49. Front.

- Lower the neck $3/4''$ at the center front.
- Reshape the neckline.
- Add a $1/2''$ extension to the center front.
- Lower the hem $1/2''$ at the center front, then blend into the side seam (prevents the blouse from raising in the front).
- Reposition the waist dart one times its width toward the side seam.
- Draw the princess style line from the armhole to the hem, blending into the waist dart.

Button placement:
- Mark the first button placement $1/2''$ down from the neck point.
- Refer to the instructions given in the Button Placement section of Chapter 7 to mark the remaining button and buttonhole placements, as shown.

Drawing 10.49

Drawing 10.50.

- Cut along the princess line, eliminating the waist dart.
- Close the side dart and reshape the side seam.
- Smooth the princess line.
- **Note:** The remaining dart on the center front piece will be eased in as it is sewn.

Facing:
- Measure in $1 1/2''$ from the neck on the shoulder.
- Measure in $3''$ from the center front at the hem.
- Draw the facing line from the shoulder to the hem, as shown.
- Trace the facing separately.

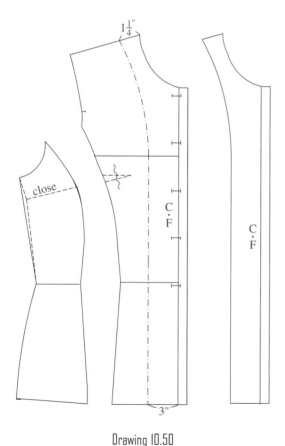

Drawing 10.50

- Trace the fitted sleeve sloper.

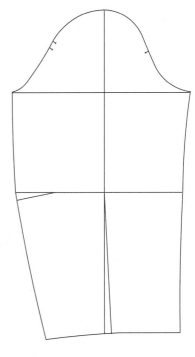

Drawing 10.51

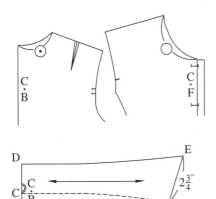

Drawing 10.52

- Measure and record the front and back necklines.
- Refer to the convertible collar instructions from Drawing 8.15 in Chapter 8 (Collars), using the following dimensions:

$$AC = 1''.$$
$$CD = 1^3/_4''.$$
$$BB' = ^1/_2''.$$
$$B'E = 2^3/_4''.$$

• Label the pattern pieces and mark the notches and
  grain lines, as shown.

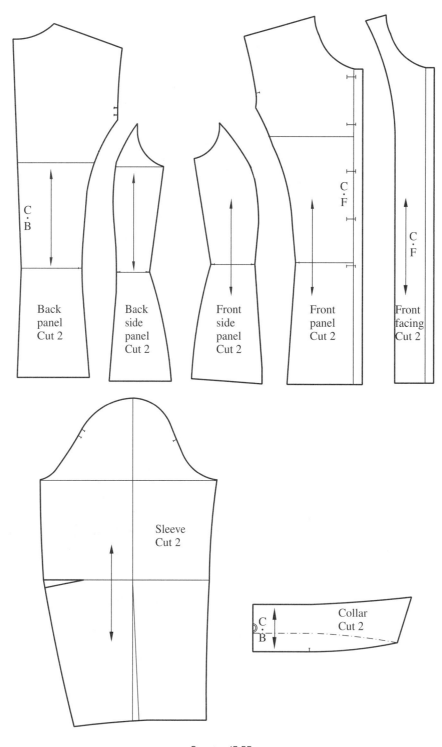

Drawing 10.53

BAND COLLAR BLOUSE

Pattern Analysis

- Waist darts are not sewn, and side seams are shaped for a semi-fitted silhouette.
- The side dart is transferred to center front and converted to shirring.
- Detail patterns developed for the band collar blouse are:

  Mandarin collar.
  Bishop sleeve.
  Wing cuffs.
  Shirt placket.

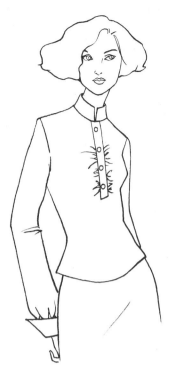

Illustration 10.8

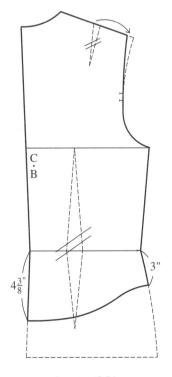

Drawing 10.54

Drawing 10.54. Back.

- Trace the back blouse foundation, but do not trace the waist dart.
- Measure in from the shoulder tip the amount of the shoulder dart intake then reshape the armhole.
- Measure down $4^3/_8''$ from the waistline at the center back.
- Measure down $3''$ from the waistline at the side seam.
- Draw the new hemline with a curved shape.

- Trace the front blouse foundation, but do not trace the waist dart.
- Measure down $4^3/_8''$ from the waistline at the center front.
- Measure down $3''$ from the waistline at the side seam.
- Reshape the new hemline, as shown.
- Measure in $^1/_2''$ from the neck at the center front and down $10''$.
- Draw the placket line.

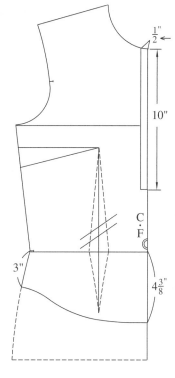

Drawing 10.55

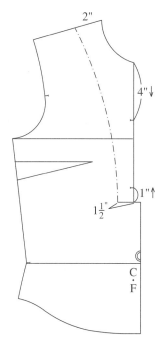

Drawing 10.56

Drawing 10.56.

- Cut along the placket line.
- Mark a notch $4''$ down from the neck on the placket line.
- Mark a notch $1''$ above the bottom of the placket line.
- **Note:** The notch placement may vary according to the desired placement of shirring.
- Mark the pattern "Right Side Up."

Facing:
- Measure in $2''$ from the neck on the shoulder and $1^1/_2''$ from the bottom of the placket line.
- Draw the facing connecting these two points.

Drawing 10.57. Placket.

- Trace the facing separately, including the notches.
- Add a 1″ extension to the placket line.
- Mark the center of the extension and label this line the center front.
- Add a 1″ placket facing.
- Transfer the notches to the edge of the placket facing.
- Flip the facing over and retrace for the left side.
- Mark the button and buttonhole placements on the center front.

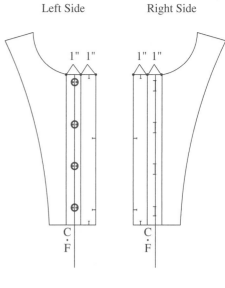

Drawing 10.57

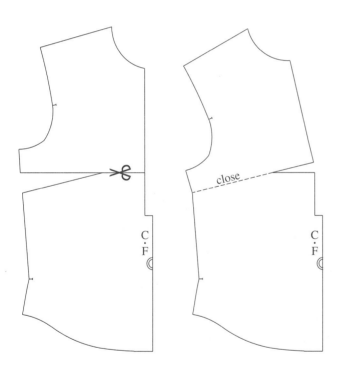

Drawing 10.58

Drawing 10.58.

- Draw a slash line, from the bust point, perpendicular to the placket line.
- Transfer the side dart to the placket line.

Drawing 10.59.

- Draw two slash lines from the placket line to the side seam, 1″ apart.
- Cut along the slash lines to, but not through, the side seam.

- Spread the slash lines a total of 4″, including the space of the dart.
- Measure out $^3/_8$″ from the slash lines.
- Reshape the placket line to this measurement with a curved lined for a smooth, contoured shape.
- Reshape the side seam.

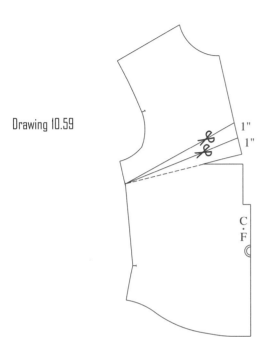

Drawing 10.59

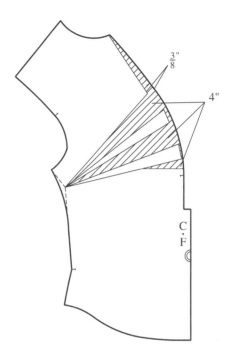

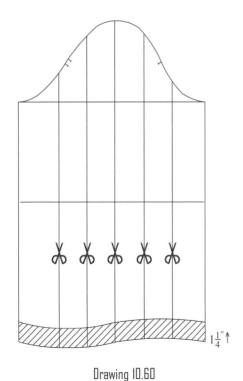

Drawing 10.60

Drawing 10.60. Sleeve.

- Trace the straight sleeve sloper.
- Shorten the sleeve length $1^1/_4$″ (the cuff height minus $^3/_4$″).
- Refer to the Bishop sleeve instructions from Drawing 9.18 in Chapter 9 (Sleeves) to complete the sleeve.

Drawing 10.61. **Placket slash line.**

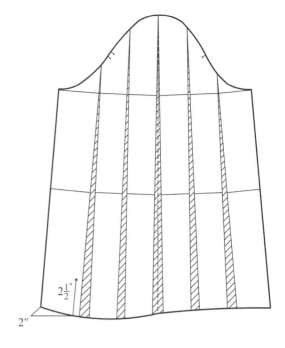

- Measure in 2″ from the back underarm seam.
- Draw the placket slash line 2¹⁄₂″ long.

Drawing 10.61

Drawing 10.62. **Wing cuffs.**

- Refer to the cuff instructions from Drawing 7.15 in Chapter 7 (Details), using the dimensions shown.

Drawing 10.62

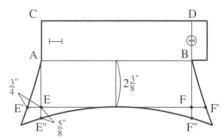

Drawing 10.63. **Band collar.**

- Measure and record the front and back necklines.
- Refer to the standing collar instructions from Drawing 8.4 in Chapter 8, using the dimensions shown.

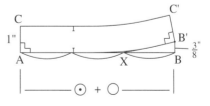

Drawing 10.63

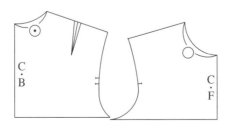

Drawing 10.64. Finished patterns.

- Label the pattern pieces and mark the notches and grain lines, as shown.

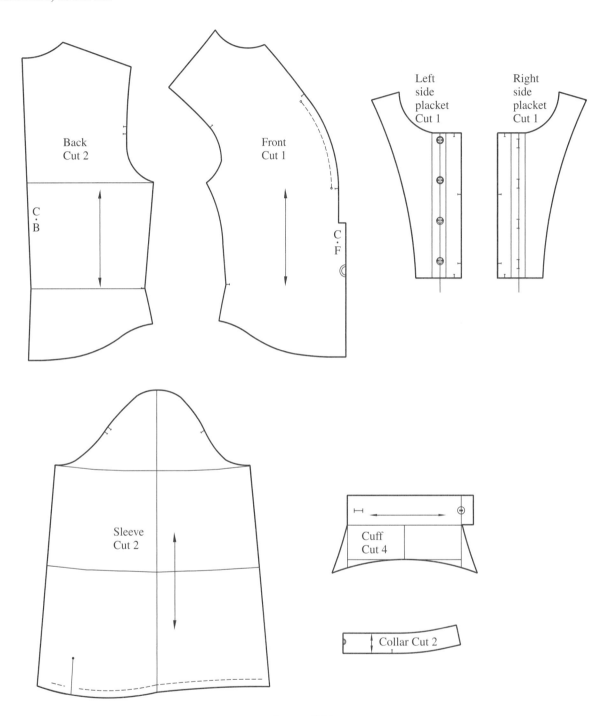

Back
Cut 2

C
·
B

Front
Cut 1

C
·
F

Left
side
placket
Cut 1

Right
side
placket
Cut 1

Sleeve
Cut 2

Cuff
Cut 4

Collar Cut 2

Drawing 10.64

PIN-TUCK BLOUSE

Pattern Analysis

- Waist darts are not sewn.
- Side and shoulder darts are transferred to the hem.
- Front and back bodice hem circumferences are made equal.
- Fullness is added at the side seam at the hem.
- Detail patterns developed for the pin-tuck blouse are:

 Pin-tucks added at front.
 Back placket.
 Peter Pan collar.
 Puff sleeve.
 Piping cuffs.
 Front and back facings.

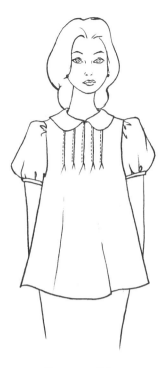

Illustration 10.9

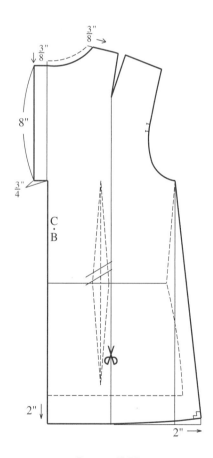

Drawing 10.65

Drawing 10.65. Back.

- Trace the back blouse foundation, but do not trace the waist dart.
- Extend the blouse length 2″ from the hip line.
- Draw the new side seam to be perpendicular to the hem.
- Measure out 2″ from the side seam at the hem then redraw the side seam.
- Lower the neck $^3/_8$″.
- Add a $^3/_4$″ extension to the center back that extends down 8″.
- Draw a slash line, from the shoulder dart point, perpendicular to the hem.

Drawing 10.66.

- Cut along the slash line to the shoulder dart point.
- Close the dart so that the slash line spreads open at the hem.
- Refer to the instructions given in the Button Placement section of Chapter 7 to mark the button and the buttonhole placements, as shown.

Facing:
- Measure in $1^1/_2''$ from the neck on the shoulder.
- Measure down 2″ from the extension at the center back.
- Draw the facing from the shoulder to the center back, as shown.
- Trace the facing separately.

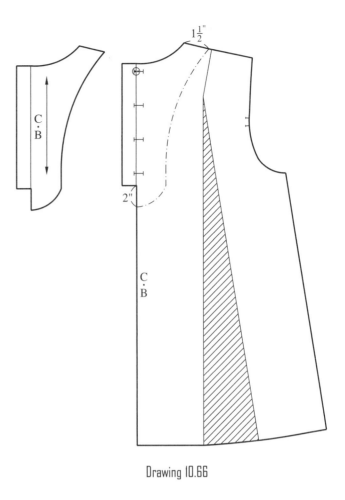

Drawing 10.66

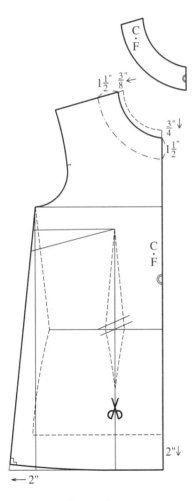

Drawing 10.67

Drawing 10.67. Front.

- Trace the front blouse foundation, but do not trace the waist dart.
- Extend the blouse length 2″ from the hip line.
- Draw the new side seam to be perpendicular to the hem.
- Measure out 2″ from the side seam at the hem.
- Redraw the side seam.
- Lower the neck $^3/_4''$ at the center front and measure in $^3/_8''$ from the neck on the shoulder.
- Reshape the new neckline.
- Draw a slash line, from the bust point, perpendicular to the hem.

Facing:
- Measure in $1^1/_2''$ from the neck on the shoulder.
- Measure down $1^1/_2''$ from the neck at the center front.
- Draw the facing parallel to the neckline, as shown.
- Trace the facing separately.

- Cut along the slash line to the bust point.
- Close the side dart so that the slash line spreads open at the hem.
- Add a $^5/_8''$ extension to the center front.
- Balance the difference in flare between the front and back bodices, referring to Chapter 4 (Drawing 4.13).

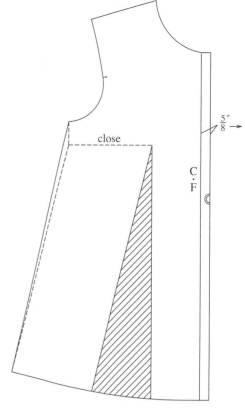

Drawing 10.68

Drawing 10.69. Pin tucks.

- Each pin tuck is $^3/_{16}''$ wide, 6″ long, and spaced $^5/_8''$ apart.
- * **Note:** Because it is placed on a fold, the first pin tuck at the center front is half of the $^3/_{16}''$.
- Measure $^5/_8''$ from the first pin tuck and draw the second pin tuck $^3/_{16}''$ wide, ending even with the first.
- Measure $^5/_8''$ from the second pin tuck and draw the third.

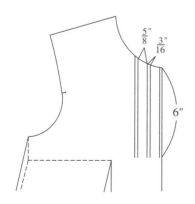
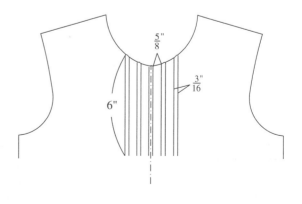

Drawing 10.69

Drawing 10.70. Peter Pan Collar.

- Refer to the Peter Pan collar instructions from Drawing 8.23 in Chapter 8, using the following dimensions:
    - Collar width = 2″.
    - Front and back shoulder tip overlap = ¹/₂″.
- Mark a notch at the shoulder on the neckline.

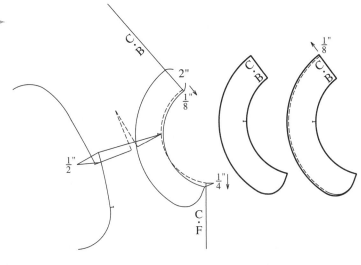

Drawing 10.70

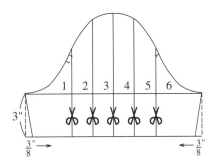

Drawing 10.71

Drawing 10.71. Puff sleeve.

- Trace the straight sleeve sloper.
- Measure down 3″ from the biceps line for the sleeve length.
- Taper in ³/₈″ at each side.
- Refer to the puff sleeve instructions from Drawing 9.9 in Chapter 9, using the dimensions shown.

Drawing 10.72.

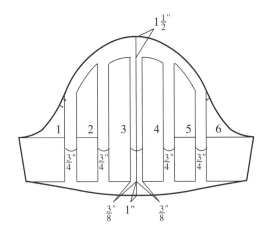

Drawing 10.72

Drawing 10.73. Cuff band.

- Refer to the piping cuff instructions from Drawing 7.19 in Chapter 7, using the dimensions shown.

Drawing 10.73

Drawing 10.74. Finished patterns.

- Label the pattern pieces and mark the notches and grain lines, as shown.

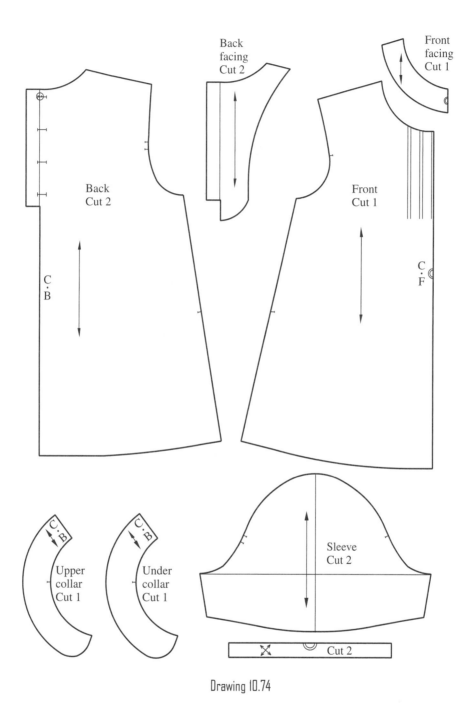

Drawing 10.74

CASCADE COLLAR BLOUSE

Pattern Analysis
- The underarm point is raised for the sleeveless armhole.
- The front and back necklines are reshaped.
- The detail pattern developed for the cascade collar blouse is:

    Cascade collar.

Illustration 10.10

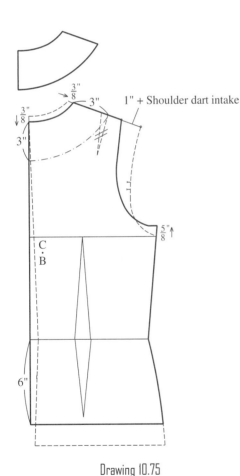

Drawing 10.75

Drawing 10.75. Back.

- Trace the back blouse foundation.
- Reshape the center back line with a straight line.
- Measure down 6″ from the waistline at the center back.
- Draw the new hemline with a straight line.
- Lower the neck $^3/_8$″.
- Raise the underarm $^5/_8$″ at the side seam.
- Measure in 1″ plus the shoulder dart intake from the shoulder tip, and mark.
- Reshape the armhole from the mark to the raised underarm with a smooth line.

Draw the collar edge:
- Measure in 3″ from the neck at the shoulder.
- Measure down 3″ from the neck at the center back.
- Draw the collar edge.
- Trace the collar separately.

Drawing 10.76.

- Add a $\frac{5}{8}''$ extension to the center back.
- Mark the first buttonhole $\frac{1}{2}''$ from the neck at the center back.
- Refer to the instructions given in the Button Placement section of Chapter 7 to mark the button and buttonhole placements on the center back line, as shown.

Facing:
- Measure in 2" from the extension edge at the hem.
- Draw the facing from the hem to the neck with a straight line.
- Trace the facing separately.

Drawing 10.76

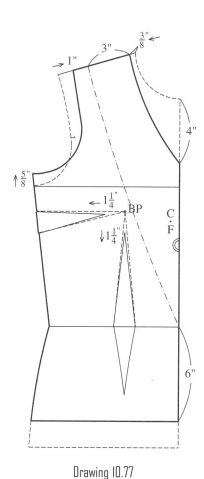

Drawing 10.77

Drawing 10.77. Front.

- Trace the front blouse foundation.
- Measure down 6" from the waistline at the center front.
- Draw the new hemline with a straight line.
- Measure in $\frac{3}{8}''$ from the neck on the shoulder.
- Lower the neck 4" at the center front.
- Reshape the neckline with a slightly curved line.
- Raise the underarm $\frac{5}{8}''$ at the side seam.
- Measure in 1" from the shoulder tip, and mark.
- Reshape the armhole from the mark to the raised underarm with a smooth line.
- Reposition the side and waist dart points $1\frac{1}{4}''$ from the bust point.

Collar:
- Measure in 3" from the neck on the shoulder.
- * **Note:** The front and back collar widths at the shoulder seam are equal.
- Draw the collar edge from the shoulder to the waistline at center front with a slightly curved line.

Drawing 10.78. Cascading collar.

- Trace the collar separately.
- Refer to the cascading collar instructions from Drawing 8.32 in Chapter 8 to develop the cascade collar, as shown.

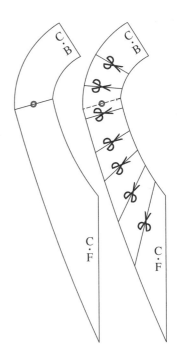

Drawing 10.78

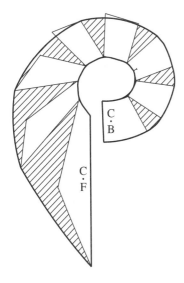

Drawing 10.79

Drawing 10.79.

- Reshape the neckline and collar edge, as shown.

- Label the pattern pieces and mark the notches and
  grain lines, as shown.

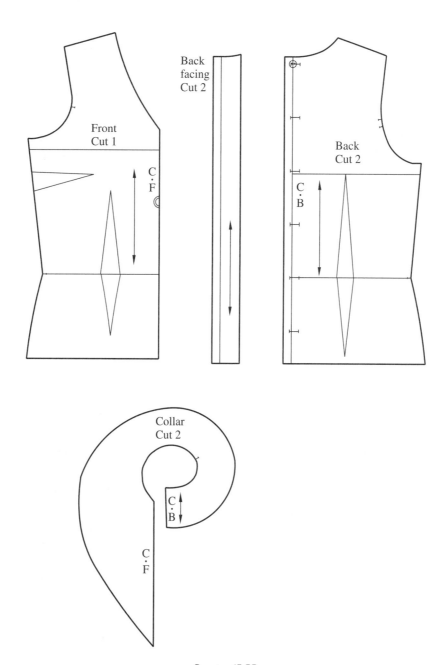

Drawing 10.80

CAP SLEEVE BLOUSE

Pattern Analysis

- The right and left front patterns are developed separately for the surplice bodice.
- Waist darts are not sewn.
- Detail patterns developed for the cap sleeve blouse are:

  Italian collar.

  Cap sleeve without armhole seam.

Illustration 10.11

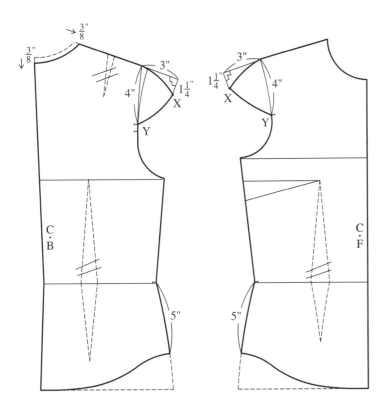

Drawing 10.81

Drawing 10.81. Back and Front.

- Trace the blouse foundation, but do not trace the waist dart.
- Measure down 5″ from the waistline on the side seam.
- Reshape the hem, as shown.
- Extend the shoulder line 3″ then square down $1^{1}/_{4}$″ and label X.
- Shape the shoulder line from the shoulder tip to point X, as shown.
- Measure down 4″ from the shoulder tip along the armhole and label Y.
- Shape the cap sleeve from point X to Y, as shown.

Back:
- Ease the shoulder dart out at the armhole.
- Lower the neckline $^{3}/_{8}$″.

Drawing 10.82. Front.

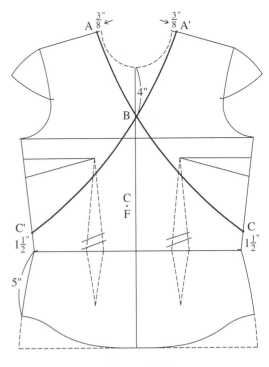

- Trace the entire front blouse foundation.

Neckline and notch:
- Measure in $^3/_8''$ from each side of the neck on the shoulder and label A and A$'$.
- Measure down 4″ from the neck at the center front and label B.
- Measure up $1^1/_2''$ from the waistline on both side seams and label C and C$'$.
- Connect point A to C, passing through B, with a curved line.
- Connect point A$'$ to C$'$, passing through B, with a curved line.
- Mark a notch at each side seam on the waistline.

Drawing 10.82

Drawing 10.83.

- Trace the left and right side separately.

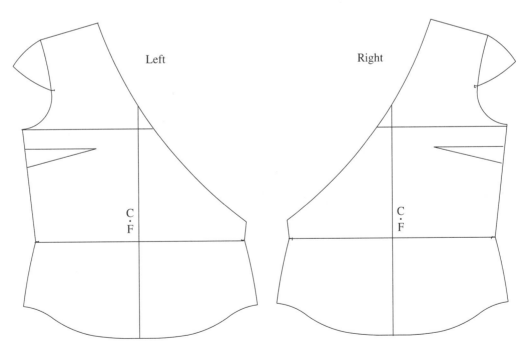

Drawing 10.83

- Measure in 3″ from point C on line AC, and label D.
- Square down from point D to the hem.

Tie and facing:
- Draw the tie strap at east 28″ long, starting from point D.
- Shape the bottom of the tie, blending with the hem.
- Separate the tie from the front bodice.
- Draw the neck facing $1\frac{1}{4}$″ wide, along the neck-line, from point A to D.
- Trace the facing separately.

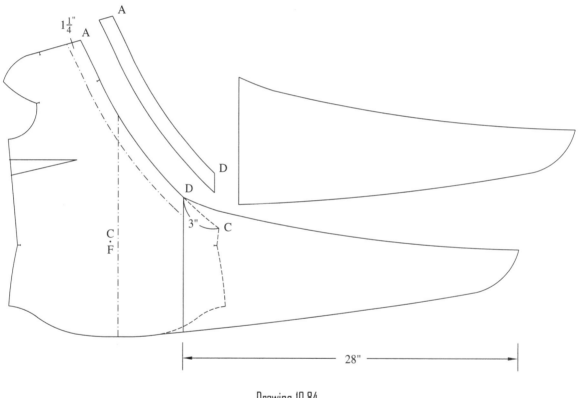

Drawing 10.84

- Draw three slash lines 1″ apart, beginning $1\frac{1}{2}″$ down from the waistline notch on the left side seam, and curving up to the bust point, as shown.

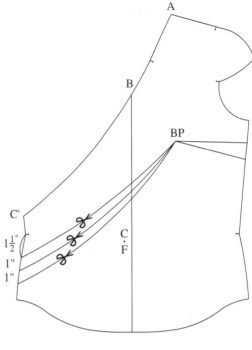

Drawing 10.85

Drawing 10.86.

- Cut along the slash lines to the bust point.
- Close the side dart and spread the slash lines $1\frac{1}{2}″$ each.
- Measure in 3″ from point C′ on line A′C′, and label D′.
- Square down from point D′ to the hem.
- Mark the pleat lines 2″ long on each slash line.
- Reshape the side seam.

Tie and facing:
- Draw the tie strap at least 28″ long, starting from point D′.
- Shape the bottom of the tie, blending with the hem.
- Mark a notch 2″ down from the notch at the waist-line, on the right side seam, for the slit.
- Draw the neck facing $1\frac{1}{4}″$ wide, along the neck-line, from point A′ to D′.
- Trace the facing separately.

Drawing 10.86

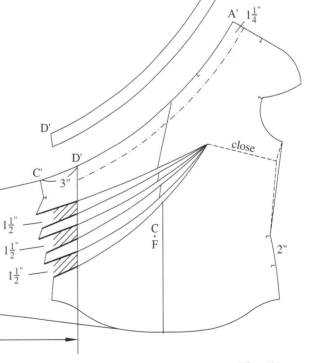

Drawing 10.87. Italian collar.

- Refer to the Italian collar instructions from Drawing 8.20 in Chapter 8, using the dimensions shown.

  AA′ = 1″.
  A′C = 1″.
  CD = 1⅝″.
  BB′ = ³⁄₈″.
  B′E = 4″.

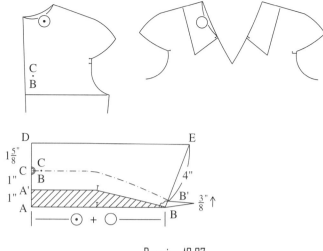

Drawing 10.87

Drawing 10.88. Finished patterns.

- Label the pattern pieces and mark the notches and grain lines, as shown.

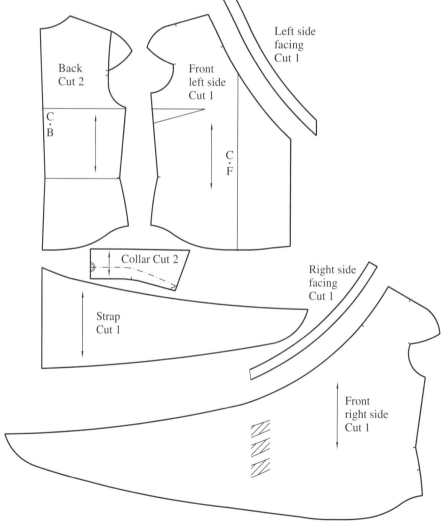

Drawing 10.88

RAGLAN SLEEVE BLOUSE

Pattern Analysis

- Waist darts are not sewn.
- Side seams are straight, creating a box silhouette.
- The neckline is lowered to accommodate pulling on the garment.
- The side dart is transferred to the neckline, then converted to shirring.
- The detail pattern developed for the raglan sleeve blouse is:

    Folklore sleeve.

Illustration 10.12

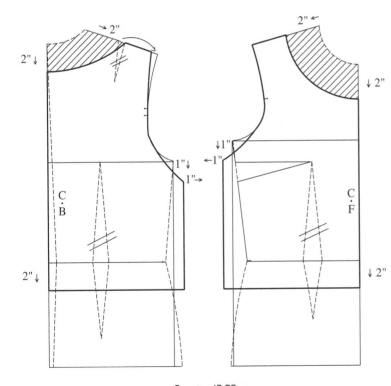

Drawing 10.89

Drawing 10.89. Back and front.

- Trace the blouse foundation, but do not trace the waist dart.
- Measure down 2″ from the waistline, and draw the new hemline straight.
- Lower the neck 2″.
- Lower the armhole 1″.
- Measure out 1″ at the underarm point, then draw the new side seam.

Back:

- Measure in the amount of the shoulder dart intake from the shoulder tip.
- Reshape the armhole to remove the dart.
- Reshape the center back line with a straight line.

Drawing 10.90. **Back raglan sleeve.**

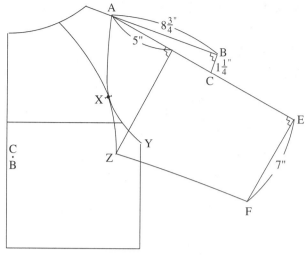

Drawing 10.90

- Refer to the raglan sleeve instructions from Drawing 9.56 in Chapter 9 to complete the raglan sleeve, using the following dimensions:

    AB = $8^3/_4''$.

    BC = $1^1/_4''$.

    Cap height = 5″.

    AE = 14″.

    EF = 7″.

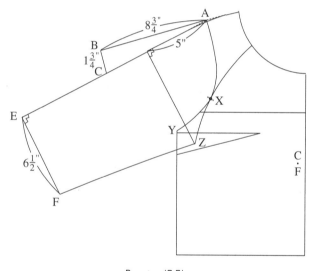

Drawing 10.91

Drawing 10.91. **Front raglan sleeve.**

- Refer to the raglan sleeve instructions from Drawing 9.60 in Chapter 9 to complete the raglan sleeve, using the following dimensions:

    A′B′ = $8^3/_4''$.

    B′C′ = $1^3/_4''$.

    Cap height = 5″.

    A′E′ = 14″.

    E′F′ = $6^1/_2''$.

Drawing 10.92. **Back bodice.**

- Separate the bodice and sleeve pattern.
- Add a 2″ extension to the center back for shirring intake.

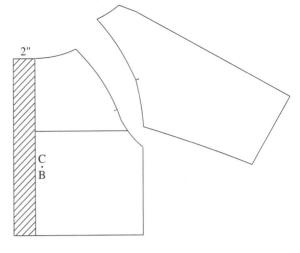

Drawing 10.92

Drawing 10.93. **Front bodice.**

- Separate the bodice and sleeve pattern.
- Transfer the side dart to the neckline.
- Add a 2″ extension to the center front for shirring intake.

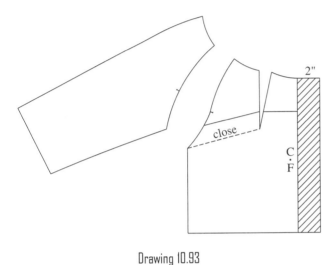

Drawing 10.93

Drawing 10.94. **Sleeve.**

- Trace the back and front sleeves, spaced 2″ apart, as shown.
- Add 1″ at the hem and ³/₄″ at the top, then reshape the sleeve.

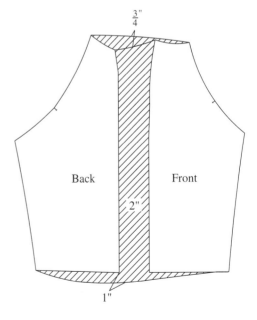

Drawing 10.94

- Label the pattern pieces and mark the notches and grain lines, as shown.

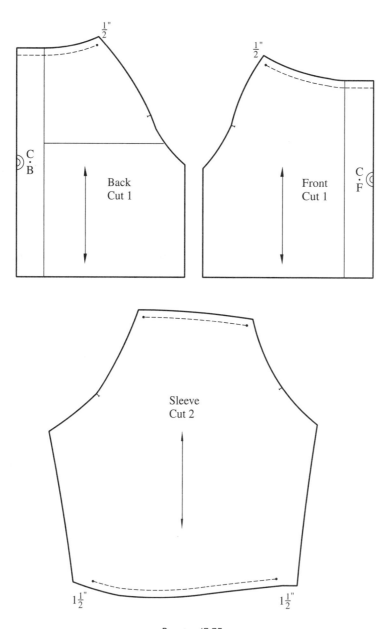

Drawing 10.95

Chapter Eleven

THE ONE-PIECE DRESS

INTRODUCTION TO THE ONE-PIECE

 he one-piece dress is one of the oldest garment designs in existence. Its pattern is unique in that the bodice and skirt are connected to form one unit. The function of a one-piece dress can range from casual to business to formal, and will have an impact on the style line and design details. The use of different types of necklines, sleeves, and collars can enhance the overall appearance and allow for different functions, as well.

One-Piece Silhouette Variations

One-piece dresses can be classified into three basic categories: straight, A-line/flare, and fitted.

Fitted
This silhouette is fitted at the waist and bust, and may be fitted or flared at the hemline.

Straight
This silhouette falls straight down from the shoulder to the hem.

A-line/flare
This silhouette flares out from the underarm seam to the hem in an A-shape.

Fitted   Straight   A-Line   Flare

Illustration 11.1

One-Piece Style Line Variations

To generate even more silhouettes, different style lines and design details (e.g., darts, pleats, tucks, flare) can be applied to any of the basic categories. Experimenting with waistline placement can result in unlimited variations of the skirt shapes of the dress, as well.

Illustration 11.2

Sheath Dress
This is a close-fitting style, owing its shape to waist darts. It is somewhat narrow at the hemline and generally features a slit at the back to allow for movement.

Shift Dress
This style falls straight from the shoulder to the hemline, which can also be flared out at the side seam.

Princess Style Line
The princess line starts from the armhole or mid-shoulder and continues over the dart point, blending into the waist dart. The darts are converted to the princess style line. Fullness can be added to each panel hem.

Natural Waistline
This style line has a seam at the natural waistline that connects the bodice and skirt. Generally, it is accented with a belt or sash.

Low Waistline
This style line is placed below the natural waistline, anywhere between the waistline and the hip line.

High Waistline
This style line is placed above the natural waistline, anywhere between the waistline and the bust line. When placed immediately below the bust line, this style is called an Empire waistline.

HIGH WAIST ONE-PIECE

Pattern Analysis

- This is an above-knee length, high waistline.
- Waist darts are transferred to the hem.
- Side darts are transferred to the waist dart.
- Marker directions are provided for garment patterns.
- Detail patterns developed for the high waist one-piece are:

    Flared sleeve.
    Scooped neckline.
    Neckline facing.

Illustration 11.3

Drawing 11.1. Back and front.

- Trace the front and back blouse foundation.
- Extend the length 12″ from the hip line.
- Measure up 4″ from the waist and draw the new waistline.
- Measure out 2″ from the side seam at the hem and mark.
- Draw the side seams from the new waistline to marks.

- Reshape the hem with a slight curve, ending square at the inseam and out seam.

Back:
- Lower the neckline $\frac{5}{8}$″ then reshape.
- Measure out 1″ from the center back at the hem and draw a line from the new waistline.

Front:
- Lower the neck 3″ at the center front, and measure in $\frac{5}{8}$″ from the neck on the shoulder.
- Reshape the neckline.

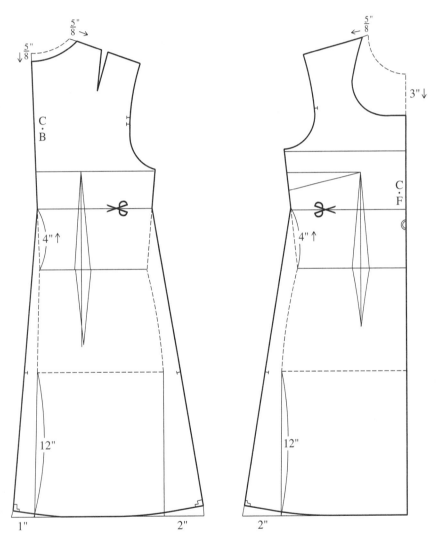

Drawing 11.1

Drawing 11.2. **Back.**

- Cut along the new waistline.
- Measure down $1\frac{1}{4}''$ from the neck at the center back, and measure in $1\frac{1}{4}''$ on the shoulder.
- Draw the facing parallel to the neckline.
- Trace the facing separately.

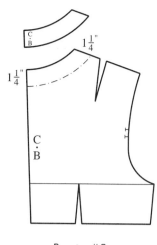

Drawing 11.2

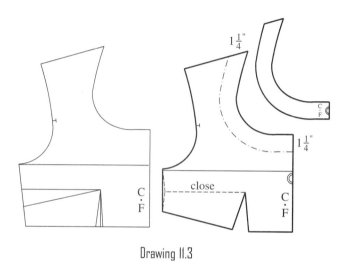

Drawing 11.3

Drawing 11.3. **Front.**

- Cut along the new waistline.
- Transfer the side dart to the waist dart.
- Reshape the side seam.
- Measure down $1\frac{1}{4}''$ from the neck at the center front and measure in $1\frac{1}{4}''$ on the shoulder.
- Draw the facing parallel to the neckline.
- Trace the facing separately.

Drawing 11.4. **Back and front skirt.**

- Draw a slash line from the dart point perpendicular to the hem.

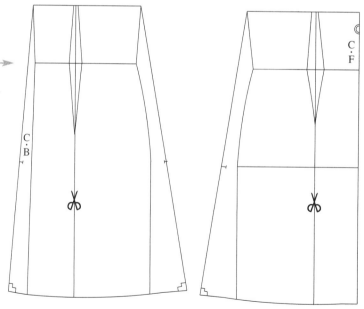

Drawing 11.4

Drawing 11.5. **Back and front.**

- Cut along the slash line.

Drawing 11.5

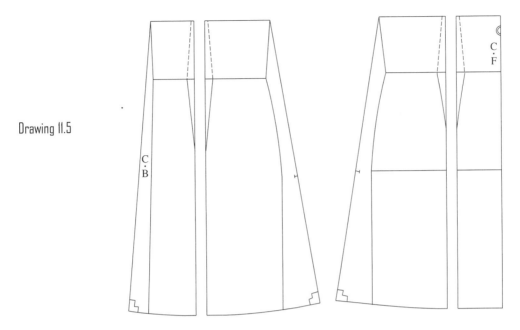

Drawing 11.6. **Back and front.**

- Match the two dart legs (dashed lines) at the waistline, and spread the slash lines 2″ at the hem.
- **Note:** This will close the waist dart. The spread
  amount can be varied as desired.
- Reshape the waistline and hem.

Drawing 11.6

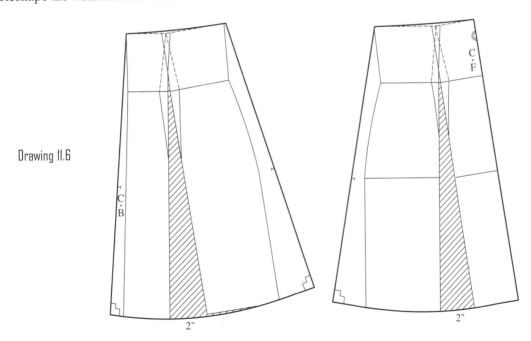

Drawing 11.7.

- Trace the straight sleeve sloper
- Measure down $1^5/_8$" from the biceps line.
- Draw two slash lines on each side of the center line, spaced 2" apart, as shown.

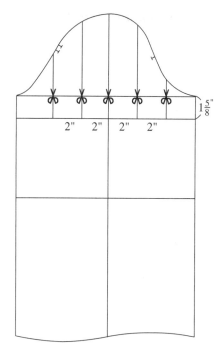

Drawing II.7

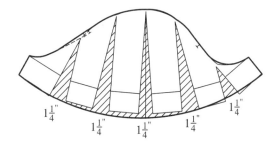

Drawing II.8

Drawing 11.8.

- Cut along the slash lines, including the center line to, but not through, the sleeve cap.
- Spread each slash line $1^1/_4$" at the hem.
- Reshape the hem.
- Draw the center line.

Drawing 11.9. Finished patterns.

- Label the pattern pieces and mark the notches and grain lines, as shown.

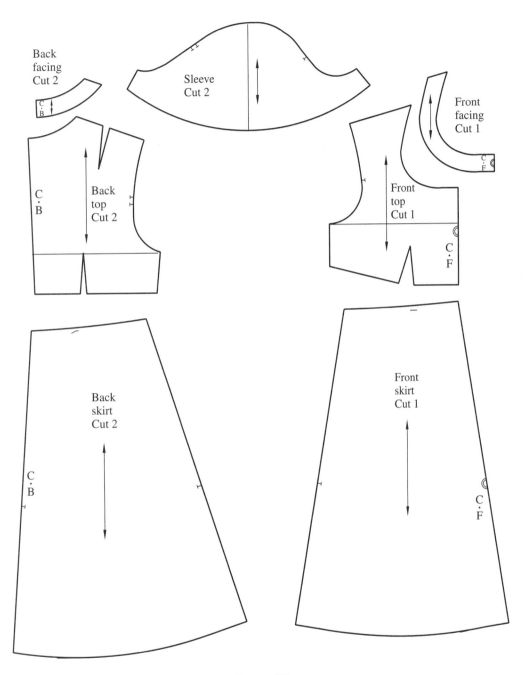

Drawing 11.9

• Add the seam allowances:
Sleeve cap, armholes, necklines, facings, and
waistline $= {}^3/_8''$.
Center back, side, shoulder seams, and sleeve
hem $= {}^5/_8''$.
Hems $= 1{}^1/_4''$.

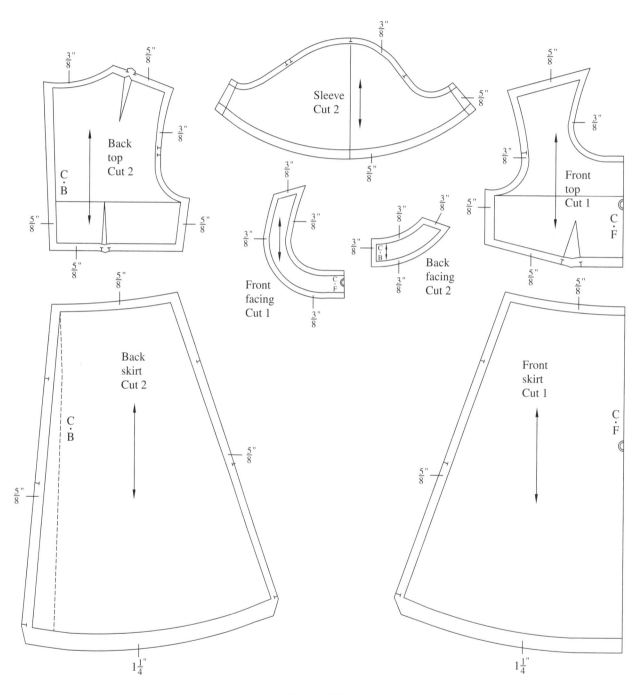

Drawing 11.10

Drawing 11.11. Garment marker.

- The garment marker is produced by laying out all of the pattern pieces on the fabric. The pattern pieces should be placed so that their grain lines match the straight grain of the fabric. The width of the fabric and sizes of the pattern pieces will dictate how the pieces are laid. Much of this process is handled by computers in industry, but it is still important to be familiar with the relationship between fabric and pattern.

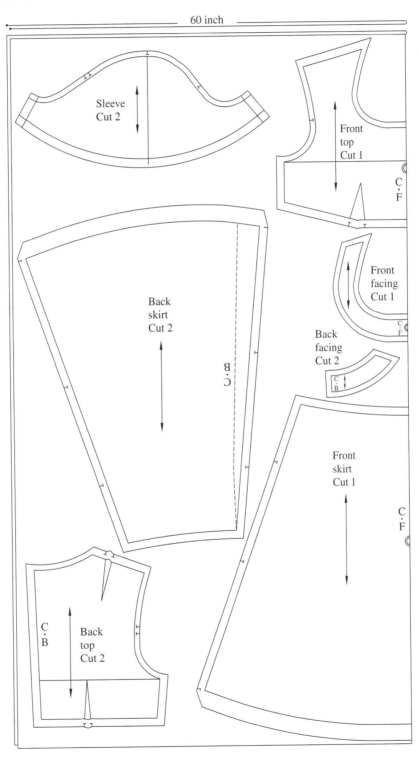

Drawing 11.11

The One-Piece Dress 439

ONE-PIECE CONSTRUCTION

Drawing 11.12. Preparation.

- Attach the interfacing to the center back zipper placement and facings.
- Apply straight tape at the front and back neckline edges.

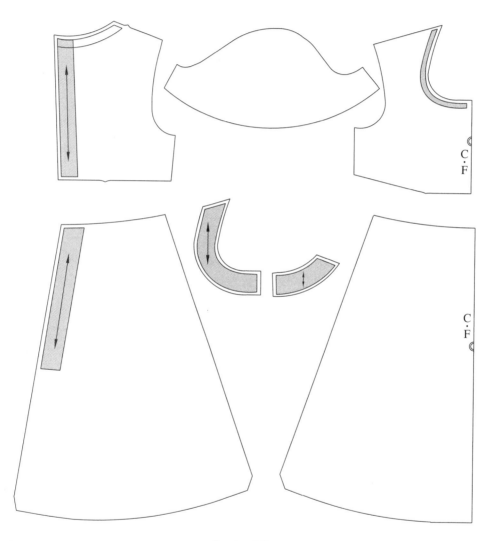

Drawing 11.12

• Serge or zigzag the seam allowances.

Drawing 11.13

Drawing 11.14. Back and front bodice.

- Sew the darts, then press toward the center back and front.
- Attach the skirt at the waistline of each panel, then press the seams open.

- Stitch the back panels together at the center back from the zipper placement to the hem notch, then press the seams open.
- Attach the invisible zipper to the center back.
- Stitch the front and back bodice shoulder seams, then press the seams open.

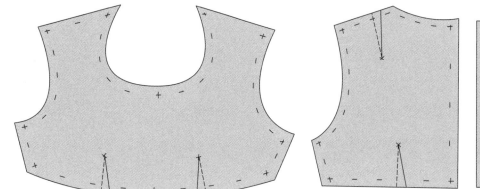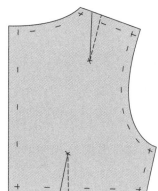

Drawing 11.14

Drawing 11.15. Invisible zipper attachment.

- Open the zipper and press to flatten it.
- On the right side of the garment, place the zipper face down with its teeth aligned on the stitch line.

- Stitch the zipper in place as close to its coils as possible, generally around $1/8''$.
- Fold the seam allowances under so that the zipper coils show slightly.
- Repeat for the other side of the zipper.

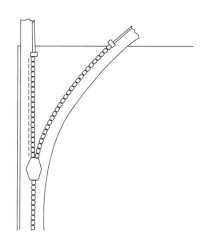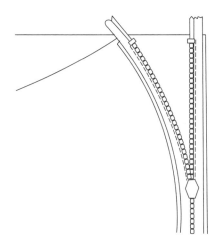

Drawing 11.15

Drawing 11.16. **Facing-to-bodice attachment.**

• Attach the front and back facing shoulder seams, then press the seams open.

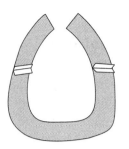

Drawing 11.16

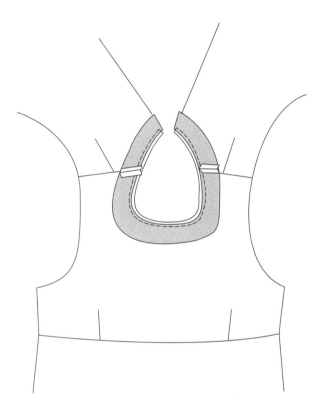

Drawing 11.17

Drawing 11.17

• Attach the facing to the bodice neckline, with the right sides together.
• Stitch around the neckline.
• Trim and clip the seam allowances.
• Press the seam allowances toward the facing, then under-stitch the seam allowance to the facing.
• Turn the facing toward the inside of the garment, then press.
• Stitch the side seams, then press open.

Drawing 11.18. **Sleeve.**

• Stitch the underarm seam, then press open.
• Roll, stitch, then press the hem.
• Place two rows of basting around the sleeve cap, between the notches.
• Shape the sleeve cap by distributing the ease evenly.
• Match the notches, underarm seam, and shoulder point, then stitch to set the sleeve into the bodice.
• Serge or zigzag the seam allowances, then press them toward the sleeve.

Drawing 11.18

Drawing 11.19. Finishing.

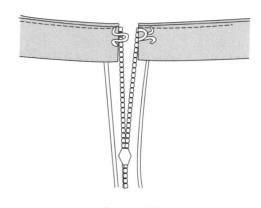

Drawing 11.19

- Fold the hem, then catch stitch the hem.
- Tack the facing to the zipper and shoulder seams.
- Attach the hook and eye at the top back of the neck opening.

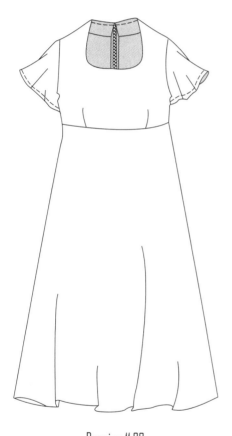

Drawing 11.20

Drawing 11.20.

- Press and finish.

BOAT NECK ONE-PIECE

Pattern Analysis

- This is a below-knee-length sheath dress.
- It has a tapered hem.
- Detail patterns developed for the boat neck one-piece are:

  Boat neckline.
  Back slit.
  Neckline facing.
  Three-quarter-length sleeve.

Illustration 11.4

Drawing 11.21. Back and front.

- Trace the blouse foundation.
- Extend the length 16″ from the hip line.
- Measure in ⅝″ from the side seam at the hem.
- Draw the new side seam from the hip line to the hem.
- Mark a notch 6″ above the hem at the center back for the slit.

Back:
- Lower the neck ⅜″ at the center back, and measure in 2″ from the neck on the shoulder.

- Reshape the neckline.
- Mark a notch 18″ down from the neck point at the center back, for zipper placement.
- Label each pattern.

Front:
- Lower the waist dart 1″ from the bust point.
- Reposition the side dart point 1¼″ from the bust point.
- Lower the neck ⅝″ at the center front, and measure in 2″ from the neck on the shoulder.
- Reshape the neckline.

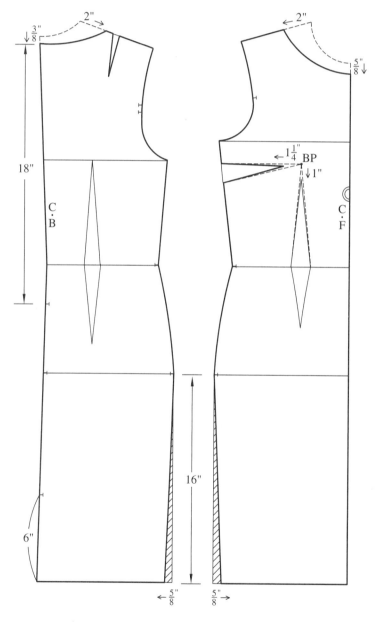

Drawing 11.21

Drawing 11.22. **Back and front facing.**

- Measure down $1^1/_4''$ from the neck at the center back and center front.
- Measure in $1^1/_4''$ from the neck on the shoulder.
- Draw the facing parallel to the neckline, as shown.
- Trace the facing separately.

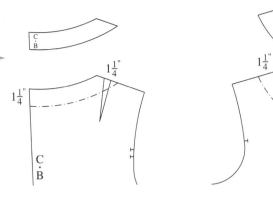

Drawing 11.22

Drawing 11.23. **Sleeve.**

- Trace the tight sleeve sloper.
- Measure down 4″ from the elbow line, and draw the new hemline.

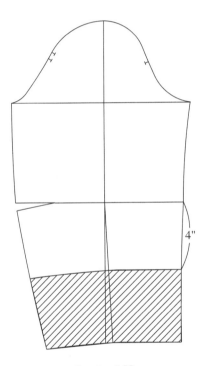

Drawing 11.23

Drawing 11.24. Finished patterns.

- Label the pattern pieces and mark the notches and grain lines, as shown.

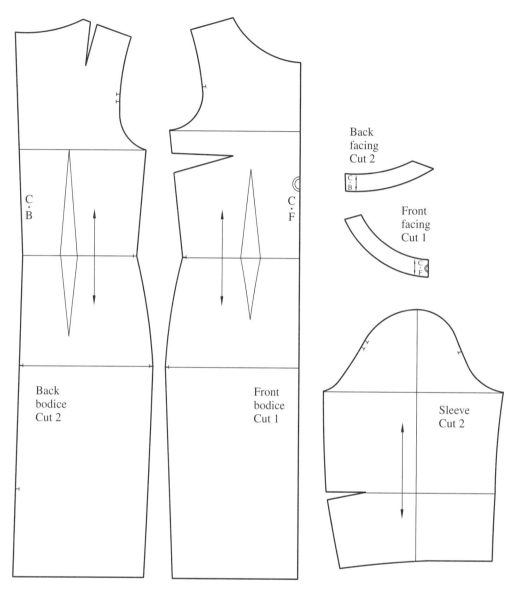

Back facing Cut 2

Front facing Cut 1

Back bodice Cut 2

Front bodice Cut 1

Sleeve Cut 2

Drawing 11.24

PRINCESS LINE ONE-PIECE

Pattern Analysis
- This is a tea-length, princess line dress.
- The armholes are raised and reshaped.
- Detail patterns developed for the princess line one-piece are:
  Square neck.
  All-in-one facings at neckline and armhole.
  Inverted pleats added between front princess lines as a slit.

Illustration 11.5

Drawing 11.25. Back and front.

- Trace the blouse foundation, but do not trace the shoulder dart.
- Extend the length 24″ from the hip line.
- Lower the neck $1\frac{1}{4}$″ at the center back and front.
- Measure in 2″ from the neck on the shoulder.
- Draw the square neckline, as shown.
- Measure out 2″ from the neck on the shoulder.
- Raise the underarm $\frac{3}{4}$″ at the side seam.

- Reshape the armhole.
- Mark the midpoint of the hip line.
- Draw a line from the waistline perpendicular to the hem, passing through the mark.
- Center the waist dart on this line.
- Draw a princess line from the armhole, blending into the waist dart.
- Mark the notches on the princess line, as shown.

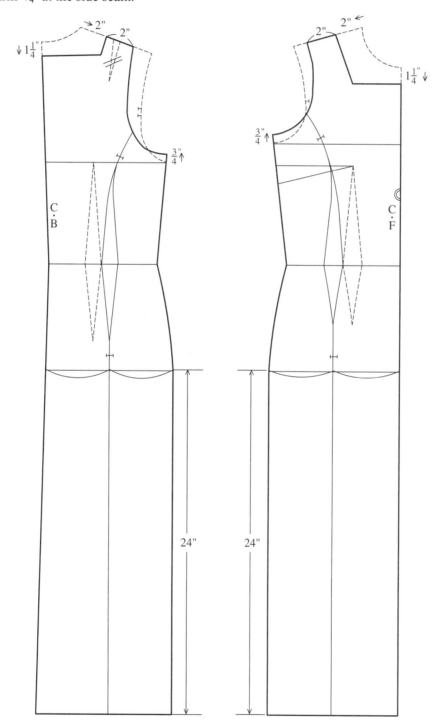

Drawing 11.25

Drawing 11.26. **Back and front facing.**

- Measure down 4″ from the neck at the center back and center front.
- Measure down 2″ from the underarm point at the side seam.
- Draw the facing from the center back to the side seam, as shown.
- Trace the facing separately.

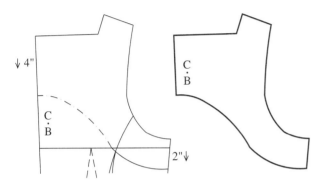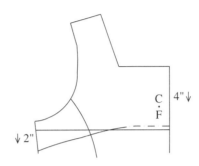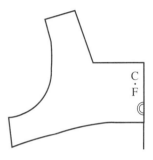

Drawing 11.26

Drawing 11.27. **Back.**

- Cut along the princess line, eliminating the waist dart.

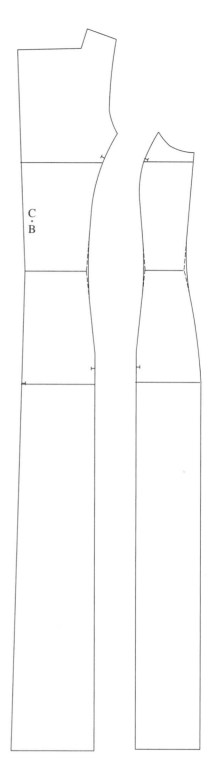

C
. B

Drawing 11.27

Drawing 11.28. Front.

- Cut along the princess line, eliminating the waist dart.
- Close the side dart.
- Measure down 10″ from the hip line, on the princess line, and mark.
- Add a 2″ pleat extension to both sides of the princess line, as shown.
- Mark the fold line on each extension, then measure down ³/₄″ and mark.
- Connect the marks to the extension edges, as shown.

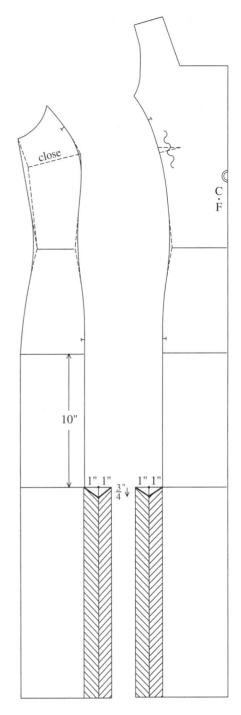

Drawing 11.28

Drawing 11.29. Finished pattern.

- Label the pattern pieces and mark the notches and grain lines, as shown.

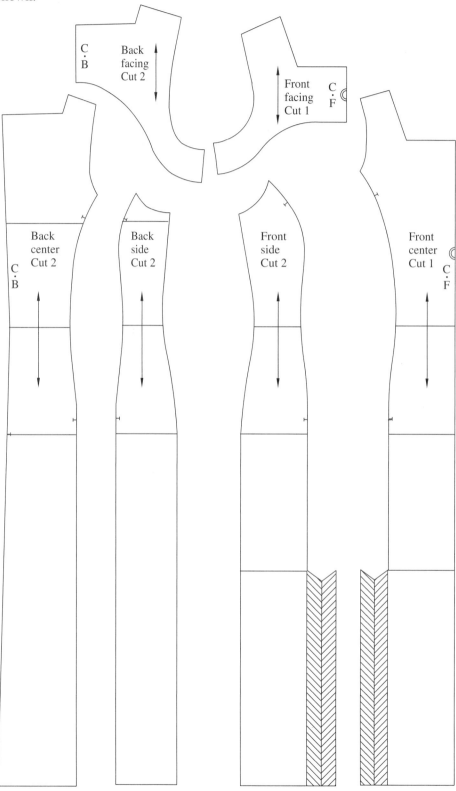

Drawing 11.29

LOW WAIST ONE-PIECE

Pattern Analysis
- This is a knee-length, low waistline dress.
- Waist darts are not sewn, creating a semi-fitted silhouette.
- It is double-breasted.
- Detail patterns developed for the low waist one-piece dress:
  Asymmetric Revere collar.
  Rolled-up cuffs sleeve.
  Low-waist waistband.

Illustration 11.6

- Trace the blouse foundation, but do not trace the waist dart.
- Redraw the center back line to be perpendicular to the hip.
- Extend the length 14″ from the hip line.
- Measure out 2″ from the side seam at the hem.
- Reshape the hem, with a slight curve, ending square to the side seam.
- Lower the waistline $2\frac{1}{2}$″.
- Measure down 2″ from the new waistline, and draw a line parallel to the waistline for a band.

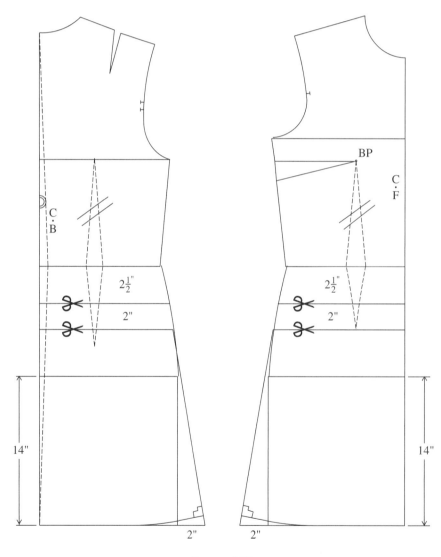

Drawing 11.30

- Separate the pattern along the new waistline and the band.
- Reposition the side dart point $1\frac{1}{4}''$ from the bust point.

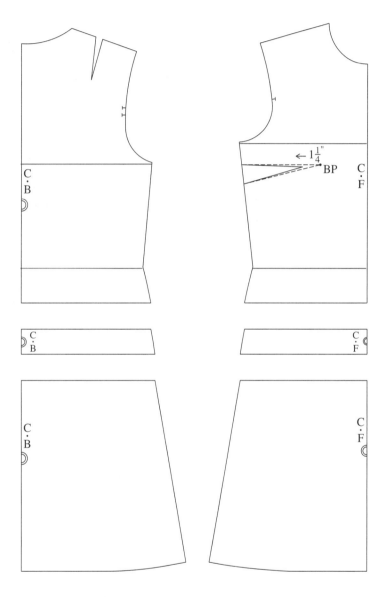

Drawing 11.31

Drawing 11.32. **Right front bodice.**

- Trace the entire front bodice, marking the center front line.
- Draw an extension line 2½" from center front.
- Label A′ at the waist.
- Measure in ⁵⁄₈" from the neck on both shoulders and label B and B′, as shown.
- Draw a 3"-long line from point B′ to the extension line and label A.
- Connect point B to A.
- **Note:** The neckline shape may vary according to design.
- Draw the desired collar style line (BXA).

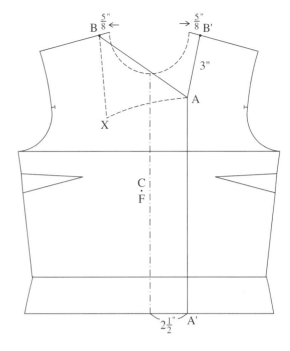

Drawing 11.32

Drawing 11.33.

- Cut along the neckline B-A-B′, leaving excess paper at the neck to trace the collar.
- Fold the paper under along line AB.
- Trace the collar style line (B-X-A) with a tracing wheel.

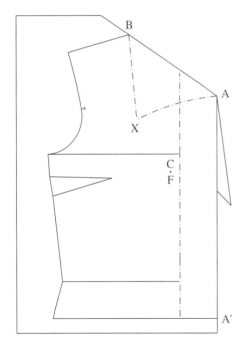

Drawing 11.33

Drawing 11.34. **Right front bodice.**

- Unfold the paper and draw the collar style line.
- Draw a buttonhole guideline $3/4''$ in from line AA′.
- Mark the first buttonhole $1/2''$ down from A.
- Mark the last buttonhole 1″ up from A′.
- Space the remaining buttonholes evenly between the first and last buttonholes for a total of seven.
- Measure the distance from the center front to the buttonhole guideline, then place the buttons that distance in from the center front line.

Facing:
- Measure in 1″ from point B on the shoulder.
- Measure in 3″ from the center front at the waist.
- Draw the facing, from the shoulder to the hem, as shown.
- Trace the facing separately.

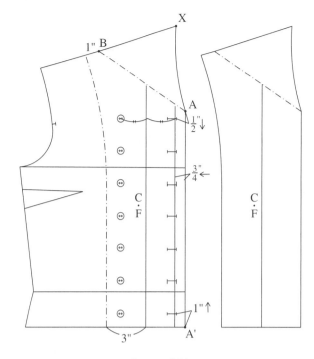

Drawing 11.34

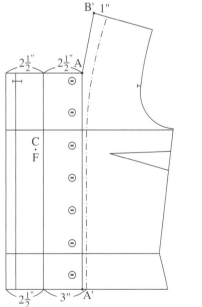
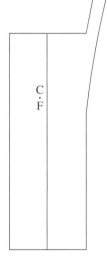

Drawing 11.35

Drawing 11.35. **Left front bodice.**

- Trace the left side pattern piece.
- Draw the center front line $2^{1}/_{2}''$ from line AA′.
- Add a $2^{1}/_{2}''$ extension to the center front.
- Draw the neckline, square to the extension from point A.
- Draw a buttonhole guideline $3/4''$ from the extension line.
- Mark one buttonhole $1/2''$ down from the neckline.
- Measure the distance from the center front to the buttonhole guideline, then place the buttons the same distance in from the center front line.

Facing:
- Measure in 1″ from point B′ and in 3″ from the center front at the waist.
- Draw the facing, from the shoulder to the hem, as shown.
- Trace the facing separately.

Drawing 11.36. Back.

- Lower the neck $^3/_8''$ at the center back, and measure in $^5/_8''$ from the neck on the shoulder.
- Reshape the neckline.

Facing:
- Measure down $1^1/_4''$ from the neck at the center back.
- Measure in $1^1/_4''$ from the neck on the shoulders.
- Draw the facing parallel to the neckline.
- Trace the facing separately.

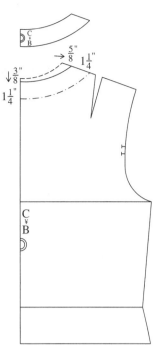

Drawing 11.36

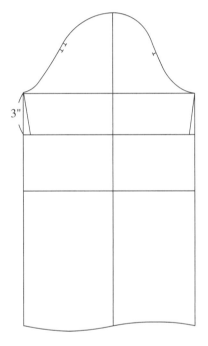

3"

Drawing 11.37

Drawing 11.37. Sleeve.

- Trace the straight sleeve sloper.
- Measure down 3" from the biceps line, then draw the new hemline.
- Taper the underarm seam.

Drawing 11.38. Cuff.

- Measure up $^1/_2''$ from the hem and mark.
- Add $3^1/_2''$ to the hem for the roll-up cuff.
- Mark the fold line of the cuff.
- Fold the cuff up then redraw the underarm seam.

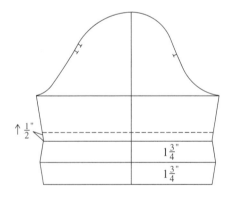

Drawing 11.38

Drawing 11.39

Drawing 11.39.

- Separate the turned back cuff.

- Label the pattern pieces and mark the notches and grain lines, as shown.

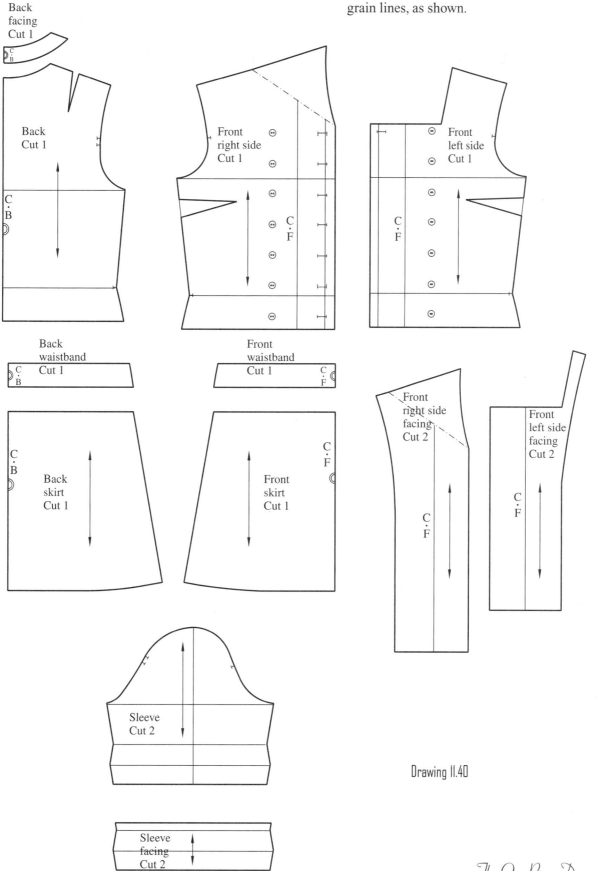

Back facing
Cut 1

C
B

Back
Cut 1

C
B

Front right side
Cut 1

C
F

Front left side
Cut 1

C
F

Back waistband
Cut 1

C
B

Front waistband
Cut 1

C
F

Back skirt
Cut 1

C
B

Front skirt
Cut 1

C
F

Front right side facing
Cut 2

C
F

Front left side facing
Cut 2

C
F

Sleeve
Cut 2

Sleeve facing
Cut 2

Drawing 11.40

Appendices

APPENDIX A DECIMAL-TO-FRACTION CONVERSION CHART

Whenever it is necessary to adjust measurements mathematically, convert the resulting decimal values to a ruler-friendly fraction, using the following chart. Begin by locating the range that contains the number that you would like to convert. Then, use the chart to translate that range to either a decimal or fractional standard.

Example: An adjustment requires that you divide $5\frac{1}{2}''$ by 3, which yields 1.833.
The decimal portion (0.8333) falls on the chart nearest decimal 0.8125 for fraction $\frac{13}{16}$.
Thus, the number used is $1\frac{13}{16}$.

FRACTIONS	DECIMAL	RANGE
$\frac{1}{16}$	0.0625	0.031–0.093
$\frac{1}{8}$	0.1250	0.094–0.155
$\frac{3}{16}$	0.1875	0.156–0.218
$\frac{1}{4}$	0.2500	0.219–0.280
$\frac{5}{16}$	0.3125	0.281–0.343
$\frac{3}{8}$	0.3750	0.344–0.405
$\frac{7}{16}$	0.4375	0.406–0.468
$\frac{1}{2}$	0.5000	0.469–0.530
$\frac{9}{16}$	0.5625	0.531–0.593
$\frac{5}{8}$	0.6250	0.594–0.655
$\frac{11}{16}$	0.6875	0.656–0.718
$\frac{3}{4}$	0.7500	0.719–0.780
$\frac{13}{16}$ ←	0.8125 ←	0.781–0.843 ←
$\frac{7}{8}$	0.8750	0.844–0.905
$\frac{15}{16}$	0.9375	0.905–0.968
1	1.0000	0.969–1.030

APPENDIX B SYMBOLS

Finished line	————————	Grain line	
Original line	————————	Bias grain	
Facing line	—·—·—·—·—	Right angle	
Close	------------	Dart	
Fold		Remove dart	
Shirring	•------------•	Notch	
Slash	—✂—	Stretch	
Pleat		Shrink	
Inverted		Ease	
Equal length		Center front	C.F
		Center back	C.B
		Bust point	B.P

Glossary

Various terms and phrases are used in this text with very specific definitions in mind. Because these definitions will not necessarily be clear from their common usage, the reader is encouraged both to review the definitions given here and periodically to recheck them when they are encountered in the text.

Blend   To merge one thing into another, such as when a style line is integrated into the body of an existing dart.
For example, "Blend the princess line into the waist dart."

Ease In   The process of not sewing a dart and then sewing the resulting excess into the finished garment. This is sometimes done by pressing the fabric to temporarily shrink it.
For example, ". . . the dart will be eased in as it is sewn."

Eliminate   Literally to cut something out of a pattern, essentially leaving a hole where it was before.
For example, "Slash the princess line, eliminating the waist dart."

Erase   To erase something from the pattern, so that it will not later be traced or sewn.
For example, "Erase the dart from the pattern."

Extend   To continue a line or edge in the same direction where it ends.
For example, "Extend a line 3" from the shoulder point."

Extension   An addition made to the leading edge of something.
For example, "Add a 3" extension to the side seam."

Lower   To measure down on or from something, such as when lengthening a hem.
For example, "Lower the hip line 3" or as desired."

Measure In   To measure from a given point toward the interior of the pattern.
For example, "Measure in 2" from the mark."

Measure Out   To measure from a given point away from the interior of the pattern.
For example, "Measure out 2" from the mark."

Raise   To measure up on or from something, such as when shortening a hem.
For example, "Raise the hip line 3" or as desired."

Remove (the dart)   The process of not sewing a dart and then removing the resulting excess from an adjacent location on the same pattern piece.
For example, "Remove the shoulder dart out at the armhole."

Reposition   To move or relocate something to a new location on the pattern.
For example, "Reposition the waist dart. . . ."

Reshape   To redraw a line, such as after moving one of its end points.
For example, "Reshape the armhole, using the marks."

Separate   To cut a section of a pattern out of the whole, such as when removing a placket.
For example, "Separate the placket. . . ."

Smooth   To redraw a line, removing any rough or angular portions in it, such as are left after a dart is eliminated from a pattern.
For example, "Smooth the princess line."

Trace Separately   To trace a pattern in whole or in part on a new piece of paper.
For example, "Trace the facing separately."

Index